The Myth of Egypt and its Hieroglyphs

ALLES VERGÄNGLICHE

IST NUR EIN GLEICHNISS

Goethe

WAS BLEIBET ABER

STIFTEN DIE DICHTER

Hölderlin

The Myth of Egypt and its Hieroglyphs

IN EUROPEAN TRADITION

BY ERIK IVERSEN

PRINCETON UNIVERSITY PRESS
PRINCETON, NEW JERSEY

PUBLISHED BY PRINCETON UNIVERSITY PRESS, 41 WILLIAM STREET,
PRINCETON, NEW JERSEY 08540
IN THE UNITED KINGDOM: PRINCETON UNIVERSITY PRESS,
CHICHESTER, WEST SUSSEX

LIBRARY OF CONGRESS CATALOGING-IN-PUBLICATION DATA

IVERSEN, ERIK, 1909–

THE MYTH OF EGYPT AND ITS HIEROGLYPHS IN EUROPEAN TRADITION / BY
ERIK IVERSEN.

P. CM.—(MYTHOS)

ORIGINALLY PUBLISHED: COPENHAGEN: GAD, 1961. WITH NEW INTROD.

INCLUDES BIBLIOGRAPHICAL REFERENCES AND INDEX.

ISBN 0-691-02124-4

1. EGYPTIAN LANGUAGE—WRITING, HIEROGLYPHIC.   2. EUROPE—
CIVILIZATION—EGYPTIAN INFLUENCES.   I. TITLE.   II. SERIES: MYTHOS
(PRINCETON, N.J.)

PJ1052.I9   1993

493′.1—DC20   93-19325

FIRST PRINCETON PAPERBACK PRINTING, 1993

1   3   5   7   9   10   8   6   4   2
TEXT DESIGNED BY ERIK ELLEGAARD FREDERIKSEN

PRINTED IN THE UNITED STATES OF AMERICA

Contents

Preface (1993)

During their many years of absolute hegemony, classical philologists were prone to consider Greek culture an autochthonous, almost spontaneous phenomenon. Any talk of an Egyptian—or for that matter any other—influence on Greece was consequently considered not merely heretical, but almost sacrilegious, a vain infringement on the pristine purity of Greek thought.

Strange to say, this general approach was to a great extent typical also of generations of predominantly positivist Egyptologists, in awe of the omnipotent classicists, who more or less openly despised Egyptian civilization as barbarous and inferior.

However, in the course of time the more tolerant attitude emerged that any culture, even the Greek, was indebted to its predecessors, and the question of the Egyptian influence on ancient Greece, and through Greece on Western culture, was then quite naturally drawn into the Egyptological debate, although the question of the extent and the scope of the influence still remains controversial.

In recent years, after the original publication of this volume, a series of important contributions to the debate have appeared. Frances Yates's fundamental book on the Hermetic revival of the Florentine Renaissance has rekindled discussion on the Egyptian origin of the tradition. Various aspects of the "myth" as it appeared in the literary and humanistic traditions have been given by Morenz and Baltrusaitis. Attempts have been made to show the Egyptian influence on Greek medicine and to prove that the classical reports on the Egyptian origin of the canon of Greek archaic art rest on solid foundations. At the same time our knowledge of the survival of archaeological, religious, and philosophical lore has been essentially furthered by the studies of Gwyn Griffiths, Leclant, and Stricker.

But as a red thread through this intricate web of direct and indirect influence runs the hieroglyphic tradition, always considered the true Egyptian heritage and, however mistakenly, the only direct link with ancient Egypt. Dying out in their homeland together with the native dynasty and the local cults with which they were indissolubly connected, the hieroglyphs saw a shortlived and strange revival outside Egypt when Roman emperors and magnates began making hieroglyphic inscriptions directly translated from Latin and made locally with barbarous signs; but very soon the tradition disintegrated, the entire system of hieroglyphic writing was forgotten and replaced by the completely wrong but most fertile myth about the hieroglyphs as a sacred writing of ideas.

Misunderstood and misrepresented, what was called hieroglyphs became henceforward synonymous with any form of allegory and metaphor, and gained as such access to all fields of literature and art, becoming to no small extent vehicles of the entire allegorical tradition.

The history of this strange, but artistically most fertile and productive, change in the conception of the hieroglyphs from their origin until their decipherment in the nineteenth century remains therefore the principal purpose and aim of this study, in which the problem, owing unfortunately to the overwhelming richness of the material, can only be traced in its broadest outlines.

Preface

The present attempt to trace the origin of the myth of Egypt and its tradition in European literature and art is not an iconological study or a study in the history of art. The author is an Egyptologist, and the book is merely an effort to present the raw-materials of the process which in the melting-pot of Neo-Platonism transformed the waning memories of ancient Egypt into a living mythos, which from the time of the Renaissance became an inexhaustible source of inspiration to European artists and mystics, and to men of letters and scientists as well.

Together with the conception of Egypt as the venerable home of all fervent piousness and true wisdom and of all occult and mystic knowledge, the allegorical expouding of the hieroglyphs spread all over Europe and made its influence felt as an often concealed, but always fertile and inspiring force in almost all departments of culture, and it is curious to observe the extent to which the changing aspect on Egyptological and hieroglyphical problems in the various epochs and periods, reflects and illustrates their changing attitude towards artistic, literary and scientific problems in general.

The material is overwhelming, and the author is fully aware that any specialist in any particular field may well be able to point out oversights, omissions, and lacunae; but if the book could merely contribute in calling attention to the importance of the tradition, and in tracing its meandering course it would have served its purpose as an illustration to the profound observation of Jean-Jacques Ampère: 'Comparer c'est comprendre. Choississez un object quelconque, observez comment il a été envisagé par différents hommes, a différentes époques, et toute une portion de l'histoire de l'ésprit humain aura passé devant vous'[1].

I am, as always, greatly indebted to Professor Černy and Mr. Henry James for their never failing help and encouragement, and also to Professor Panofsky for his readiness to read, and weed, my manuscript, and improving upon it with constructive criticism and valuable suggestions. Special thanks are due to the members of the staff of the Royal Library in Copenhagen for their untiring patience and helpfulness, and to the Danish State's Research Foundation for a generous grant for the publication of the book.

1 La Grèce Rome et Dante, (ed. 5ième, Paris 1865, p. 169)

9

1. The System of Hieroglyphic Writing

All systems of writing such as they have developed in Egypt and China, in the Far and the Near East, and in the Americas, have insofar a common origin, as all of them evolved more or less directly from the fundamental urge of primitive man at a certain stage of his development, to reproduce the conceptions of the world surrounding him, in pictorial representations, mainly for magical and religious purposes. The rock-drawings found in the deserts of Egypt and Sahara, and on the cliffs of Scandinavia, the paintings from the caves of Southern Europe, and the decorative scenes occasionally found on prehistoric Egyptian pottery and on tomb-walls, represented undoubtedly a primitive form of writing, insofar as each picture and each representation told a story of its own, and had a definite message to convey.

Each of the objects reproduced, the human beings as well as the animals, the pictures of the celestial bodies, as well as those of the ordinary worldly implements of daily life, were in the belief of their primitive creators endowed with life, and had a magical existence of their own. By no means did they merely serve decorative or 'artistic' purposes; but the fundamental belief in the magical reality of his art, enabled primitive man to use his artistic representations as magical means, by which he could influence the dynamics of his cosmos, alter their course, determine their outcome, and control the dark and mysterious forces by which he felt himself surrounded and threatened.

The meaning of each individual representation could only be visually conceived and could never be expressed in any fixed or established sequence of words or sentences, but each of them had nevertheless a specific message to convey, and a definite event or sequence of events to describe or enact.

This magical conception of the aim and purpose of art lived on throughout the course of Egyptian history, and to the Egyptian mind statues and reliefs as well as paintings and drawings were always things alive, conveying messages and fulfilling magical aims, and only secondarily did they serve ornamental and decorative purposes.

The art of writing is in its origin a natural development of these narrative and magical propensities of primitive art, and the hieroglyphic writing of the Egyptians retained throughout its history strong and ineffable reminiscenses of its artistic and religious origin.

The turning point at which true writing in our sense of the word was created and separated from pictorial art was reached when it was realized that artistic representations of individual objects could convey not only visual associations, but also associations of sound, which could be 'read' and understood as words, an elementary mental observation which necessarily had to precede the invention of phonetic writing.

Throughout the history of the world several different systems of writing have been constructed separately and independently and at different places and periods. Their origin and the time of their first appearance are generally shrouded in misty uncertainty, but in Egypt we are able to date the invention of the hieroglyphs with a fair amount of certainty to the time immediately preceding the unification of Upper and Lower Egypt into one Kingdom, an event which took place about 3200 B.C. and inaugurated the history of the country as a people and a nation. We shall see that the basic functional principle of Egyptian phonetic writing was that hieroglyphic pictures of ordinary material objects were used as graphic elements with the sound value of the Egyptian word for the object they represented; and this very idea that pictorial representations could, in fact, be used to transmit values of sound, was in itself a mental achievement which is unique and revolutionary to such an extent that it must necessarily be the result of invention rather than development or evolution, a conception of the origin of hieroglyphic writing which is supported by the abruptness of its appearance, and the fact that it was undoubtedly from the very outset essentially phonetical in character and function[1].

The time of their first appearance can, therefore, with great probability be taken as the time of their invention, and phonetical hieroglyphs are for the first time found on decorative slate-palettes and on seals dating from the latest prehistoric times or the very beginning of the dynastic period[2]. (Pl. I, 1, 2, 3).

On these early monuments they are almost exclusively used for the writing of titles, proper names and place names, but their phonetic functions are unquestionable. The approximate time of their origin can also be corroborated by a closer consideration of the actual objects they represent. It has been pointed out that if we surmise that one of our contemporaries should endeavour to construct a new script in which the ordinary implements and objects of daily life were to be used by the way of letters, the forms and appearances of these implements would in themselves indicate the period when the system was created. Utensils and weapons, dresses and ornaments, animals and plants, would obviously be represented by the ordinary contemporary models of our daily existence, and not by those of bygone ages and periods, and later generations would, consequently, be able to base their dating of the invention and introduction of the new writing on solid archaeological evidence.

It is Scharff's great merit to have pointed out that to a certain extent this is also the case with Egyptian hieroglyphs[3], and that a simple comparison between the individual sign-forms of the early hieroglyphs and the archaeological evidence of the objects they represent, tends to show that the shapes and forms of the former are characteristic of the latest prehistoric and the early dynastic periods, and that this was, therefore, undoubtedly the time when Egyptian phonetic writing was invented, and the use of Egyptian hieroglyphs first introduced.

The question of where in Egypt this intellectual achievement was completed is unfortunately more difficult to answer. It has been demonstrated that the specific employment of certain signs would seem to become more clear and understandable, if a Lower Egyptian origin of the script was surmised. The throne □ occurs in the name of the old Delta town of Buto. The scepter ⌐ is found in the hands of the Lower Egyptian God Andjeti from Busiris, and the picture of the Lower Egyptian Horus became the ordinary sign for God, just as the picture of the Lower Egyptian Snake-Goddess Edjo was used for the word Goddess. The two emblems and , which originally represented the Western and the Eastern Delta respectively, became the ordinary signs for West and East, and the fact that 'West' in Egyptian means 'right' and 'East' 'left', has also been used to support the assumption that the inventors of the hieroglyphs were oriented from the North towards the South. On the other hand, arguments for an Upper Egyptian origin of the script have also been adduced with reference to the fact that the general political and cultural impetus of the period would seem to have come from the South, and that the names of the Northern kings orthographically seen were treated as foreign names. Unfortunately both sets of arguments are in themselves inconclusive and unsatisfactory, and the question about the Northern or Southern origin of hieroglyphic writing must at present be left open and undecided[4].

This is also the case with the question of whether the hieroglyphic system as such represents an autochthonic invention or whether it has been constructed under direct or indirect influence of Sumerian cuneiform writing[5]. It has been pointed out that the original sound values of such hieroglyphs as 'the eye', ⊂⊃, 'the ear', , and 'the hand' ⊂⊃, correspond to the Semitic names of these parts of the body[6]. This has been taken as a proof of a Semitic influence at early stages of the script, at which a connection with Sumerian writing might be possible, and attention has also been drawn to certain concords and similarities in the elementary ideas of the two systems.

But apart from the fact that a certain basic conformity of principles seems to be characteristic of almost all systems of writing at early stages of their developments, these arguments seem to carry little weight against the incontestable fact that hieroglyphic and Sumerian writings in their final developments and forms present entirely different solutions of the functional problems involved, and represent two equally important, but widely different, achievements.

Turning to the governing principles of hieroglyphic phonetic writing, it has already been mentioned that they are based on the mental observation that pictorial representations of material objects could convey associations of sound, derived from the names of the objects represented, as well as visual 'ideographic' impressions of the objects as such. The hieroglyphic picture of a mace ⎨, did not only convey the idea of a mace as a specific instrument of striking, but also the sound value of the Egyptian word for mace *ḥḏ*, in such a way that the combination of the letters *ḥḏ* became associated with the picture of the mace, as a quality beside or apart from the ideographic or pictorial significance of the sign.

Throughout their history each hieroglyphic sign had, therefore, two independent functions. They could be used 'ideographically' to denote the object they represented as when the sign ⎨ was used to designate 'a mace', and in this function they were frequently accompanied by a vertical stroke |, placed after the hieroglyph itself to signify that it was to be understood as the actual material object it delineated. But each sign could also be used as a 'phonogram', as a purely phonetic element conveying the sound value expressed in the name of its prototype. ⎨ could, therefore, be used to express the fixed sequence of the letters *ḥ* and *ḏ* in whichever word this combination might occur.

It could be used in the writing of *ḥḏ* 'white', 'bright', in *ḥḏ* 'silver' (the white metal, in Coptic alphabetic writing '*hat*'), in *ḥḏ.t* 'white cloth' (the *t* is a feminine ending), and in *ḥḏj* 'damage', 'destroy', in Coptic '*hite*'. The system involved has been aptly compared to that used in our rebus, where for instance the picture of a man can be used to denote any occurrence of the sound compact m-a-n[7].

The fact, however, that the same sign is used in the spelling of the word 'silver' '*hat*', and in the word 'damage' '*hite*', reveals a fundamental constructional deficiency from which hieroglyphic writing suffered throughout its history: that it was only able to account for the consonantic skeletons of the words, and left the vowels unconsidered.

The same deficiency is found later in such Semitic alphabets, as Hebrew and Arabic, and it has been explained from certain structural concords between the Egyptian and the Semitic languages, in which the meanings of the various words are inseparably connected with the consonantic skeletons of their radicals, while the vowels denote changes and formal alterations arising from grammatical inflexion and declension[8]. In hieroglyphic writing it had the advantage of giving the individual signs a wider orthographical employment, since a sign like ⎨ *ḥḏ*, at any rate theoretically, could be used for any conceivable combination of any vowel and the two consonants *ḥ* and *ḏ*, such as* *ḥeḏ, eḥḏ, eḥḏe, eḥeḏe* etc, but it made the script as such a very imperfect medium to express the vocalization of the underlying language, a deficiency obviously much less felt by the ancient readers conversant with Egyptian, than by us who only know the language in its hieroglyphic reflection.

It will be seen that each hieroglyph was insofar an ideogram as it represented a tangible material object, but it is of fundamental importance for the understanding of the script to realize that phonetic values and functions were from the very outset of their history inseparable from the ideographic use of the signs.

Already in the earliest inscriptions, such as we find them on the palettes and the ivory tablets of the first two dynasties, the basic system of the script is fully developed, and displays all graphic elements and all systematical potentialities of its more advanced stages, even if in their rudimentary and embryonic forms. The subsequent evolution was, therefore, the result of the further development of inherent systematical possibilities more than an actual improvement of the system as such; and the main result of the growing technical command and the increased employment of the writing was a rapid increase in the number of hieroglyphs, the basic nucleus of which was fully developed in the time about the fifth and sixth dynasties (about 2580-2250 B.C.).

In the twelfth dynasty (2000-1780 B.C.), the classical period of script as well as of language, about 700 signs were in more or less constant use and they remained fundamentally unchanged in their forms as well as their functions right down until Ptolemaic times (from about 323 B.C.) when the final decadence set in, and new orthographic principles were introduced. It is obvious that no theoretical or systematical problems were involved when it came to creating new hieroglyphs representing ordinary material objects, as any pictorial representation of any object theoretically seen could be used as a hieroglyph, ideographically representing the object itself, and phonetically representing the sound-value expressed in its Egyptian name.

The introduction of new signs was, therefore, a continual and natural process, and the hieroglyphic pictures of the horse and the chariot were introduced contemporarily with their factual appearance about the 18th dynasty, just as pictures of the stela ⎕, the pyramid △ and the obelisk ▯ had followed the introduction of the corresponding architectural elements.

But not every word of the language or concept of the mind could be expressed pictorially, and special means had to be adopted to write abstract nouns and verbs, and such words as pronouns and prepositions, which could not in themselves be directly expressed by hieroglyphic representations of concrete material objects.

This problem was solved by two different approaches, one dependent on the phonetical, the other on the ideographical possibilities of the script. In the former case the vocalizations of the words in question was quite simply reproduced in ordinary phonetic spelling in accordance with the principles mentioned above, as illustrated by the use of the hieroglyph ▯ in the spelling of the word *ḥḏ* 'white', 'bright'. This was the method used in the rendering of pronouns, prepositions, and other grammatical elements of the language, but in other cases recourse was had to ideographic writing, and a great variety of abstract nouns and verbs were expressed by specially con-

15

structed ideograms used with a conventional, slightly transferred meaning, depend-end on certain elementary associations of ideas.

A man steadying a basket on his head could be used as an ideogram for the word *fʒj* 'carry', or for the word *ʒtp* 'load'. Two arms holding a shield and an axe was read *cḥʒ* 'fight'. A forearm and a hand holding what is probably a conical loaf was used for the word *dj* 'give', while the picture of an old emblem of divinity representing a piece of cloth wound on a pole was used for the word *nṭr* 'God'. In the same way the picture of a sail could signify the word 'sail' and the word *nfw* 'skipper', but also the words 'breath', 'wind'; and the picture of a hill over which are seen the rays of the rising sun , was used for the verb *ḥcj* 'appear'. A seated man which was generally the ideogram for the word *sʒ* 'man'; could in a similar way under certain circumstances be used for the pronouns 'I', 'my', and a picture of the sun ⊙ could be used for the word *hrw* 'day', as well as in its original ideographic sense *Rc* 'sun', and so on.

In those cases where the signs could be used for various words with different vocalizations and meanings, the proper readings were generally indicated by phonetical complements such as ⊙ *R*+*c* for *Rc* 'sun', and ⊙ *h*+*r*+*w* for *hrw* 'day'.

We have seen that the phonetical elements of writing were nothing but ordinary ideograms which had been endowed with certain phonetic values and functions, and as phonetic units it has in modern Egyptology become customary to classify them according to the number of consonants they represent.

About fifty, the so-called triliterals, represent a sequence of three consonants, such as *nfr*, *ḥtp*, *ḥpr*, and *nḏm*, and a slightly larger number are biliteral, combining a sequence of two, such as *mn*, *mj*, *ms*, *km*, *pr*, *ḏd* etc.

The most frequently used signs are the uniliterals, which were derived from words with only one essential consonant, and they constitute the nearest hieroglyphical approach to what we should call alphabetic letters. They had an extensive use in the writing of abstract words, names, grammatical endings and formative elements, and they were used as phonetic complements to indicate some or all of the individual consonants of bi- and triliteral signs.

In spite of their extensive use and their particular functions, the Egyptians nevertheless did not consider the uniliterals as forming a group apart from the other signs, nor did they regard them as alphabetic letters in our sense of the word. They remained in the strictest sense of the word one-consonant signs or uniliterals, and we have no evidence that alphabetical conceptions such as we understand them, or a conception of separate individual letters, were ever developed.

In the scanty sign-lists preserved, the signs are arranged occasionally in vague groups according to what they represent, so that for instance pictures of Gods, human beings, animals and plants represent so many separate groups. In other cases they are

PLATE I

1. Hieroglyphs used for the writing of town names on pre-dynastic slate palette.

2. Early hieroglyphs from the annals of King Djer. Ist dynasty.

3. Hieroglyphs from the funeral stela of King Djet. Ist dynasty.

arranged vaguely according to their shape, and in word-lists we find occasionally that the individual words have been classified according to their initials, in accordance with what is generally known as the 'acrophonic' principle. Texts are found where words with an *h, j,* or *k,* are put together in lists, but neither the sequence of the individual initials nor the sequence of the individual words seem to be governed by any fundamental alphabetical principle.

The following list gives the ordinary uniliteral signs in their conventional modern sequence, together with their ideographic meanings, their transliterations and their phonetic values.

Egyptian vulture
Neophron percnopterus   Aleph ꜣ   Unvoiced explosive laryngal. Can be compared to the glottal stop heard in French words beginning with a mute *h,* as in 'histoire'. As a medial it creates a hiatus such as heard after the first syllable in the word cooperation.

Flowering reed   *i*   Weak consonant with an affinity to the vowel *i.* As a consonant it corresponds to Hebrew yod and English *y* in 'yesterday'. At the beginning of words it is sometimes supposed to correspond to ꜣ. Hence its transliteration *ỉ.* At the end of words it is in Middle Egyptian replaced by 𓏭 or \\.

Forearm   Ayin ꜥ   Presumably voiced fricative laryngal with no Indo-European equivalent. Corresponds to the glottal stop in Danish and Scotch.

Quail-chick   *w*   Weak consonant with affinity to the vowel *u.* As a consonant it corresponds to Hebrew Waw and English *w,* as in 'war'.

Foot   *b*   Voiced explosive bilabial. Like English *b* in 'bad'.

Stool   *p*   Unvoiced explosive bilabial. Engl. *p* in 'pay'.

Horned viper
Cerastes cornutus   *f*   Probably an unvoiced fricative labiodental like English *f.*

Owl
Tyto alba alba?   *m*   Voiced nasal bilabial like English *m.* In certain words pronounced with a strong nasalization and, therefore, left unwritten as in *rt* for *rmt.* From about the XVIII dynasty ⸺ is used for *m.*

17

Water	∿∿∿	*n*	Voiced nasal dental like English *n*. Occasionally used also for *l*. In certain words pronounced with strong nasalization and left unwritten as in ḥḳ.t for ḥnḳ.t. From dynasty XVIII ⸬ is used for *n*. The original value of the sign was *m*.
Mouth	⊂⊃	*r*	Probably voiced apical *r*, articulated with the tip of the tongue as in English. Occasionally used for *l*.
Reed-shelter	⊓	*h*	Unvoiced fricative laryngal pronounced as *h* in 'house'.
Wick of twisted flax	৪	*ḥ*	Unvoiced fricative laryngal articulated more emphatically than *h*.
Placenta?	⊘	*ḫ*	Unvoiced fricative velar pronounced as *ch* in Scotch 'loch' and German 'ach'.
Animal's belly with teats	⇒	*ẖ*	Unvoiced fricative palatal. Perhaps like *ch* in German 'ich'. Interchanges occasionally with *ḫ*.
Bolt	—•—	*s*	Originally a voiced sibilant dental corresponding to English *z*. Very soon after the Old-Kingdom indistinguishable from *ś*.
Folded cloth	∏	*ś*	Unvoiced fricative dental like English *s*.
Pool	⊏⊐	*š*	Unvoiced fricative palatal corresponding to *sh* in English 'shape' or *ch* in French 'chaise', German *sch* in 'schön'.
Hill-slope	△	*ḳ*	Unvoiced explosive velar, something like *q* in 'queen' or 'quench'.
Wickerwork basket	⌣	*k*	Unvoiced explosive palatal like *c* in English 'coast', French 'cable', and *k* in German 'Krone'.
Ring-stand for jars	Ⓐ	*g*	Voiced explosive palatal like the hard *g* in English 'garden'.
Loaf	⌒	*t*	Unvoiced explosive dental like English *t*.
Tethering rope	⇒	*ṯ*	Unvoiced fricative dental something like *ch* in English 'cheek'.
Hand	⊂⊃	*d*	Voiced explosive dental like *d* in English 'dream'.
Snake	⌇	*ḏ*	Voiced fricative dental something like *g* in English 'Germany'.

18

By their invention of the uniliteral signs the Egyptians had actually created the theoretical background for the abolition of all other graphic elements, phonetical as well as ideographical, and theoretically seen it would have been possible for them to discard all of them by using the uniliterals as ordinary letters in a proper consonantic alphabet, exactly as it was done much later in early Semitic writing. Strangely enough they never took this natural consequence of their own discoveries, but retained all the complexities of the original system throughout their history.

We can only guess why, but it was undoubtedly connected with their traditional conception of the word as the final element of the language, which impeded the development a universal alphabetic system with one specific sound-sign for each particular phone, and made them dependent on standardized graphic word-pictures in their conception of the written word.

Beside their use in the spelling of abstracts, the principal aim of the uniliterals was, as already mentioned, to indicate the correct reading of ideograms, and to facilitate the reading of bi- and triliteral signs by indicating their individual consonants.

Written by itself, a 'naked' ideogram, as ⊙ 'sun', could be vocalized and interpreted in different ways, but when phonetic complements were added in such writings as ⬭ $r + $ ' or 🔲 🐦 $h + r + w$; it was always clear when hrw 'day' and Rc 'sun' should be read. When used as complements to bi- or triliterals they could be placed before after, or on either side of the signs, and the foregoing example could therefore be written either 𐤟, 𐤟, or 𐤟. In all cases the added consonants were only indicators, and each orthographic group whether $h + d + hd$, $h + hd + d$ or $hd + h + d$ is only to be read hd. In spite of these deliberate efforts to 'phoneticize' and to indicate the proper vocalization, the consonantal character of the system would nevertheless frequently have made it impossible to distinguish between words derived from the same root, or possessing an identical consonantic skeleton. All such words would necessarily in their orthographic appearance become reduced to one single pattern which would make them indistinguishable and make them lose their semantic individuality. Seen from an orthographical point of view it would, as an example, be impossible to decide whether, 𐤟 hd was the writing of the word hd 'bright', or the word hd 'silver', the word $hd.t$ 'white cloth', or the word hdj 'damage'.

To overcome this basic deficiency which in itself would have been serious enough to prevent the script from being developed into a universal system of writing, a new and ingenious graphic element was introduced, the so-called determinatives.

When placed as mute indicators after some words, certain ordinary ideograms were given a particular function. They lost their phonetic values, as well as their specific ideographic significance and were used to indicate or 'determine' the ideological group or category to which the preceding word belonged. A seated man 𐤟, which was the ideogram for the word $sʒ$ 'man', indicated, when placed as a determinative behind proper-names, titles, and words denoting crafts and professions, that the preceding word was either the name of a man, or an occupation reserved for a male person. The sign 𓀜 – from about the eighteenth dynasty generally replaced by 𓂝 – was originally an ideogram for the word *ḥwj* 'strike', but as a determinative it was used to indicate words denoting actions or states involving the exertion of bodily strength, such as 𓈖𓏏 𓀜 *nḫt* 'strong', 𓈎𓂝𓂋𓅆𓀜 *ḥꜥḏꜣ* 'plunder' 𓈖𓅓𓅆𓀜 *nḥm* 'rescue', and characteristically enough also 𓋴𓃀𓏭✶ 𓅆𓀜 *sbꜣ* 'teach', as it, to the Egyptian mind, took much beating to learn. The sign 𓈖, the ordinary ideogram of 𓈗 *mw*, 'water', was used to signify all things of a fluid and viscous nature, and so on.

An elaborate system of about 150 categories was established, and an appropriate determinative became eventually an indispensable appendix to the orthography of most Egyptian words.

The various categories were not always well defined, and the Egyptians were not always consistent in their use, but the fundamental importance of the determinatives as orthographical elements will be apparent from their employment in the above mentioned words with *ḥ* and *ḏ*, all of which become neatly separated and unambiguously differentiated when provided with their appropriate determination. 𓌉⊙ is *ḥḏ* 'bright', with ⊙ used to denote qualities or functions of the sun; 𓌉𓋜 is *ḥḏ* 'silver', with the necklace 𓋜, used as determinative of precious metals and what is made from them, 𓌉𓏤 is *ḥḏ.t* 'white cloth', as indicated by 𓏤, which represents a strip of cloth indicating textiles, and 𓌉𓅽 is the word *ḥḏj* 'damage', with the bird 𓅽 originally the ideogram of 𓇋𓅽 *nḏs* 'small', but as a determinative used to denote everything small, bad, and disagreeable.

The 'transferred' sense in which the sign 𓅽 is used as a determinative is also characteristic of signs such as 𓃰, an animal's skin, used to signify all mammals or quadrupeds, and to a certain extent also of ı ı ı and \\, when used to denote plurality and duality respectively. The sealed papyrus roll 𓏛, was used to denote what we should call abstracts, in the Egyptian conception such words that could not be ideographically expressed but had to be phonetically reproduced.

Any determinative could occasionally be replaced by an oblique stroke \, mainly used when the scribes wanted to avoid a rare sign or signs difficult to draw or write, such as 𓅓𓐠𓎛\ *mśḥ*, instead of 𓅓𓐠𓎛𓆊 *mśḥ* 'crocodile'. – Fundamentally seen these principles and elements remained essential for hieroglyphic writing throughout the nearly three thousand years of its history, but this did not exclude certain evolutional changes, at first mainly dependent on a growing command of the very art of writing itself and, later on, on the introduction of certain formal modifications made necessary by linguistic and orthographic developments.

The time from the first to the third dynasty was the embryonic period of the script, during which the command of the technical and practical difficulties was gradually achieved, a process which can be traced from the primitive indications of names and titles on the palettes through the annalistic records of the first two dynasties with their sporadic use of verbs and prepositions, to the first continuous inscriptions, the biographical texts of the third dynasty.

The systematic use of phonetic complements and uniliterals took speed towards the end of the second dynasty, and the rigidly stunted wordpictures of the earliest inscriptions, devoid of all indications of grammatical endings, and indications of gender, were developed into 'spelled' graphic units provided with their appropriate endings and marks[9]. Pluralis and dualis, which hitherto had been indicated by writing the sign or sign-group in question thrice or twice, could from now on be expressed by the graphic determinatives ı ı ı and \\, and the use of determinatives was slowly increased, although they did not become universally established as indispensable graphic elements until the twelfth dynasty.

During the Old Kingdom, – the period including the third and the sixth dynasties from about 2800 to 2250 B.C. – the script obtained its highest development in the inscriptions of the fifth and the sixth dynasties, among which the so-called Pyramidtexts are the most important, but even here the full mastery of the new invention was not yet obtained, and the struggle to develop the hieroglyphs into an adequate and universal system of writing was by no means ended.

The inscriptions bear evidence of a marked preference for the use of the simplest graphical elements, the uniliterals, and they abound in careful phonetical spellings, in which a certain amount of uncertainty is perceptible, and a neophytic fear of not being clear and unambiguous.

Phonetic complements are liberally used to facilitate the correct readings of ideograms as well as of bi- and triliteral signs, and grammatical endings are conscientiously accounted for. Definitive efforts were made to create something like a standard orthography, but determinatives were used sparingly and with apparent reluctance until the sixth dynasty. However, the full mastery of the inherent possibilities of the system was not achieved during the Old-Kingdom. The inscriptions remained unmistakably old-fashioned and archaic, although their very awkwardness and their abundant use of phonetic elements, give them a strangely 'advanced' appearance, when compared with those of later periods. To make the hieroglyphs a fully developed instrument of writing was reserved for the scribes and scholars of the twelfth dynasty. It was accomplished mainly by a harmonious and well-balanced coordination of the various elements of the script, and in the establishment of certain graphic rules, responsible for the nearest approach to an established orthography ever achieved in the history of Egyptian writing. The spellings of the individual words became standardized into a more or less consistent sequence of ideograms, phonetic elements, and determinatives. The use of the latter was systematized and for the first time fully developed, and each word became, to a certain extent, a distinct graphic unity, forming a characteristic word-picture on which subsequent periods based their orthography.

It was, however, the final as well as the highest development of the script, and no serious efforts were ever made to alter or improve the fundamental principles of the system as such, except for the introduction of syllabic-writing, to which we shall revert later.

What followed was, therefore, decline, which began sporadically as early as the eighteenth and nineteenth dynasties (ca. 1546-1200 B.C.). The origin of various signs was at this stage already forgotten, with a resulting confusion in their employment, and deliberate attempts to improve on the established word-pictures, in order to make them conform with the linguistic evolution, led to an increasing orthographic confusion. The decline gathered momentum from the twentieth dynasty and gained only a short respite through the reforms of the twenty-sixth dynasty (663-525 B.C.).

The unfortunate war with Assyria had ended with the conquest of Egypt (671 B.C.) and the destruction of the Egyptian Monarchy; but as a natural reaction it had also given rise to a violent resurgence of Egyptian nationalism. Domestic Assyrian troubles and Grecian mercenaries, made it possible for the powerful rulers of the Delta to regain their independence as the so-called Saïte Dynasty, the twenty-sixth. But only for a short while could they stem the tide, and the final dissolution of the independent national Egyptian state was drawing near.

But as long as it lasted it was obviously in the interest of the new rulers to encourage the national revival, and to use the national resurgence in their political efforts to reunite the country under the ancient monarchical idea of the King-Gods, which had always been the fundament upon which the political and religious unity of the Egyptian state had been based. They undertook, for this purpose, a grandiose reorganization of the cultic and political machinery of state, which pays the greatest credit to their historical insight as well as their knowledge and erudition. But the political and cultural centre of the reunited kingdom was no longer the traditional capital of Imperial Egypt, Upper Egyptian Thebes, now distant and remote, but Saïs the home-town of the new dynasty in the Delta, which was closer to the new political centre of the world, Asia Minor and the Eastern Mediterranean. The pattern which they chose for their reorganization was strangely enough not the Egypt of the Empire, but the old Egypt of the pyramid-builders, probably because the Imperial traditions of the eighteenth and nineteenth dynasties were inextricably connected with Thebes, and therefore had to be avoided for political reasons. We are unable to judge the profundity of the reform, which to some extent seems comparable with the pathetic efforts of the late Roman empire to revoke what it considered the virtues and the ideals of the Republic, but its outward symptoms are almost everywhere observable: The offices of state were reorganized, and Old Kingdom titles were substituted for those which had been in use since the New and Middle Kingdoms. Ceremonial dresses and costumes were made to conform with the fashions of the fifth and the sixth dynasties, and in art and decoration it became customary to copy the monuments from the Old Kingdom with such minuteness that it is often difficult to distinguish the periods. The texts from the pyramids of the sixth dynasty reappeared in private tombs, and the growing interest in ancient literature gave rise to the development of historical and linguistic studies, which excelled in commentaries and explanations of ancient texts.

As far as the hieroglyphs are concerned, they experienced a renaissance as a natural consequence of the architectural activity of the dynasty. The signs were reformed and brought in accordance with the models of the monumental inscriptions from the Old and the Middle Kingdoms, and decided efforts were made to reform spelling and orthography after the same patterns.

However, the reforms do not seem to have resulted in any true spiritual rebirth or 'renaissance', and they were probably changes of form more than of spirit. The creative forces of the country were ebbing out, and the prolonged period of final stagnation was inaugurated by the Persian conquest (525 B.C.), which resulted in the final loss of political and national independence, and an unbroken sequence of foreign domination, lasting right down until the emergence of modern Egypt into a sovereign state. Hieroglyphic writing as such survived the catastrophe of Persian rule, and lived on throughout the subsequent Greek occupation right down until Roman times. But it underwent considerable changes, which distinguish it from the writing of earlier periods, and makes 'Ptolemaic' writing, as it is generally called, appear as an orthographic system of its own.

In reality it was not subject to any systematic alterations at all, and its altered appearance was due entirely to formal changes arising from the introduction of new signs, new orthographic rules, and new word-pictures accompanied by a deliberate corruption of the old ones.

We can only guess at the reasons for this change, but its background was probably to a certain extent psychological, and depended on the altered cultural conditions of the country under foreign domination.

In the independent Egyptian state the hieroglyphs had always represented the highest and the most authoritative medium through which kings and priests had transmitted their most solemn and serene proclamations to Gods and men, and it is unquestionable that they were seemingly used for the same purpose on the walls of temples and tombs during the rule of the Macedonians. But the significance of the messages they conveyed had changed. The new masters, whose political and cultic position they proclaimed, were foreigners, believers in foreign gods, and their dependence on the old mythical cult was a political convention or fiction more than a religious reality. The inner dynamics which in the greatest periods of Egyptian history had harmoniously combined the political and the religious forces into the divine kingship of the Pharaohs broke down forever. The priestly bearers and formers of the old political religion of state became subservient to foreign masters, and became representatives of a cult which had sunk down to become the creed of a 'native' polulation, subdued and suppressed by a ruling class of foreigners. No longer were they the proud mediators between kings and Gods, framing the religious and political destiny of their people, but the humble guardians of a stagnant cultic tradition.

Their very existence as a professional body in the state became from now on exclusively dependent on their sacerdotal position, and on their mythic and cultic knowledge, which naturally furthered a tendency to guard it jealously, and to monopolize it as a professional secret inside their own circles and ranks.

The knowledge of the hieroglyphs was undoubtedly one of these professional secrets, since hieroglyphic inscriptions still served the political purpose of proclaiming the fiction that the old state-religion was still alive, and the foreign rulers still the Pharaonic king-gods; but it became subject to material changes in the hands of its priestly guardians, who wanted it to be primarily an instrument of displaying their professional mythical knowledge, and took deliberate pains to make the actual writing more complex and intricate, so as to add to the exclusiveness of their art.

It has already been pointed out that this transformation was not achieved by systematic changes, but by simple orthographic reforms. The established orthographic rules were changed, and the old word-pictures abolished in favour of new spellings, mainly obtained by the introduction of the already mentioned acrophonic principle in accordance with which an increasing number of hieroglyphs were used as uniliteral letters, with the alphabetic value of their initials or their principle consonant.

The sign ⟨glyph⟩ *fꜣj*, for instance, was accordingly used for *f*. ⟨glyph⟩ Neith was used for *n*, and ⟨glyph⟩ *imw* for *m*, and so on.

Several new ideograms were introduced, such as ⟨glyph⟩ for *prj* 'go out', ⟨glyph⟩ for *ꜥḳ* 'enter', ⟨glyph⟩ for *mk* 'protect'. For verbs denoting actions we find new signs such as a man playing the harp for *ḥs* 'sing', a man carrying a child for *fꜣj* 'carry'.

Old ideograms got new transferred meanings, often dependent on subtle mythical or speculative explanations, as when the baboon ⟨glyph⟩ greeting the sun, was used for *nfr* 'good', or the bee ⟨glyph⟩ for *kꜣ.t* 'work'.

Certain graphic peculiarities were introduced or developed, such as a tendency to combine different hieroglyphs into one single sign. 𓅯 is written for *f₃*, ⚬𓌅 for *bḫ*, 𓌺 for *ḥdd*, 𓋴𓏤 *r + šw* for *ršw*, and so on. Ideograms and determinatives were occasionally combined in the same way, as in 𓋀𓏤 'East and West', 𓍿 *kd* 'engrave', 𓏏𓊖 *sm₃* 'unite', and new graphic groups were created accordingly, mainly for calligraphic reasons such as 𓋹𓎟 for *nb ʿnḫ* 'Lord of life' or 𓅐𓊹 for *mwt nṯr* 'Mother of God.

In certain inscriptions this play with the orthographical and pictorial possibilities of the script were carried almost to its utmost limits, and developed into an utterly barbaric and abnormal graphic style.

A still greater number of new uniliterals were introduced, with a resulting increase in the general graphic confusion. The single consonant *m* could hence forward be written 𓆭, 𓃀, 𓄎, 𓈖, 𓅓, 𓏺, 𓂝, 𓅓, 𓌅, or 𓆟, and the sign to be used in any particular case was left entirely to the discretion of the individual scribes[10].

Several new biliterals were also invented and introduced, some of which were phonetic in origin such as the cat 𓅓 *mj*, used phonetically for biliteral *mj*. Others were based on profound mythical considerations, as when the sign for the God Thoth 𓅞, or 𓅤, was used for *ib* 'heart', because the God Thoth in the theological systems was considered the heart of the Sun-God; or when the picture of a female figure representing Nut, the Goddess of heaven, bending over the earth, was used for *p*, acrophonically derived from *p.t* 'heaven'.

Completely wild writings are also found, as when the word *nfr* 'good', 'beautiful', was written by a monkey *nfr*, riding on a horse, which in itself could also be used for the word *nfr*, and holding the old sign *nfr* 𓄤 in its hands.

The signs derived by mythical speculation acquired a regrettable influence on the later tradition because it furthered the erroneous conception of the 'symbolic' significance of the hieroglyphs, and the belief in their mystic origin and nature.

In this stagnant and decadent form, hieroglyphic writing lingered on as an obsolete and dying tradition throughout the Ptolemaic domination, and it survived the Roman occupation, as the spiritual property of a small and exclusive body of scholarly priests, but it was obvious that its final decline was imminent.

The inscriptions became shorter and their content more and more stereotyped, and the artistic and craftsmanlike skill necessary for their proper execution deteriorated rapidly. In their execution the hieroglyphs of the period are, therefore, generally crude and barbaric, and the old aesthetical and canonical rules responsible for the shape of the individual signs were to a great extent abolished and forgotten. In the elaborate protocol of five official names with which the Greek and Roman rulers in accordance with the old Pharaonic traditions were provided in their capacity of Kings of Egypt, we can see how the Ptolemies and their queens retained their Greek proper names, which appeared in their original Greek forms merely transcribed into imperfect hiero-glyphical vocalizations. The other ceremonial names, apparently provided by Egyptian scribes, were generally Egyptian, and their various Greek epithets were generally translated into Egyptian. The Romans, on the other hand, introduced such Greek and Roman titles as Autocrator and Caesar directly into their hieroglyphic nomenclature without any attempt to translate them.

It is almost symbolic that the last Roman emperor whose name is found in a hiero-glyphic inscription in Decius († 251 A.D.), who tried in vain to revive and reorganize the pagan cult of the empire in an effort to stem the rising tide of Christianity, but died on the banks of the Danube in pursuit of the advancing Goths.

In Southern Egypt, which remained the last stronghold of Egyptian religion, the tradition lingered on somewhat longer, and the latest hieroglyphic inscriptions are found on the island of Philae near the first cataract, and date from the year 394.

What has been said above about the systematic and constructional principles of hieroglyphic writing are valid for all periods and for all its various forms, but we shall see that the actual hieroglyphic pictures, such as they appear as actual pictorial re-presentations of human beings, animals, and material objects, were not the exclusive notation of the script. They were undoubtedly its fundamental and original charac-ters, but in the course of history their use became restricted to monumental, sacred, and official inscriptions, and their sacred and exclusive character is expressed in their very name.

In the Egyptian tradition the signs themselves are called ⌂◖⌂↶, and hierogly-phic writing as such was called 𓉐𓉐 ⌂ 𓊌, 'the writings of the House of Life', which was an academic centre of cult and administration, or 𓉐 ∼∼∼ 𓏞, 'the writing of the divine word'. The Greeks called originally the signs ἱερα γράμματα 'sacred letters', and in later times quite simply τα ἱερογλυφικα (sc. γράμματα) 'the sacred carved letters or sculpturings', from which our word hieroglyph is derived.

They were originally written in vertical columns, but horizontal lines were intro-duced already in the early part of the Old Kingdom, and became henceforward the most common notation. The normal direction of writing was from right to left, and the front of the individual signs was almost invariably pointed towards the beginning of the line. Inscriptions running from left to right were by no means uncommon, how-ever, and even isolated examples of boustrophedon writing are occasionally found, in which the direction of the signs was changed at the beginning of each line like the course of a plough in successive furrows, whence the name, which means in the man-ner of an ox-turning[11].

Owing to the ornamental character of the script no fixed rules for its direction were ever established, as graphic considerations would always have to yield to artistic demands, especially the marked partiality for symmetrical arrangements which was a prevalent characteristic of Egyptian decorative art.

It cannot be stressed enough that in their craftsmanlike execution the hieroglyphs were always artistic representations and reflected the artistic spirit and the technical skill of the various periods, and in their outward appearance and shape the individual signs were always represented in accordance with the general laws governing Egyptian art, with its particular conception and solution of perspective problems.

They were consequently dependent on the general fluctuations of art and craftsmanship, and the style and quality of its sign-forms are therefore, important criteria for the dating of any inscription[12]. (Pl. II, 1–2).

In the early periods of their history the hieroglyphs were, as we have seen, used for all purposes, and not exclusively for monumental inscriptions. They were consequently not only incised with chisel or bodkin on hard surfaces, but also drawn or written with black or red ink, by means of a reed-brush, – in Egyptian   –, on papyrus –found as a finished material already from the first dynasty,–on potsherds or limestone slabs–the so-called ostraca –, or occasionally on wooden tablets or on hide. When written with ink on smooth surfaces the hieroglyphs rapidly developed cursive forms, giving only the characteristic outlines of the signs; and the first examples of these linear or cursive hieroglyphs are found as early as the first dynasty[13]. It is, however, not until the third dynasty that sufficient material is available to establish that written hieroglyphs were fairly common phenomena. They appear as faithful reductions of their hieroglyphic prototypes, and like these they were generally written separately sign by sign, without ligatures or abbreviations. The flowing ductus of an ordinary written hand had not yet been developed, and from a graphic point of view the signs were in the strictest sense just hand-written hieroglyphs; but even as such they developed into a special calligraphic style, and were reserved for special purposes. (See cover).

From the end of the Old Kingdom they were regularly used for the writing of religious texts on sarcophagi, and, somewhat later, they were adopted for the writing of funerary papyri containing versions of the so-called Book of the Dead, generally written in vertical columns from the right, a practice which was continued right down until the XXIst dynasty. In later periods they were also occasionally used for the writing of religious texts, and their influence on the characteristic 'round-hand' used in Greek and Roman periods is unmistakable.

From a historical point of view they obtain their principal importance by forming the indispensable intermediary link between the hieroglyphs themselves, and that which should become the next, most important, stage in the graphic development of the script.

The propagation of the art of writing and the extension of its use, which took place between the third and the fifth dynasties, resulted for the first time in the history of mankind in the development of an ordinary chirography or handwriting, which in its original form appears almost fully developed in the course of the fifth dynasty, and is generally known as hieratic. (Pl. II, 3).

The term – derived from Greek ἱερατικός 'sacerdotal' or 'priestly' – is first applied by Clement of Alexandria (born about 150 A.D.), and it was created at a time when hieratic writing in itself had been supplanted for most purposes by a still younger notation, demotic.

For the most important period of its history, and at any rate down to the XXIInd dynasty, 'hieratic' is, therefore, a most misleading and confusing designation for a script which was explicitly developed to conform with the graphic demands of ordinary daily existence. However, the term has gained admittance once and for all and will probably remain, so much the more so, as no special Egyptian name for hieratic writing is known.

It would be entirely outside the scope of the present volume to attempt any history of hieratic writing as such, but a short outline of its main characteristics, and a brief summary of its development will be indispensable for the indication of the course of the graphic tradition. We have seen that the direct prototypes of the individual hieratic signs in the great majority of cases were the handwritten, cursive reproductions of the hieroglyphs. The hieratic signs were characteristic reductions of the cursives, just as the latter were reductions of the hieroglyphs, and they represent, at any rate in their origin, something like a shorthand reproduction of these. The difference between the two systems of notation was, therefore, exclusively graphic and there was no other difference between hieroglyphic and hieratic writing as such, than there is between our typed and handwritten letters. But as a natural consequence of its very nature as a handwriting, hieratic had obviously much less formal stability, and was subject to much more rigorous and abrupt changes in form and appearance than the hieroglyphs, and it was much more dependent on the personal style of the individual scribes.

Until about the XXIInd dynasty three more or less well-defined stages of its development can be discerned: I, an archaic period from the Vth to the beginning of the XIIth dynasty; II, a classical period from the XIIth to the early parts of the XVIIIth dynasty during which the basic classical style of hieratic writing was brought into existence, from a calligraphic as well as from an orthographic point of view, and III, a post-classical period from about the middle of the XVIIIth to the XXIInd dynasty, during which the results of the previous periods were brought to practical perfection, and a complete command of the technicalities was obtained[14].

Quite apart from the differences due to the individual hands of the various scribes we are able to follow right back to the Vth dynasty the first traces of a tendency, which eventually was to become responsible for the development of special graphic styles for the various categories of documents, such as the elaborate calligraphy used in official decrees and letters, the sober and conscientious book-writing found in literary and scientific texts, and the easy and hasty hand used in private communications and business documents such as contracts and accounts, and each of these styles had to a certain extent a tradition of its own.

In the course of time a fundamental distinction was established between the conservative traditional literary writing and the common business style, used for the everyday purposes of correspondence and commerce. In its origin this distinction can be traced back to the new Kingdom, and the separating tendencies gained impetus through the general orthographic deterioration at the end of the period. The separation was fully established already in the XXIst dynasty, and from then on the two graphic styles followed separate and entirely different lines of tradition.

The book-writing stagnated, ceased to develop, and became subject to certain archaizing tendencies. It became exclusively reserved for the writing of religious and scientific texts, and overtook, generally speaking, the functions which had hitherto been reserved for the cursive hieroglyphs, and it became thus for the first time exclusive and 'hieratic'. As such it remained in use right down into the second century of our era, standardized into a characteristic 'roundhand', clear-cut and beautiful, but impersonal like the Italian cancellaria of the Renaissance.

The business hand developed with increasing rapidity. We have very little material permitting us to follow the early stages of its development which was determined by the gradual abolishment of that basic principle which had hitherto been fundamental for all true hieratic writing: that each sign and each graphic element, however cursive and contracted, should represent a transcription of an individual hieroglyph[15].

This rule began to lose its validity about the XXIst dynasty, and the result was what is generally known as abnormal hieratic, a notation best known from Theban documents from the XXVth and the XXVIth dynasties (about 700-500 B.C.). It abounded in ligatures and contractions, formed new word-pictures and new orthographic rules, and emerged finally in its Lower Egyptian form as a new graphic system generally known as demotic[16]. The name is derived from Greek δημοτικός meaning 'popular' or 'common', and it was first used by Herodotus in his account of the Egyptian systems of writing. (Pl. III, 1).

Seen from a systematic point of view, the new notation retained a basic connection with the old scripts, continued to operate with a combination of phonograms, ideograms and determinatives, and was always written in horizontal lines from the right; but formally, and as a graphic instrument, it represents undoubtedly a new achievement, and in most respects a simplification and practical improvement, at any rate when compared with abnormal hieratic.

The individual signs were in most cases directly derived from hieratic, but they were even more simplified and stereotyped, almost to the extent of becoming a system of conventionalized 'letters' or standardized word-groups. New signs were introduced, some of which were derived from late hieroglyphs, while others had no direct hieroglyphic prototype at all, being developed from hieratic ligatures or sign-groups. Entirely new orthographic rules were introduced, so that the graphic pictures of the words were completely changed. Ideographical writings were still used, but there was a marked preference for phonetic spellings, for which extensive use was made of uniliterals and of old biliterals used as acrophonic letters. Certain texts display indisputable indications of intended vocalization. The language of the demotic texts is undoubtedly the vernacular of the period, basically probably that of the XXVIth dynasty, although later stages of linguistic evolution are discernible in contracts and other profane documents. The language remains under all circumstances pure Egyptian in all texts, and even in the latest periods Greek foreign words are few and rare. A special demotic epigraphy was evolved in the Ptolemaic period for official inscriptions on stone.

The development and expansion of demotic was furthered by the growth of trade, characteristic of the XXVth dynasty and the following period, and to a great extent dependent on the resulting demand for written records and communications, but a literary demotic style was developed in Roman times and used for religious texts as well as for profane literature. The script as such remained to a great extent commercial and administrative, and the increasing Greek influence in these fields was responsible for the ultimate decline of demotic, which faded away when Greek in Roman times became the predominant business language and the idiom of the administration.

As a literary script demotic shared the general decline of paganism and died away slowly towards the fourth century.

In the pagan stronghold of Philae, where Nubian tribes maintained and defended the cult of Isis against invading Christianity, the latest graffiti written in demotic dating from 452 A.D., are to be found.

The advance of Christianity became the ultimate fate of all hieroglyphic traditions.

The violently fanatic Christian neophytes could never forget the pagan origin of the old native systems of writing, and they considered them always with suspicious aversion as dangerous manifestations of a cultural and religious tradition, the destruction and annihilation of which they considered their sacred religious duty. Even as demotic, that is in its simplest and most easily accessible form, the script was probably also too complicated and too impractical for the simple followers of the new faith, and it became, therefore, a serious problem for the early Christian propagandists of how to create a new uncontaminated and uncomplicated notation, by means of which the Christian messages could be transmitted in the native tongue. The problem was solved in the most radical and practical manner. Already as early as the beginning of the second century A.D. tentative efforts had been made to use Greek letters for the writing of Egyptian words, mainly in incantations and magical spells, and these efforts were now systematically pursued, with the result that the Egyptian language for the first time in its history, and at the latest stage of its development, in which it is generally known as Coptic[17], was written by means of the ordinary letters of an established alphabet, which, moreover, was not merely consonantic in character, but reproduced the full vocalization of the words. (Pl. III, 2).

The alphabet consists of 31 letters – in the Bohairic dialect of 32 – 25 of which are directly borrowed from Greek, while the remaining 6, expressing sounds particular to Egyptian, are derived from demotic. The alphabet was used for the writing of all Christian literature, whether translated into or composed in Coptic. To this day Coptic is still the liturgic language of the whole of the Coptic church, which includes the Christian communities of Egypt and Abyssinia, and the 6 supplementary letters of its alphabet, all of which through demotic can be traced back to a hieroglyphic prototype, are consequently the last elements of the hieroglyphic tradition still alive and in use. Otherwise the hieroglyphs never became articles of exportation. They were harmonious offsprings of Egyptian civilization and culture and adapted for its particular demands, as well as for those of the Egyptian language, but the inherent shortcomings and deficiencies of the system became immediately apparent as soon as its natural limits were transgressed, as when the hieroglyphs were used for the writing of foreign words and names of non-Egyptian origin. Its influence outside Egypt was, therefore, comparatively small, and only in Nubia did it directly influence the graphic conditions and give rise to new graphic traditions.

Generally speaking Nubia is a rather vague and primarily geographic designation for the Nile valley, such as it extends from the first cataract near Assuan down to the confluence of the Blue and the White Niles.

In antiquity it was inhabited by various tribes of Negro and Negroid origin, and as the most easily accessible territory among the borderlands of Egypt, it became at a very early period a natural goal of Egyptian expansion. Its northern confines were invaded and conquered already by the kings of the Old Kingdom, and the early Pharaohs of the XIIth dynasty occupied the country right down to the fourth cataract, and appointed an Egyptian governor. It regained its independence in the dark periods following the XIIth dynasty, but was reconquered by the belligerent Pharaohs of the XVIIIth dynasty, who made it a closely connected dependency of Egypt governed by an Egyptian viceroy.

The northern parts of the country, at any rate down to the fourth cataract, became from a cultural and administrative point of view very soon completely Egyptianized, but in the South, where the sway of Egypt was maintained with greater difficulty, lo-

31

cal chiefs acquired from about 1000 B.C. sufficient power, influence and wealth to gain their independence, and to found a local royal dynasty and a kingdom of their own, the mysterious Ethiopian kingdom of the later tradition.

We know very little about its early history, but its original capital was the city of Napata, situated in the plains bordered by the huge S created by the bend of the Nile. As far as its organization and its administration are concerned, it was undoubtedly deliberately modelled on the theocracy of Egyptian Thebes, such as it developed in the time after the XXIst dynasty. Ammon was venerated as the official God of the State, and was considered its theoretical ruler, whose oracles were law. The official language, such as it appears in the hieroglyphical inscriptions of the temples and the official records was Egyptian, and it is obvious that the Ethiopian rulers took great pride in, and directly boasted of their dependence on Egyptian culture.

During the general state of national degradation and political dissolution which characterized Egypt under the so-called XXIInd, XXIIInd, and XXIVth dynasties, the Ethiopians became 'plus royalistes que le Roy', affected to disdain the Libyans and the petty dynastic rulers of Egypt, and proclaimed themselves the sole guardians of the true Pharaonic traditions.

During the reign of their king Kashta (about 742 B.C.) they began to invade Egypt, which was eventually conquered by Kashta's successor Piankhi, and he and his successors from now on ruled Egypt as the XXVth dynasty (712-661 B.C.). They were eventually expelled by the Assyrians and forced to retreat to Nubia where the Ethiopian kingdom survived for nearly a thousand years, until it was finally destroyed by the king of Axum in the fourth century of our era. About 300 B.C. the capital was removed somewhat further South to Meroë, but the Egyptian tradition lingered on after all direct ties with Egypt itself had been severed, right down until the first century before Christ, and gave rise to the development of a local script known as Meroïtic writing, found in official inscriptions on temples as well as on potsherds and leather rolls from about the first century B.C. until the end of the third century A.D.

The language in which these records are written is unfortunately an almost entirely unknown local idiom. It is probably related to Nubian, but we are unable to read it, although the script as such has been completely deciphered. Its crude and barbaric signs and symbols are undoubtedly modelled on Egyptian hieroglyphs but constitute an entirely different graphic system.

Its basic Egyptian origin reveals itself in the rudimentary and rare use of ideograms and maybe also in the direction of the script which runs from right to left, although the individual signs, unlike the hieroglyphs, face backwards. The script is essentially phonetic in character, and operates with an alphabet consisting of 23 characters of which 17 are consonantal signs, 4 vowel signs, and 2 syllabic. The individual words are generally separated by dots and the whole system seems to have been efficient and practical. It was used for ornamental inscriptions on stone, as well as for writing on potsherds, wooden tablets and leather rolls[18].

Owing to our ignorance of the language we are unfortunately only able to read single words such as the names of Gods and persons and to a certain extent place names and titles, but the script is important to our knowledge of the history of writing as it represents the only other system developed under the direct influence of the hieroglyphs. It must not be forgotten, however, that our own graphic tradition is probably also connected with that of the hieroglyphs.

It is a well-established fact that our Latin alphabet of today is derived from the Ionic form of the Greek alphabet. The latter is no indigenous invention in itself, but was – probably some time between 1100 and 900 B.C. – borrowed from the Phoenicians, which had developed a phonetic alphabet based on the current North-Semitic graphic traditions[19].

So far the course of the tradition is fairly clear, but the problem of the origin of the early Semitic alphabets is unfortunately still obscure and has been subject to much strife and many controversies. Several basic problems are still unsolved, but the finding of the so-called Sinai inscriptions would seem to indicate where the solution might sometime be found. The peninsular of Sinai – in the Old Testament famous for the mountain of the Covenant – forms a triangle between Egypt, Palestine and Arabia. It was always considered Semitic soil and its population was of Semitic origin, but it was from time immemorial an important centre of communication. One of the oldest trade routes, connecting Egypt and Palestine runs through its northern parts, and, like Nubia, it was from the earliest dynastic times an object of Egyptian expansion, mainly because of its valuable quarries and rich copper mines, which were exploited by Semites as well as Egyptians. About the year 1905 some hitherto unknown inscriptions written in an unknown script were found in the vicinity of one of these quarries, together with a variety of ordinary hieroglyphic inscriptions, which made it possible to date them with great certainty at a period not later than 1500 B.C.

Unfortunately it has not yet been possible to decipher them with certainty, and various theories have been propounded concerning their origin and nature. The most ingenious of these is undoubtedly the one formed by Gardiner[20], who pointed out that some of the signs were undoubtedly borrowed from Egyptian and represented debased Egyptian hieroglyphs with changed sound-values. He gave some very probable decipherings of some recurrent word-groups, demonstrating that the script was apparently phonetic in character, and that the sound-values of the individual letters were derived acrophonically from the Semitic names of the objects represented. If Gardiner's readings should be confirmed by subsequent discoveries, and his theories supported by new material, the consequences would indeed be far-reaching.

Not only would the Sinai inscriptions represent the earliest known Semitic alpha-

33

bet, but if it could be proved the prototype of the later ones, it would become the source of the whole of the subsequent graphic tradition. In this case the Egyptian hieroglyphs used as its letters would become the remote, but nevertheless legitimate ancestors of our own.

Syllabic Writing

Before we can bring the present account of hieroglyphic writing to its final conclusion it will be necessary to consider a couple of its offshoots, which by influencing the course of its evolution added to the complexity of its appearance. The most important of these is undoubtedly the so-called syllabic script, which represents the only deliberate attempt to change the basic character of hieroglyphic writing by the introduction of new phonetic principles.

Several problems concerning the historical background of the new notation are still unsolved, and the exact functions and phonetic values of the individual signs have not yet been established with certainty in all cases, but to the present writer there is no doubt that Albright's[21] explanation of the nature of the new script is fundamentally correct in all essentials, and the following résumé is consequently based on his studies and interpretations, with one formal reservation. The basic characteristic of the new orthography was that it aimed at substituting the phonetically seen imperfect and skeletal 'word-pictures' of the older script, by phonetic renderings of the words as pronounced and spoken. As far as possible each individual sound, consonants as well as vowels, was represented either by separate letters, group-letters or syllabic signs, but the syllabic element was always only one graphic element amongst the others, and it might, therefore, be advisable to stress the alphabetic rather than the syllabic character of the script. This would also make it unnecessary to maintain the rather unnatural distinction between what is generally called 'the new orthography', and syllabic writing, and make both of them represent two, frequently overlapping, stages of one orthographic evolution.

Already in the inscriptions from the Pyramid age we find occasionally that certain hieroglyphic signs have been assigned particular phonetic functions when used in Semitic loan-words, so that for instance 𓅽 was used for the rendering of the Semitic *r* (*reš*) in the word ◿ 𓅽 𓅽 (*kȝm* 'garden' (Heb. *kerem*). At the same time we find also isolated cases in which biliteral signs such as 𓅠 and 𓏮 are used at places where in ordinary orthography the use of the uniliterals 𓏤, *s*, and ◠, *t*, would be expected[22]. Whether the latter spellings at this early date should be explained merely as an irregular employment of the acrophonic principle, or whether orthographic improvements were actually aimed at may be doubtful, but it seems indisputable that the particular orthography developed already during the first intermediate period and extensively used for the rendering of foreign names in the texts from the XIth dynasty, represented a deliberate effort to obtain better, that is phonetically more correct, hieroglyphic transcriptions, than could be achieved by the conventional employment of the signs. Also in this new notation, generally known as the new orthography, ⟦𓅭⟧ is constantly used for Semitic *r* or *l*, while Semitic Aleph is rendered by ⟦𓇋⟧, and we find an extended use of the signs for the weak consonants, which seems to indicate that, in some cases at any rate, they were already used as vowel-indicators[23]. If so, it is only natural to assume that biliteral groups such as ⟦𓈖⟧, ⟦𓄿⟧, and ⟦𓏏⟧, had also begun to obtain syllabic qualities[24].

During the Middle and New Kingdoms the spellings of 'new' Egyptian words such as ⟦𓇋⟧ 'but', ⟦𓂋⟧, 'outside', and ⟦𓇋⟧ 'together with', also became influenced by the new orthography, which undoubtedly was introduced as a deliberate reform in order to overcome certain practical difficulties arising from the purely consonantic character of the old script. The introduction of what is called syllabic writing was probably only one more step in the same direction.

It would seem to have been invented some time before the middle of the XIIth dynasty[25], and operates with a combination of the ordinary uniliteral consonants, a specific use of the uniliteral signs for the weak consonants, certain biliterals mostly ending on ⟦𓅭⟧, ⟦𓂋⟧, ⟦𓅱⟧, or ⟦𓇋⟧, and certain 'groups' such as ⟦𓇋𓏭⟧, ⟦𓄿⟧, ⟦𓏏⟧, and ⟦𓈖⟧. Certain biliterals such as ⟦𓏏⟧, ⟦𓅓⟧, ⟦𓊪⟧, ⟦𓅯⟧, and ⟦𓅆⟧, were generally accompanied by the vertical stroke ⟦𓏤⟧, in ordinary orthography indicating the ideographic employment of the signs. This seems to indicate that the phonetic values they obtained as syllabic elements somehow or other were derived from the Egyptian word for the object they represented.

The word for the bird ⟦𓅯⟧ was presumably pronounced something like *biꜣ and the syllabic value of the sign became consequently *bi*, just as the lion ⟦𓃭⟧ *ruw was used for *ru*, and so on. Of the uniliterals ⟦𓇋⟧ was used for Aleph, while the group ⟦𓇋𓄿⟧ represented *ꜣa*. ⟦𓇋𓅭⟧ stood probably for *ꜣi*, which could also be expressed by ⟦𓏏⟧, or more rarely by ⟦𓇋𓏭⟧. ⟦𓇌⟧ was used for *y*, for *ya*, and, more rarely, for *yi* or *yu*. The other uniliterals retained their ordinary phonetic values, but could be combined with one of the signs for the weak consonants, which then indicated the presence of a vowel and intimated its phonetic timbre or quality so that for instance ⟦𓉔𓅭⟧ was written for *ha*, ⟦𓉔𓏭⟧ for *hi*, and ⟦𓉔𓅱⟧ for *hu*. Theoretically seen it would, therefore, have been possible to discard the use of the biliteral signs altogether, and write ⟦𓇋𓏭⟧ instead of ⟦𓅯⟧ or ⟦𓅆⟧, but this was never done, and the biliterals remained characteristic features of the script throughout its history, but always coordinately with the use of the uniliterals.

Certain details are still obscure and it seems to be a question whether the biliterals

35

were not occasionally used as acrophonic uniliterals, especially when preceded by a written vowel, but the remarkably correct renderings of Semitic loan-words such as ⟨hieroglyphs⟩ *ma-ir-ka-bu-ti(t)* for the Semitic word *markabat(a)*, 'chariot', and ⟨hieroglyphs⟩ *tu-lu-ta* for sult(a), 'flour', demonstrate indisputably the alphabetical, vowel-indicating, nature of the script, which perhaps, as already stated, aught to be stressed more than its syllabic character. The growing intercourse with the East which during the Middle and the New Kingdoms became a dominant feature in the political as well as the cultural development extended the possibilities for the application of syllabic writing.

It was used with increasing frequency for the hieroglyphic rendering of Asiatic place names such as ⟨hieroglyphs⟩ '-s -*ka-lu-na*, Askalon, and ⟨hieroglyphs⟩ '-r-an?-*tu*, Orontes, for the names of Asiatic Gods and Goddesses, such as ⟨hieroglyphs⟩ *ba-al*, Baal, and ⟨hieroglyphs⟩ '-s-*ta-ar-ta(t)*, Astarte, and above all for the names of the ever increasing number of Asiatic princes and individuals who entered into the searchlight of Egyptian policy and were introduced into its annals as friends or foes.

Orthographically seen it would seem to have attained its perfection about the time of Amenophis III, and it was still in full use during the XIXth dynasty[26]; but following the general political and cultural decline which became fatal for the classical orthography it deteriorated rapidly after the XXIst dynasty.

Enigmatic Writing[27]

While group-writing undoubtedly represented a deliberate orthographic reform, and an effort to change some of the fundamental principles of hieroglyphic writing, the so-called enigmatic or cryptographic script was merely a learned play with certain graphic possibilities, compared to that of the Renaissance scholars, who displayed their erudition and their newly acquired knowledge of the Greek letters in writings as: 'nella φδφνρ la β', for 'nella fideltá finira la vita', or 'μφδμλ' for 'mi fideltá mi lauda'.

Seen from a systematic point of view the enigmatic inscriptions involved no changes of the basic graphic rules, and their strange and bizarre appearances were entirely due to the peculiar rebus-like way in which they were written, and in their strange and irregular orthography.

Why this complicated, and from a graphic point of view most unsatisfactory, style was invented, is doubtful.

The texts involved are mostly well-known from ordinary inscriptions written in the conventional orthography, and they are even not infrequently found properly written, right next to the enigmatic ones. It seems hardly possible, therefore, that the intention was merely to conceal the content of the text from the profanes. It is possible that the inscriptions may in some cases have served special magical purposes, but above all it was probably quite simply considered a learned accomplishment to be able to invent new writings, and much erudition and profound mythological knowledge were undoubtedly displayed in the subtle and speculative choice of the enigmatic signs and symbols.

One of the elementary means employed to alter the orthographic appearance of the words was the well-known acrophonic principle, and new spellings were frequently obtained merely by substituting ordinary uniliteral signs by bi- and triliterals, used with the phonetic value of their initial consonants.

The picture of the red crown of Lower Egypt *Nt* was used for *n*, and so was the sign [] generally used for the writing of the name of the goddess Neith of Sais. *tf* 'spit' was used for *t*, and *ḥwj* 'strike' for *ḥ*, and so on. In certain cases signs generally used as determinatives were used as ideograms, such as used for the word *nb* 'master', 'lord'. Several new 'allegorical' ideograms were introduced such as the picture of a man swimming in a pond for the verb *nb* 'swim', or the picture of a running hare for *wnj* 'hasten', 'pass by'. The ordinary spelling of the word *nḏ* 'save', 'revenge', is occasionally substituted by a new hieroglyphic picture representing a woman grinding corn, because the words 'grind' and 'save' were homophones, and the ordinary word *ḫftj* 'enemy' is substituted by a picture of the mythological animal of the God Seth, because Seth was the reputed enemy of Osiris and his son Horus. A new hieroglyphic picture of a chicken inside its egg was used for the ordinary word *imj* 'being in', and a strand of hair was used for the ordinary preposition *ḥrj tp* 'upon', because the original meaning of the latter is 'being upon on the head of'.

As the same writings and pictures are found in a great variety of enigmatic inscriptions we are, in fact, justified in speaking of a specific orthography, and some of them gained admission even to ordinary texts, and became current orthographic features already comparatively early such as the enigmatic writing of the preposition *m ḫnw* 'in the interior of' written with the picture of a bowl ☺ above the ordinary sign for water 〰, because the sentence 'water below bowl' in Egyptian sounds like the preposition.

In other cases these orthographic 'puns' were obviously invented for one specific text only, as when the name of one of the princes from the XXVIth dynasty, Montuemhat–in ordinary orthography written , and signifying something like 'the God Montu is the principal one', – was written merely with the hieroglyphic picture of the God Montu, carrying a sail, because the sentence 'Montu with a sail' sounds like the name Montuemhat.

Generally speaking these efforts are interesting merely for their curiosity, but they did acquire a certain importance for the later orthographic development owing to their unquestionable influence on Ptolemaic writing.

II. The Classical Tradition[1]

As one of the supreme and most original manifestations of the Egyptian genius, and the principal vehicle of Egyptian culture, the hieroglyphical traditions were necessarily doomed with the dissolution of the Egyptian state, and the subsequent disintegration of the nation's religious and political forces.

The script disappeared as a practical instrument of writing and fell victim to the relentless destruction of all reminiscences of pagan cult and belief characteristic of early Christianity.

The tradition died with its priestly bearers, but unlike other systems, which had suffered a similar fate, it continued to occupy the minds of men in a persistent and peculiar way, and left something like a living myth behind it.

From their very first encounter with it, Egypt and Egyptian culture had fascinated the Greeks and aroused their curiosity and interest. The discovery of an age-old civilization, indisputably developed independently of all Hellenic traditions and far away from Hellenic shores, puzzled and intrigued them, because what they learnt about it was hardly compatible with their general conceptions of foreigners (barbar-oi), and conflicted with their often somewhat insular confidence in their own cultural supremacy.

Already the Saïte dynasty (663-525 B.C.) had seen a lively intercourse between Hellas and Egypt. Greek mercenaries had served in the army of Amasis (569-526 B.C.) against the Persians, and as a reward, the Greek merchants had their privileges confirmed and extended in their various settlements in the Delta, amongst which Naucratis was the most prosperous and important.

However, the intercourse between the two countries was by no means merely commercial, and we have ample evidence clearly demonstrating the importance of Egyptian influence on the early development of Hellenic science as well as art.

The Greeks themselves by no means concealed their dependence on a certain Egyptian influence, – they admitted it, in fact, a great deal more willingly than many modern classicists – and we have several reports of Greek artists and scholars visiting Egypt to learn and study[2].

Not all of these can be verified, but authentic evidence remains of the admiration with which several of the most outstanding and prominent representatives of Greek philosophy and thought regarded the knowledge and the wisdom of the Egyptians, and the veneration they felt for their piety and the ancientness of their traditions is clear and unambiguous. The general attitude of the ordinary Greeks towards Egypt and its culture has been aptly compared to that of bygone European generations towards China, and it found a typical expression in Herodotus' remark that the Egyptians "made themselves customs and laws of a kind contrary to those of other men";[3] but the basic differences, which prevented a direct spiritual contact between the two cultures and made it difficult for one to understand the other, went deeper, and were undoubtedly more than conventional.

In most accounts of Greco-Egyptian relations, and above all in the efforts to trace the Egyptian influence on Greek philosophy and religion, it has been insufficiently stressed that it was probably just as difficult for the post-Platonic Greeks to understand Egyptian mentality and the Egyptian way of reasoning, as it is for us. This difficulty cannot be explained merely by pretending that the Egyptians were more 'primitive' than the Greeks, or represented an inferior stage of mental development. It can only be understood when it is realized that there was a basic and fundamental difference in the Egyptian and the Greek conceptions of the phenomena and their nature, and that the former followed different courses from the latter in their efforts to understand and explain them.

It is obvious that the Egyptians had exactly the same means, and the same abilities, for empirical observations of the objects and the phenomena of their world as we have in ours, and fundamentally seen their mental faculties were neither inferior nor different from those of the Greeks or our own, but they had, due to their all-pervading belief in the magical nature of things, and in magic as a basic and ever active force of nature, an entirely different conception of the dynamic processes of the cosmos.

They were perfectly able to follow empirically, and to account for, any ordinary sequence of cause and effect, but the ultima ratio, the dynamic force which originated any process, was in their conception always magical in its nature; and this basic belief influenced the very chain of their reasoning and made it dependent on laws of logic which are incompatible with ours and those of the post-Platonic Greeks from which we have inherited them.

The difficulties arising from these fundamental divergencies are accentuated by another peculiarity of Egyptian thought: its reluctance to form and use abstract concepts, and its characteristic use of concretions, that is tangible concrete words and pictures, to express what we should consider abstract notions and ideas, which again resulted in its dependence on concrete mythical representations in all efforts to form and express a theoretical conception of the nature of things.

Every object and creation had to the Egyptian mind beside its ordinary existence in the material world a mythical existence of its own, dependent on the mythical object or being with which it was identified and the explanations of it expressed in the appropriate legends, and only as mythical manifestations did the material things to the Egyptian mind reveal their true nature.

Visual phenomena, such as the celestial bodies and their movements, could therefore be empirically observed and registered, and the results used for ordinary practical purposes, but a conception of their true nature, and a theoretical explanation of their functions, could only be given in mythical form, as narratives and legends about their mythical counterparts and manifestations. The enormous and ever increasing mythical material of Egyptian theology became consequently the background of all 'theoretical' Egyptian thought. It gave in mythical form the final formulation of all problems, and offered at the same time, in a way which we can hardly fathom or comprehend, their solutions. All Egyptian reasoning, therefore, became necessarily theological speculation, which left no possibility open for the development of an independent logic and an empiric science in our sense of the words. The truth aimed at throughout the whole history of Egyptian thought remained always a concrete mythical truth, expressed in the mythical representations and legends, never, as with the Greeks and ourselves, a scientific or philosophical one, based on empirical observations and logic deductions.

To the post-Aristotelian Greeks in whose systematic thinking remnants of the mythical thought of earlier periods only lived on as archaic rudiments, this Egyptian way of reasoning was just as difficult to understand as it is to us; and in order to conceive and express in their own tongue the Egyptian conceptions of religious and philosophic problems, they had to translate them into the terms of their own logic, and this process invariably involved an interpretation, based on utterly un-Egyptian premises.

This procedure, which is of fundamental importance for the proper understanding of the Greek traditions of Egypt, is very clearly illustrated by the Greek attitude towards the Egyptian mythical material. In Platonic and post-Socratic philosophy the Egyptian myths were always considered in the way in which the Greeks had become accustomed to consider their own, which means that the relationship between myth and reality was considered as being of a symbolic and allegorical nature.

But the establishment of this symbolic relationship was a fundamental misinterpretation of the very basis of Egyptian thought, and substituted the mythical truth of the Egyptians, with its indissoluble magical identification of myth and matter, by an utterly un-Egyptian interpretation created by Greek philosophy and poetry; and nothing makes it more difficult to obtain a true and unbiased picture of the Egyptian influence on Greek philosophy and thought. It is an undeniable fact that the latter right down to its very last days continued to seek inspiration in the study of what it

PLATE II

2. Ornamental hieroglyphs from the time of Ramesses III. XIXth dynasty.

1. The name of Tuthmosis III in cartouche. XVIII dynasty.

3. Section of a page from hieratic text recording the deeds of Ramesses III.

PLATE III

I

1. Section of demotic agreement for the sale of land with banker's receipt in Greek. 163 B.C.

2

Ψαλμος με.
ΠΕΝΝΟΥ†ΠΕΠΕΝ
ιεεεε Ψωτπεεεεπχοιι ''
Πεπβοηθοςπε 2εππεπθλ+Ψι
σε τετχεε τεπεεεεχω ''
Gθβε Ψειπεπερερ† · εqω
πεq ϣεποϥθορ τεπηχεπκε2γ''
Ουο2η τυτοοω τεβπ χεπ τω
υτ·2εππεμ†π τε πεεειου ''
Δτωεγουο2γτεγ θορτερ πχεπι
εειου '' δτεϣορ τεπηχεπ τω
οτ 6εππε Ψειεει ''
Νιοτοιπ τε Ψιεροςεωρσπθκιε
Ψ†οτπο†'' δητυτ βοειτ
ϥεεεληϣω πιπχε Ψκελδος ''
Ουο2 Ψ†ηπε ϥκιεε 2επτε
εεπ† '' Εϥετερβοπθιπεπε σε2
πχεΨ† ''

SYL-

3

PSALTERIUM DAVIDIS.   I

Arab.	Psal. I. David.	Copt.
	Latin. ad verbum de Copt. expreſſ.	
المزمور الاول لداوود		Ψαλμὸς τῷ Δαυίδ ά.
للرجل الذي ١ لم يتبع راي الفاقين ولم يقف في طريق الخاطيين ولم يجلس في مجالس المسخرين ٠	BEATUS ille Vir qui non abiit in conſilio non cultorum Dei, neque ſte- tit in via com- mittentium pec- catum, nec ſedit in cathedra pe- ſtilentium.	OTMAKAPIOCΠE ι ΠΙΡΩΜΙΕΤΕΜΠΕϤ ϢΧΕΧΕΝΠϢΟϢΧΝΙ ΝΤΕΝΙΑϹϹΕΒΗϹ·ϤΟΤ ΔΕΜΠΕϤΌΙΕΡΑΤϤΙϤ ΜΩΙΤΝΤΕΝΙΡΕϤΕΡΝΟ ΒΙ·ΟΤΔΕΜΠΕϤΕΜ ϢΙΤΚΑΘΕΔΡΑΝΤΕ ΝΙΛΟΙΜΟϹ·፥

3. Coptic text printed with Greek letters from Th. Petraeus, Psalterium Davidis, Leyden 1663, an exeedingly rare print containing recommendations from Brian Walton, Isaac Basire and Edward Pococke.

2. First text printed in Coptic with founts made for the Propaganda Fide in 1629.

PLATE IV

1 a

1 b

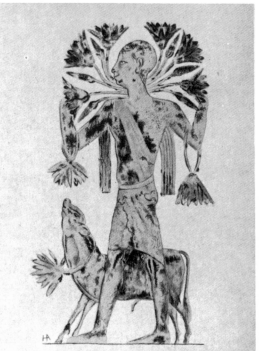

1 a-b. Painted reliefs from the tomb of Petosiris, showing Egyptian art succumbing to Greek influence. About 300 B.C.

2

2. Egyptian landscape from Roman mosaic.

PLATE V

1. Alexandrine Serapis from the Cairo Museum.

2. Roman statue in Egyptian style from the villa of Hadrian at Tivoli. During the Renaissance the general conception of Egyptian art was based mainly on such Egyptianizing Roman sculpture. See plate XIX,3.

3. Statue of Isis from Pompeii.

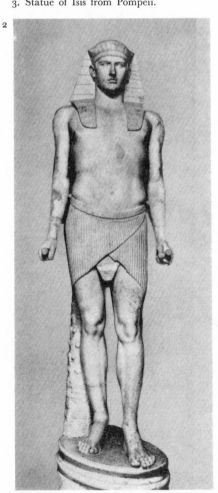

PLATE VI

1. Part of the Isiac table with representations of Osiris, Isis, Thoth, and the Apis. The various decorations of the table recur with great frequency among the Egyptian motives of the Renaissance and the Baroque.

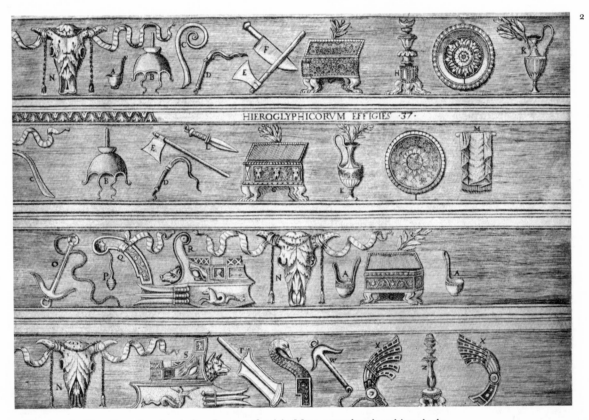

2. The temple frieze from the church San Lorenzo fuori le Mura reproduced as hieroglyphs.

considered the wisdom of the Egyptians, and it is the conviction of the author that it continued to be directly inspired, influenced and stimulated by it to a much greater degree than is generally acknowledged, and only the strange laws governing the relationship of the two cultures make it difficult in most cases to demonstrate and recognize the transformed Egyptian material.

But in no field is the strange cultural relationship between Egypt and Greece better illustrated, and nowhere else are the fatal consequences of the Greek symbolic interpretation of Egyptian facts made more apparent than in the Greek conception of hieroglyphic writing and the subsequent development of the so-called hieroglyphic tradition. Already Herodotus had shown a certain interest in Egyptian writing. He mentioned that the Egyptians wrote from right to left, and that 'they use two kinds of writing, one called sacred (ἱερά), and the other common (δημοτικά)'⁴, and in the last statement he is in accordance with almost the entire subsequent tradition.

None of the Greek writers had any first-hand knowledge of the hieroglyphs. Few of them, if any, spoke Egyptian⁵, and their reports on the writing of the Egyptians were in all cases based on more or less superficial hearsay evidence. None of them had taken the trouble to get acquainted with the practical and theoretical problems of the system, and, irrespective of their insufficiency, certain conceptions were generally accepted and acknowledged and uncritically handed over from one author to another.

In accordance with these conceptions the Egyptians were supposed to have used two different scripts, a sacred, symbolical or allegorical one, by which the Greeks always understood the actual monumental hieroglyphs, and an ordinary one, which they called demotic, epistolographic or enchorial – of ἐγχώριος 'indigenous' –, used for all ordinary purposes of daily life. By the latter they probably always understood what we call demotic, ignoring the existence of what we understand by hieratic.

Porphyry mentions in an otherwise very obscure passage 'three kinds of Egyptian letters'⁶, but Clement of Alexandria⁷ is the only ancient authority who gives a fairly clear indication of the fact that the Egyptians used three different kinds of writing, which he calls epistolographic (i. e. demotic), hieratic, and hieroglyphic, and he gives us a fairly sensible account of the particular functions of each, to which we shall revert later.

As a general rule it may be said that none of the classical authors knew what they were writing about as far as the hieroglyphs were concerned, although most of them, maybe more or less unconsciously, tried to cover their ignorance with the pompous cloak of a learned 'philosophic' terminology.

But the charming scene in Apuleius' 'Golden Ass' describing Lucius' initiation into the mysteries of Osiris gives in its 'naïveté' and unpretentious simplicity what is probably a truer picture of what the average Greek knew and understood about the hieroglyphs than most of the learned and pretentious elucidations. We are told how the old priest: 'brought out of the secret place of the temple certain books written with unknown characters, partly painted with figures of beasts, declaring briefly every sentence, partly with letters whose tops and tails turned round in fashion of a wheel, joined together above like unto the tendrils of a vine, whereby they were wholly strange and impossible to be read of the profane people'[8].

However, it was not by all Greeks that the hieroglyphs were considered merely as strange and foreign objects of curiosity, and there was in particular one problem which fairly early made the Greek philologists consider with true scientific interest the relations between the Greek and the Egyptian systems of writing, the question about the origin of their own alphabet. But even those did not take the trouble to make themselves properly acquainted with the systematic problems of the script, and their ideas about its nature were always very vague and mostly erroneous. It is nevertheless a pleasure to observe the true scientific spirit in which they openly acknowledged their graphic dependence on their 'barbaric' predecessors, and to see how close their conceptions of the graphic traditions in certain respects came to what has later been established as the truth.

Already Plato tells us in the Philebus how 'a certain Theuth' – if I understand the obscure text rightly – was the first to observe that the 'infinity of sound' could be divided up into distinctive categories, such as vowels, consonants, and what are termed 'mutes'[9]; and in isolating the individual elements of sound in each of these categories 'until he knew the number of them', he became the discoverer of the concept of letters, not necessarily as graphic, but as phonetic elements.

The same Theuth is also mentioned in the Phaedrus[10], where we are explicitly told that he was an ancient Egyptian God, 'the one whose sacred bird is called the Ibis', so as to exclude all doubt about his identity. He is said to have been the inventor of numbers, of arithmetic, geometry, and astronomy, of the games of draughts and dice, and 'most important of all, of letters'.

It is obvious from the context that Plato here speaks about letters as graphic elements, but his use of the word 'letters' (γράμματα) does not necessarily imply that he considered Thoth the inventor of a proper alphabet in our sense of the word.

On the contrary, a comparison with corresponding accounts from other Greek authors on the same subject makes it pretty certain that he quite simply considers him as the inventor of writing as such.

It is obvious that his account is based on a genuine Egyptian tradition, because the Ibis-headed Thoth was, in fact, the Egyptian God of science and letters and the reputed inventor of the hieroglyphs.

Plato's explanation was generally accepted by most subsequent scholars although with certain modifications. The Egyptian Thoth, – who in Greek literature is considered as a God, or Demi-God, or quite simply as an ancient Egyptian philosopher, and frequently appears in the texts under the name of Hermes or the Egyptian Hermes, – was universally considered the original inventor of the art of writing, and was accepted as such also by the Romans, who called him by his Latin name Mercurius[11].

A few authors, Pliny[12], for instance, seem inclined to assign the priority to Accadian cuneiform writing, but seem unable to support their divergent views with actual evidence, and Diodorus[13] speaks in a vague and obscure way about Ethiopian hieroglyphs as being older than the Egyptian ones, but otherwise the Egyptians were throughout antiquity acknowledged as the true and original inventors of writing, although not always of phonetic writing.

The question about the introduction of phonetic letters, the invention of true phonetic writing, and the ensuing problem about the origin of the Greek and Latin alphabets, remained subject to some disagreement and much discussion.

Almost all classical writers agree unanimously as to the important part played by the Phoenicians in the transmission of the fundamental principles of an alphabet consisting of phonetic letters, which became the direct prototype of the Ionian alphabet; and there was even a tendency to credit them with the invention of it.

Lucan tells us: 'These Phoenicians first made bold, if report speaks true, to record speech in rude characters for future ages, before Egypt had learned to fasten together the reeds of her river, and when only the figures of birds, beasts, and other animals, carved in stone, preserved the utterances of her wise men'[14].

However, the most concise account of the graphic evolution, and that which comes closest to what modern science has taught us to be the true one, was given by Tacitus[15]: 'The Egyptians, in their animal-pictures, were the first people to represent thought by symbols: these, the earliest documents of human history, are visible today, impressed on stone. They describe themselves also as the inventors of the alphabet: from Egypt, they consider, the Phoenicians, who were predominant at sea, imparted the knowledge into Greece and gained the credit of discovering what they had borrowed'.

It will be seen that insight into the nature of the hieroglyphs as such, and knowledge of the practical problems of the script were of secondary importance for these historical investigations, but the focus of interest shifted as time went on, and speculations concerning the meaning and the true nature of the signs came, in an ever-increasing way, to occupy the minds of the Greek scholars. However, even in their most serious efforts to become informed, the Greeks were invariably impeded by their ignorance of the Egyptian language, which made it impossible for them to understand the basic principles of the script, and made them victims of certain fundamental misconceptions as to its nature.

They refused to acknowledge the phonetic functions of the signs, even in those cases where they explicitly spoke of them as 'letters', and they ignored entirely the distinction between the various elements of the script, such as ideograms, determinatives and phonetic signs, and many a mistake in their interpretation of the meaning of hieroglyphical inscriptions are quite simply due to their ignorance of the difference between determinatives and ideograms[16]. Another source of frequent misunderstandings was the fact that they did not always distinguish between ordinary hieroglyphs and the iconographic representations frequently accompanying the inscriptions, and several otherwise enigmatic 'hieroglyphic' interpretations become understandable when it is realized that they are not based on hieroglyphic inscriptions at all, but are iconological explanations of reliefs, ornamental motifs, or conventional religious symbols[17].

The information they acquired from their Egyptian hosts concerning Egyptian writing was, therefore, always received with preconceived ideas, and only partly understood. It was obviously impossible for the former when asked to explain a representation or an inscription to interpret its meaning, and at the same time explain the technical principles of iconography and writing. When informed about the meaning of any hieroglyphic group or any iconographic representation, the Greeks would consequently remain ignorant about the true relationship between words and pictures.

When told for instance that the picture of an old man leaning on a stick was used to express the word 'old', they were unable to conceive the true graphic significance of the sign, and the phonetic implications involved.

But, what they did not understand they would interpret in their own manner; and in accordance with their general conception of the natural relations between form and substance, matter and idea, they would quite naturally also here, establish an allegorical connection between word and sign, and consider the latter a 'symbolic' expression of the former. We find this symbolic or allegorical conception of the nature of the hieroglyphs clearly expressed already by Diodorus[18], who states that: 'their – the Egyptians' – writing does not express the intended concept by means of syllables joined one to another, but by means of the significance of the objects which have been copied, and by its figurative meaning which has been impressed upon the memory by practice. For instance they draw the picture of a hawk, a crocodile . . . . . and the like. Now the hawk signifies to them everything which happens swiftly, since this animal is practically the swiftest of winged creatures. And the concept portrayed is then transferred, by the appropriate metaphorical transfer, to all swift things and to everything to which swiftness is appropriate, very much as if they had been named. And the crocodile is a symbol of all that is evil.'

This metaphorical and symbolical conception of the hieroglyphs was unanimously accepted by all subsequent writers on the subject, and it was as a matter of fact their

44

supposed allegorical qualities which henceforward to an ever increasing extent intrigued and fascinated the Greeks.

It is true that Clement of Alexandria[19] about 200 A.D. gave an account of the hieroglyphs which in certain respects would seem to be based on a less conventional conception of the system, and suggested the existence of phonetic signs. But the metaphorical and allegorical qualities of the hieroglyphs are at the same time explicitly mentioned, and his examples are expounded in the same symbolic way as those of earlier writers, among which those of Plutarch are of special interest.

In his treatise on Isis and Osiris, which is one of the most instructive sources for our understanding of the Greek conception of Egyptian religious ideas, he mentions the hieroglyphs and their metaphorical and mythological significance in several places.

One paragraph in particular is important for the understanding of his conception of their nature[20]. He gives an extensive list of distinguished Greeks who at different times were supposed to have visited Egypt, and amongst them is also mentioned Phytagoras whose admiration and dependence on 'the symbolic and occult teachings' of the Egyptians is emphasized and illustrated by a comparison of the allegorical method used in the so-called Pythagorean precepts, and 'the writings that are called hieroglyphs'[21]. In these precepts ordinary proverbial expressions were expounded allegorically, so that the simple phrase 'do not poke a fire with steel' gets the secret meaning of 'do not provoke an angry man'. 'Abstain from beans' means that a man should keep out of politics, and 'do not put food in a slop-pail' signifies that it is not fitting to put clever speech into a base mind. In Plutarch's opinion the allegorical method used in these expoundings illustrated the basic principle of hieroglyphic writing, which actually in his conception, was not ordinary writing at all, but pictorial, rebus-like, expressions of divine ideas and sacred knowledge.

Knowledge easily presented and acquired was not esteemed in antiquity, because, as Clement[22] has expressed it somewhat later, 'the mysteries of the word is not to be expounded to the profane,' and 'all things that shine through a veil show the truth grander and more imposing.' The mysterious symbolic qualities with which Greek ignorance of their true character endowed the hieroglyphs, became, therefore, their main charm and attraction. They became, in an ever-increasing way, recurrent topics in the philosophical debate of the times, and the final wording of what henceforward should become their accepted canonical definition was framed by Plotinus (204 or 5-270 A.D.) through the intervention of whom the subsequent hieroglyphic studies of Western science and philosophy became inextricably bound up with Neo-Platonism, right down until the eighteenth century.

It was Plotinus'[23] opinion that the Egyptians, either by exact science or spontaneously, had arrived at a method by means of which they could write with distinct pictures of material objects, instead of ordinary letters expressing sounds and forming words and phrases. These pictures were not merely ordinary images of the things they represented, but were endowed with certain symbolic qualities (sophia), by means of which they revealed to the initiated contemplator a profound insight into the very essence and substance of things, and an intuitive understanding of their transcendental origin, an insight which was not the result of reasoning or mental reflection, but was acquired spontaneously by means of divine inspiration and illumination. As artistic representations of the phenomenal objects, they revealed, in fact, the ideal world of the soul.

In this interpretation, and with Plotinus' authority behind them, the hieroglyphs ceased to be mere objects of curiosity or historical interest.

They became illustrations of a Neo-Platonic conception of the allegorical nature of things, and as such they remained integral elements of the philosophical discussions of the period until the interest in them waned away, characteristically enough together with Neo-Platonism itself, which ceased to exist as a living philosophical system towards the beginning of the sixth century.

But in the intervening period after Plotinus, the interest remained as great as ever in Neo-Platonic circles, and quite an extensive hieroglyphic literature arose written in Greek, which, together with the socalled Hermetic writings[24], and books such as Iamblichus'[25] treatise on the Egyptian mysteries, bear illuminating evidence of the widespread Hellenistic interest in what was supposed to be Egyptian philosophy and mysticism[26].

With one important exception all works dealing specifically with hieroglyphic questions have been lost, but the existence of quite an extensive literature on the subject can be established with certainty from quotations and references found in the works of various subsequent authors.

We know that the renowned Alexandrian scholar Chairemon was the author of a treatise on the hieroglyphs, to which several references are found in contemporary literature[27], and from which the Byzantine grammarian Tzetzes[28], who lived in Constantinople sometime during the twelfth century, has taken the material for a digression on hieroglyphs, found in his commentary on the Iliad.

Chairemon[29] lived in the first half of the first century of our era, first as a priest and pedagogue in Alexandria, and after 49 A.D. in Rome whither he was summoned to become the tutor of Nero. He was well known as the author of several works on grammatical, historical and astronomical subjects, was especially interested in Egyptian matters, and famous for a history of Egypt, unfortunately lost.

His cultural background was undoubtedly Hellenistic and not Egyptian, and as far as we are able to judge from Tzetzes' excerpts, his conceptions of the hieroglyphs did not differ essentially from those of other classical authors on the subject, which is obvious from the very use Tzetzes makes of them. In this commentary Tzetzes went in for an allegorical expounding of the Iliad, and quotes Chairemon's hieroglyphs only to prove that his allegorical method is identical with that of Homer, and that the latter had become acquainted with it through hieroglyphical studies. The examples do not give the faintest indication of any knowledge of the phonetic qualities of the signs, and they are explicitly chosen to illustrate the allegorical nature of the script. Chairemon describes 19 hieroglyphs followed by an explanation of the allegorical significance of each in strictest conformity with the methods we have already met with in the works of Diodorus and Plutarch. It is obvious, however, that Chairemon must necessarily have had access to, or consulted an authority with a proper knowledge of the script, because all his allegorical explanations are, in fact, based on an element of truth, and often derived from the actual significances of the signs in their various uses as ideograms or determinatives in hieroglyphic texts. A weeping eye is said to designate the concept 'misfortune', and the hieroglyph 𓁸, representing an eye with flowing tears, is, in fact, used as a determinative in the verb 'weep' and related words. Two empty hands extended are said to express negation, and the hieroglyph 𓂜, with which the ordinary negation of the classical language is generally written, represents, in fact, two arms with the hands in the gesture of negation, with the phonetic value *n*. A snake crawling out of its hole is said to signify the rising of a star, while the same animal entering a hole is said to mean its decline, and the two hieroglyphs in question 𓂻 and 𓂺 are, in fact, late ideograms for the two verbs 'go out' and 'enter', in astronomical texts used as terminological expressions for the rising and setting of stars.

Generally speaking we find the same theoretical conceptions and the same methods applied in the only true hieroglyphic treatise preserved from classical antiquity, the 'Hieroglyphics' of Horapollo. (Pl. X, 1).

Nothing can be said with any amount of certainty about the origin of the book, or about its author. The manuscript, which was found in Greece in the early fifteenth century, contains a few introductory lines stating that the book was originally written in Egyptian by Horapollo from Nilopolis, and subsequently translated into Greek by one Philippos. The author cannot with certainty be identified with any known scholar by the name of Horapollo, the translator is entirely unknown, and his Greek is bad, but if the tradition is true, it would be the only existing case in which a book is known to have been translated from Egyptian into Greek in its entirety.

There are certain indications that it was written not before, and not very long after, the fourth century A.D., and the translation is probably not very much younger[30].

It consists of two books, one containing 70 chapters, the other 119, each dealing with one particular hieroglyph[31]. Each chapter has a short heading describing either the hieroglyph itself in simple terms, as for instance 'the explanation of the picture of a falcon' (I.6), or else stating the nature of the allegorical subject to be explained, such as 'how to signify eternity' (I.1), or 'how to signify the universe' (I.2). The relations between sign and meaning were according to Horapollo always of an allegorical nature, and it was always established by means of exactly the same sort of 'philosophical' reasoning which we find later in the Physiologus and the bestiaries of the Middle Ages[32].

We are told that the goose is used to express the word 'son' (I.53), because this animal more than any other is supposed to love its offspring. The vulture is used to express the concept 'mother' because male vultures do not exist, and so on; but in spite of this misconception of the nature of the script, there is nevertheless in the greater part of his explanations a fundamental element of truth. Almost all of the allegorical expoundings can more or less directly be traced back either to the actual hieroglyphical meaning of the signs, or be explained from one of their specific employments as graphic elements, exactly as we have seen it to be the case in Chairemon's commentary.

In ordinary hieroglyphic writing the word 'son' is actually written with the picture of a goose, because the words for son and goose are homonymous in Egyptian, and the word 'mother' is written with the picture of a vulture for the same reason. We are told (I.47) that the ear of an ox signifies 'hearing', and the hieroglyphic picture of an ox's ear is, in fact, used as a phonetic element in the word 'hear' and as an ideogram for the word 'ear' itself. The hare is said to be used for 'what is open' (I.26), and the picture of this animal is actually used as a phonetic element in the word 'open'.

If, as a matter of fact, Horapollo had confined himself to state quite simply that the pictures of the goose, the vulture, the ear, and the hare were used in the writing of the words for 'son', 'mother', 'hear', and 'open', he would actually have been right in all cases[33].

It is unfortunate that we are entirely ignorant of the sources from which Horapollo's information was obtained, but it is obvious that somehow or other they must, either orally or literary, be connected with true hieroglyphical traditions from a period in which a first-hand knowledge of the system was still alive; and it is significant that the information given, implies a knowledge of the late as well as the classical orthography[34]. But it is equally characteristic that he never ventures to combine his individual hieroglyphs into sentences or phrases[35], and quite a considerable part of his actual information is undoubtedly directly erroneous.

Like Plutarch he gives a description of pictures which were not of hieroglyphic origin at all, but ordinary religious representations and illustrations[36]; and he describes a substantial number of professed hieroglyphical motifs which were never represented in any form or shape in Egyptian art or writing such as 'a lion eating a monkey' (II.76), or a 'horse's carcass' (II.44). These, together with others which would seem difficult to depict – although the Renaissance artists did, in fact, succeed with some of them such as 'a man eating the hours', 'a blind beetle', and 'crocodile's blood', – are presumably of Horapollo's own invention, but the deficiencies and misconceptions of his book were never discovered by antiquity.

In the subsequent tradition of the Renaissance the book became, as we shall see, the canonical authority on all hieroglyphic questions, and was regarded with something like a sacred awe, as the only 'authentic' evidence of the hieroglyphic wisdom of the Egyptians.

It was among the very first books printed after the invention of the art, and we shall trace its influence on European art and literature in the following chapters. For the development of Egyptology the book became fatal, because its contorted, but from a speculative, artistic as well as literary, point of view fascinating, conception of the hieroglyphs, impeded the rediscovery of their true nature for centuries.

The tenacity with which the classical authors stuck to their erroneous interpretations and, as it were, deliberately disregarded all evidence which could conflict with their preconceived allegorical ideas, is indeed astonishing. Several of them must undoubtedly have been acquainted with such texts as the bilingual decrees frequently issued in Ptolemaic times, and often inscribed on stelae carrying identical inscriptions in Greek and Egyptian. (Pl. XXII). Many must have known about the existence of an extensive Egyptian literature frequently mentioned in classical sources, and including many subjects and genres known to the Greek themselves, and it is hard to believe that they should have considered it possible that all this could have been expressed by means of allegorical symbols alone. The explanation is, that what interested the Greeks was not Egyptian writing at all; but from their own 'Platonic' interpretation of the relation between sign and meaning in Egyptian hieroglyphs, grew the idea of the existence of a true symbolic system of writing in which abstract notions and ideas could be expressed by means of concrete pictures of material objects[37].

This was the idea which fascinated the Greeks and occupied their fantasy and imagination, and the hieroglyphs as such interested them only insofar as they could be used to manifest and illustrate it. But in the very midst of this strange and unpenetrable jungle of errors and misconceptions we find, like the delicate shoots of original corn growing amongst the weeds in an abandoned field, isolated and sporadic traces of a better and truer tradition in the scanty remnants of Greek translations of original Egyptian texts, among which the rendering of the inscription from one of the Roman obelisks found in the history of the Roman historian Ammianus Marcellinus is the most extensive and the most important[38].

Ammianus, who lived from about 325 A.D. to sometime after 391, was a Greek who wrote in Latin an extensive history of the Roman empire, covering the period from the accession of the emperor Nerva (96 A.D.) until the death of Valerianus in 378 A.D.[39].

Only the last eighteen books are preserved, giving a detailed account of the period between 353 and 378, and the seventeenth includes the history of the obelisk which the emperor Constantine in the year 357 erected in the Circus Maximus; the obelisk gave Ammianus an opportunity to display his erudition in a short digression on obelisks and Egyptian writing in general[40]. His account of the latter subject is couched in conventional terms: 'For not as nowadays when a fixed and easy series of letters express whatever the mind of man may consider, did the ancient Egyptians also write, but individual characters stood for individual nouns and verbs; and sometimes they meant whole phrases'[41]. This brief explanation is accompanied by a couple of examples displaying the usual metaphorical conception of the signs. But in the course of his enumeration of the other Roman obelisks, he also mentions 'the ancient obelisk which we see in the Circus'[42], and its inscription, of which he quite unexpectedly gives an extensive translation into Greek, said to be quoted 'from the work of Hermapion'. Nothing is known with certainty about the latter author or his work, but he was probably one of the numerous Hellenistic scholars living in Rome about the time of Augustus[43].

It cannot be established with absolute certainty that his text is actually a translation of the Flaminian obelisk[44], but it was undoubtedly an authentic translation of a genuine Egyptian inscription. (Pl. VIII).

The Greek text has suffered pitifully in the course of its tradition, and it is only partly preserved, but although it is by no means a literal, or even a careful philological translation, the original text has nevertheless been followed closely enough to permit a reconstruction of substantial parts of the original text by comparing it with that of the closely related Flaminian obelisk. It is obvious that the meaning of many stereotyped Egyptian passages could only be rendered approximately and in a paraphrased way in Greek, and the translation displays indisputable errors and misunderstandings, but the correctness of several phrases are proved from their identity with those of official Greek translations found on monuments such as the Rosetta stone, where the original hieroglyphic text is also preserved. There can be no doubt that the translation, in spite of its shortcomings, gives a fairly adequate picture of the original text, and it must undoubtedly have been made by somebody conversant with the fundamental principles of the script and able to read and understand the signs, and we have, in fact, irrefutable evidence of the existence and the activity of such hierogrammates living in Rome and Italy, hierogrammates who were not only able to read hieroglyphic texts and translate them, but were even able to compose conventional hieroglyphic inscriptions.

All of them are anonymous, but most of them were probably Alexandrine Greeks brought over to the new 'temple of all the world', in the train of that strange cultural development which, at the late eve of its history, should make Egyptian religion ex-

PLATE VII

1. The Pyramid of Cestius in Rome which right down until the eighteenth century served as a model for most representations of Egyptian pyramids.

2. The Vatican obelisk now standing in front of St. Peter's in Rome, in its original position next to the old church. It was the only Roman obelisk still standing at the beginning of the Renaissance.

3. The Pamphilian obelisk at the Piazza Navona was originally erected by Domitian. Its hieroglyphic inscription, celebrating the emperor and the Flavian family was the first to be used on a public monument outside Egypt.

PLATE VIII

The Flaminian obelisk on the Piazza del Popolo seen from Monte Pincio. It was the first Egyptian obelisk transported to Rome by Augustus, and its inscription is probably the one translated in the history of Ammianus Marcellinus.

pansive and cosmopolitan, and make it exert a momentous influence on the classical world: the spread of the cults of Isis and Serapis[45]. (Pl. V, 1 and 3).

Isis belonged to the oldest creations of Egyptian theology, and occurs frequently in the Pyramid-Texts of the Old Kingdom. Mythologically seen she was always considered the devoted sister-wife of Osiris, and the ardent loving mother of his son Horus. Her popularity and religious significance grew steadily through the ages, and when the gradual decline of the old religion of state, centered around the Gods Rē and Ammon, gained speed after the dissolution of the Egyptian empire, the importance of Osirianism increased proportionately. In later periods he had undoubtedly become the dominant factor in the religious life of the country.

From the King of the dead, Osiris became the God of the living[46], and the religious importance of Isis rose accordingly. Little by little she absorbed and assimilated most of the religious and cultic functions of the other goddesses, and from the last centuries before our era her position as the great mother-goddess of Egypt was unchallenged. She was universally revered throughout the country, and the ascent of the Ptolemaic dynasty meant the final acknowledgement of her official position in the new state cult.

Policy and religion had always been inextricably connected throughout the history of Egypt. The predominant political influence of monarchy, and the fundamental belief in its divine origin and in the divine nature of the king, gave a religious aspect to all political problems.

In accordance with the general principles of mythical thinking, all political events, and above all the ascent of a new dynasty, had to be mythically motivated and registered. Its religious acknowledgement was generally achieved by an adjustment of the mythical position of the tutelary deity of the dynasty, or the God of whom the new king considered himself a relation or a manifestation. This had happened in the case of Horus, Rē, and Ammon, and we have seen how the original state religion of the latter had lost its importance and raison d'être with the dissolution of the Theban empire it reflected.

In the period of foreign domination it carried on a shadowy existence amongst the fanatic clergy of remote Thebes, with its ruined and impoverished temples and its memories of ancient glory, henceforward the traditional centre of nationalistic revolts and religious disturbances.

From the very outset of their rule the Ptolemies were, therefore, faced with enormous problems of a political as well as a religious character. Their ascent had raised the Greeks to a privileged ruling class and reduced the Egyptians to the status of subject natives; but certain efforts to reconcile the religious divergencies of the two new classes were nevertheless considered necessary for the maintenance of the balance and the political unity of the state. Religious means should once more serve political ends by the introduction of a new religion of state, and it was only natural that the re-

51

forming efforts should be based on the cult of Osiris as the most influential religious movement of the country, and not on Rē or Ammon, compromised by their connection with the national reaction. It is probably also significant that the manifestation chosen to represent Osiris in the new creed connected him directly with the old God Ptah from Memphis, who from the very outset of Egyptian history had a particular relation to the monarch and the monarchical idea. The sacred bull of Memphis, the so-called Apis, was in Memphite theology considered a manifestation of Ptah, but with the spread of Osirianism the dead bull, became more and more considered a manifestation of Osiris, and was henceforward worshipped separately under the name of Usar-Hapi. This Usar-Hapi or, as the Greeks called him, Osorapis, was in grecized form made the central figure in the new cult.

The Greek God Pluto of Sinope was said to have appeared to Ptolemy in a dream, and his statue was transported from Sinope to Alexandria to represent the new god, henceforward known under the name of Serapis. The centre of his cult was his temple Serapeum in Alexandria, his liturgic language as well as his canonical appearance was Greek, and as such he was never introduced into the orthodox Egyptian temples where he was always considered a form of Osiris, but he became tremendously popular and was fervently worshipped and revered not only in Egypt but all over the Hellenistic world and in Rome, generally together with Isis, with whom he, as a manifestation of Osiris, was intimately connected. (Pl. V, 1).

The cult of Isis had already at a much earlier period begun to spread outside Egypt, and she was worshipped in the Syrian part of Asia Minor already about the seventh century B.C. As the tutelar deity of Egyptian sailors and merchants her influence rose steadily with the growth of trade, and spread to most of the principal ports and trading centres of the Mediterranean. From Byblos and Crete she had come to Athens probably as early as the fifth century; but from the time of her connection with Serapis the two cults spread together with irresistible force and rapidity, first all over the Greek world and eventually, in the last centuries before Christ, also in Italy, Rome, and the empire.

The progress of the new cult was not always welcomed by conservative and orthodox circles, and in the days of the late Roman republic the goddess and her priests were on several occasions expelled from the city. But her influence could be neither quenched nor stemmed.

Caligula (37-41 A.D.) built her a temple in Rome itself, although outside the sacred precincts of the city, but Vespasian (69-79 A.D.), Domitian (81-96) and Hadrian (117-138), all favoured the cult of the goddess and Serapis, and Caracalla (211-217) built her a temple on the Quirinal hill, which inaugurated her final acknowledgement as one of the official deities of Rome and the state.

Henceforward her position was only challenged by Christianity, and it is significant

52

that the temple of Isis on the island of Philae was almost the last pagan temple in use until it was forcibly closed by Justinian (527-565). As long as their cults flourished, the priesthood attached to the temples of Isis as well as of Serapis, was to a great extent made up of Egyptians or Greco-Egyptians, many of whom were probably of Alexandrine origin, or at any rate educated at the Serapeion there, and the local sanctuaries became, therefore, as many enclaves of Alexandrine culture. In spite of their bad reputation, many were undoubtedly true initiates and scholars, conversant with hieroglyphic writing and able to read the texts.

A certain Harnouphis, accompanying the Roman army in the official capacity of a priest of Isis during the reign of Marcus Aurelius (161-180 A.D.), is explicitly called 'an Egyptian scholar' on the altar which he dedicated to Isis in the city of Aquileia[47], and it is undoubtedly in circles such as these that the hieroglyphic traditions of the early empire were kept alive, and from which originated the curious fancy for things Egyptian which had spread all over Italy as a genteel fashion already during the later years of the republic. Almost everywhere, from Pompeii and Herculaneum to the villa of Hadrian at Tivoli, and even in Rome itself, we find evidence of this Egyptian influence on art and decoration, from now on abounding in Egyptian motives, Egyptian ornaments, and sculptural representations imitating Egyptian forms and style. (Pl. IV, 2. V, 2. VII, 1).

It is evident that certain artists and craftsmen must have specialized in this particular style, and some of them had even acquired the necessary technical skill to carve hieroglyphs and make hieroglyphic inscriptions, for which there was quite a demand in the first couple of centuries after Christ, owing to the imperial fashion of erecting and dedicating obelisks. Augustus (30 B.C.-14 A.D.) was the first to undertake the immense task of transporting original Egyptian obelisks to Rome, and in so doing he created a precedent, and spurned the architectural ambitions of his successors to such an extent that Rome was eventually said to possess no less than 42 obelisks, apart from those mentioned by Pliny and Ammianus Marcellinus[48]. Very soon it became difficult or even impossible to find any more original Egyptian obelisks with inscriptions, and to supply the demand new ones had to be quarried either in Egypt or in Italy. (Pl. VIII).

These were obviously without inscriptions, but uninscribed obelisks were apparently considered inferior and in a deplorable way less ostentatious than inscribed ones. It became customary, therefore, to provide uninscribed obelisks with new inscriptions, apparently executed by local craftsmen in Rome itself. The so-called Sallustian obelisk is a typical example. Its origin is obscure, but it is supposed to have been quarried in Egypt, brought to Rome by one of the earlier emperors, and to have been placed in the Circus of Sallustius. In modern times (1792) it was re-erected opposite the church of Trinità dei Monti.

It is provided with a hieroglyphic inscription, but its unorthodox appearance, and the rude and barbaric character of its signs puzzled the early Egyptologists, until it was established that the inscription was a Roman fake, representing an old copy of the text of the Flaminian obelisk, evidently made by Roman artists some time during the early empire. It is obvious, however, that a copied inscription could only serve decorative and ornamental purposes and in no way contribute to the fame and glory of the dedicator. From the time of Domitian (81-96 A.D.) it became customary, therefore, to order original dedicatory inscriptions made by Egyptian scholars either in Alexandria or in Rome, and to have them executed by local craftsmen. Such is the case with the Pamphilian obelisk, employed by Domitian for his magnificent extension of the Serapeum on the Campus Martius, and since 1651 placed on the Piazza Navona. (Pl. VII, 3).

We do not know the composer of the text, but he was undoubtedly a competent scholar, able to write and read the hieroglyphs and conversant with the style of dedicatory inscriptions of original Egyptian obelisks.

His inscription is dedicated to the Sun-God Harakhte, called 'the father of Domitian', and the text is strictly conventional in its use of the appropriate titles and epithets, which are in true 'Pharaonic' style, and in part copied from the inscriptions of Ptolemaic obelisks which the author must have been able to read.

It contains a few topical allusions, such as a reference to the Flavian family, to Vespasian the father of the emperor, and to Titus his brother. The hieroglyphs are barbaric, flat and strangely extended in breadth, and to a certain extent reminiscent of those found on Roman monuments in Egypt, but utterly un-Egyptian in style and appearance. But they retain all the main characteristics of the traditional signs, and were undoubtedly made in Rome and by Roman craftsmen[49].

But it was apparently not the temples of Rome alone which could boast of hieroglyphic scholars, and the tradition seems to have been alive also at the minor sanctuaries of the provinces.

It would seem highly improbable that a provincial citizen like that Lucilius Rufus, who in the year 88 A.D. dedicated two minor obelisks to the emperor Domitian and erected them at the temple of Isis in his home town of Beneventum, should have procured the text for his dedicatory inscription directly from Egypt. As a matter of fact we can probably take it for granted that they were made by a member of the local college of priests[50]. Nevertheless they are amazingly true to style and remarkably correct, the hieroglyphs even being less barbaric than those on the emperor's own obelisk. However, the tradition declined with remarkable rapidity. The obelisk called Barberinus, now placed on Monte Pincio, is by less than half a century separated from that of Domitian, but the difference between the two monuments is unmistakable. It is dedicated to Harakhte by Hadrian (117-138) in commemoration of his favourite Antinous, who had committed suicide by drowning himself in the Nile (130 A.D.), presumably to avert an evil omen from the emperor. In the excess of his grief Hadrian took excessive and exceptional steps to commemorate the deceased who was deified and worshipped at different places, mainly in Greece and Egypt. A new city, Antinoöpolis, was founded near the place of the accident, and a magnificent tomb or cenotaph was erected in his honour in Rome, and adorned with the obelisk in question. As was generally the case with Roman obelisks, it was dedicated to Harakhte by the emperor in his official capacity of 'Son of the Sun' and 'King of Egypt', but contrary to ordinary practice not as a monument of Hadrian himself, but of 'Osiris Antinous'.

As far as the official titles and epithets of the king and the various Gods are concerned, the text is still correct and conventional, but its eulogy on the deified favourite is unique, and represents a definite break with all traditional obelisk inscriptions. Antinous speaks in the inscription as a resurrected God, and asks Harakhte to bless the reign of Hadrian. He has been granted eternal youth by Thoth, and been received as an equal amongst the Gods of Egypt. The establishment of his official cult is recorded and accepted, together with the consecration of his temple in Antinoöpolis, which is said to have been built in accordance with the traditions of the Egyptians as well as the Greeks, to account for the characteristic Greco-Egyptian style, typical of late temples. All this about a non-Egyptian who was not the sovereign, is entirely new and exceptional. It is entirely out of keeping with the fundamental rules and the practice of orthodox Egyptian theology, and in its spirit, as well as in its conception of the religious problems involved, the text is decidedly Greco-Roman, and only very superficially Egyptian. Its orthography is, even for a late text, preposterous, and the signs themselves are no longer made in accordance with the accepted rules, but represent frequently more or less free elaborations on the old patterns.

The end of the tradition was obviously near at hand, and chance has provided us with yet another curious relic illustrating the next and final stage of its dissolution, the formerly widely famous Isiac table, now after many hazardous peregrinations safely harboured in the Museum of Turin[51]. (Pl.VI, 1). It is a rectangular table (1.28×0.75 m.) richly engraved with mythological pictures and hieroglyphic ornaments, centred around a picture of the enthroned Isis. Nothing is known about the origin or history of the monument until it suddenly turned up in Rome at the beginning of the sixteenth century, and was acquired by Cardinal Bembo. The late and rather barbaric style of its decorations makes it doubtful whether it was made by an Egyptian or an Alexandrian craftsman, and whether it was made in Egypt or abroad. Iconographically seen its representations are undoubtedly associated with genuine Egyptian traditions and refer to genuine Egyptian religious ideas, and the table as such is certainly a genuine cult-object, probably from some Italian temple or shrine of Isis. It is lavishly adorned with hieroglyphs, narrow lines of which separate the various pictures, which are also provided with vertical lines of short hieroglyphic 'legendae', such as we find them in the classical representations of Egyptian art. It is obvious that the individual signs of these 'inscriptions' have been copied from genuine hieroglyphs, but it is equally obvious that they are devoid of any meaning, and have no graphic significance whatsoever[52]. They have once and for all ceased to represent 'letters' and graphic elements, and have become reduced to simple ornaments and mute decorative patterns. The hieroglyphs of Egypt had ceased to speak, and the time had come for the fulfilment of the prophecy of Hermes Trismegistus on Egypt, in its tragic passion and true pathos one of the most profoundly moving documents from dying antiquity: "There will come a time when it will be seen that in vain have the Egyptians honoured the deity with heartfelt piety and assiduous service, and all our holy worship will be found bootless and ineffectual. For the Gods will return from earth to heaven: Egypt will be forsaken, and the land which was once the home of religion will be left desolate, bereft of the presence of its deities ... Do you weep at this Asclepius? There is worse to come. Egypt herself will have yet more to suffer ... O Egypt, Egypt, of thy religion nothing will remain but an empty tale, which thine own children in time to come will not believe; nothing will be left but graven words, and only the stones will tell of thy piety. And so the Gods will depart from mankind"[53]. (Pl. IV, 1 a–b).

III. The Middle Ages and the Renaissance[1]

We have seen how the religious vacuum created by the disintegration of the ancient mythical state-religions of the Near East was filled by Christianity, the message of which by no means appealed merely to the poor and the oppressed. The strong influence of Greek philosophy and thought all over the Hellenistic world had prepared the way by undermining the very foundation of the older systems, the myths, which, from a philosophical point of view, had come to appear irrational and out of keeping with Hellenic logical reasoning.

In more enlightened circles, logic and reason was, therefore, decidedly on the side of Christianity in its fight against the myths, an argument continually stressed by Christian preachers and propagandists.

The rapidity of the process which led to the victory of Christianity is indeed remarkable. Religious systems which had lived on and dominated the minds of men for millenniums, crumbled up and disintegrated with very little inner resistance in so many centuries, and one of the early historians of the new faith, Eusebius, could already about 300 A.D., in a treatise which also contained an extensive digression on the hieroglyphs and their use, proclaim the final victory within reach, even in Egypt, the professed stronghold of national intolerance and religious fanaticism: 'See what blessings God's Christ came to bestow on us since through His teachings in the Gospels he has redeemed even the souls of the Egyptians from such a disease of lasting and long continued blindness, so that now most of the people of Egypt have been freed from this insanity'[2], i. e. the belief in the old Gods. He even felt secure and powerful enough to preach indulgence, – a sentiment not frequently cultivated by the early fathers – and to admonish his triumphant brethren in the faith: 'Laugh not in future at their Gods, but pity this thrice wretched human race for their great folly and blindness'[3].

The Christian victory was so complete that almost from the very beginning it was able to satisfy more than the religious demands of the country. Also the national political forces, which had become homeless during the foreign occupations rallied around it, because they found a new centre of gravitation in the strong organization of the new church, which rapidly developed into a powerful instrument through which they could gather and exert political strength and influence.

The result was the development of a national Coptic church, the administrative and political centre of which was Alexandria, from whence it vigorously asserted itself, with stubborn resistance against Rome as well as Byzantium in ardent religious and political feuds, culminating at the famous Robber-Synod of Chalcedon in 451, after which the Egyptians broke away from the mother church.

They adopted the monophysite doctrine concerning the nature of Christ, in accordance with which he was declared non-consubstantial with humanity, his human qualities being considered entirely transmuted into his divinity which, in monophysite conception, made him the supreme manifestation of the word – logos – and essentially God. In spite of this religious schism, and except for a short Persian domination from 616–626, the country remained under the sway of Byzantium to which it had fallen in 395 after the division of the Empire; but political and religious controversies caused continual internal strife between the Melchites, supporting the creed and authority of the emperor, and their nationalistic monophysite opponents.

The divergencies grew to such an extent that nationalistic circles encouraged and facilitated the Arab conquest in 640, which resulted in a decisive break with all previous continuity. It inaugurated an entirely new era for the country, and the end of its existence as a homogeneous national state. The Egyptian people were once more to suffer the painful experience that the devil had been cast out by means of Beelzebub, and that the blind fanaticism of its leaders, in their fanatic struggle for power and independence, had only made them exchange one hard and tyrannical master for another.

The original policy of the new conquerors, which at the beginning had aimed at nothing more than a military occupation, was soon changed into a deliberate and ruthless attempt at colonization. To counterbalance the native elements, Arabic immigration was encouraged, the economic extortions were intensified, and from about the beginning of the eighth century, the relations between the Copts and their new masters had become strained to such an extent that the resentment of the former broke out in an almost uninterrupted sequence of sanguinary revolts, lasting until the year 832, when the Coptic nation was finally forced into submission after an unsuccessful insurrection crushed by Afshin, the general of the caliph Mamun, in a general massacre and persecution. From now on the native population was pacified, but from a national point of view it was the pacification of death.

Greek disappeared as the official language, and was very soon supplanted by Arabic for all official purposes. The old native tongue, from now on known as Coptic, survived as a fossil patois in the dispersed and scattered Christian communities leading an isolated and submissive existence in an otherwise entirely Moslem state. That Egypt which Hellenism and Christianity had conquered for the West was rapidly reconquered by the East and its new Islamic culture. Of ancient Egypt even the memory was dead, also in the West, where the vague and hazy reminiscences of its past were based, almost exclusively, on the biblical stories and legends and the mostly polemic accounts of the ecclesiastical authors. But an almost mystic veneration for the wisdom of the Egyptians lived on, and the various classical records and accounts of Egypt were read and copied by the monastic scholars responsible for the continuation of the classical traditions, together with the works in which they were contained. We have seen how Tzetzes as late as the twelfth century was able to quote works of Chairemon[4] which have subsequently been lost, and how Horapollo's Hieroglyphica was continually copied right down until the fourteenth century. But with Tzetzes as the sole exception, the Egyptological material was never studied for its own sake, for the information it provided about Egypt and Egyptian culture, but exclusively for philological reasons. In the didactic literature of the period the hieroglyphs are occasionally mentioned in conventional terms borrowed from the classics, such as in Martianus Capella's 'Marriage of Mercury and Philology' (II,136)[5], which dates from the fifth century and throughout the Middle Ages remained one of the canonical works on the liberal arts trivium and quadrivium.

They are also mentioned by Isidorus of Seville (about 570-636) in his Etymologies[6] written about the turn of the century as a compendium of human knowledge, and surviving as one of the encyclopedias of the Middle Ages; but even these faint offshoots of the hieroglyphical traditions were undoubtedly confined to very narrow circles.

The current ideas and the general knowledge about Egypt before the classical revival of the Renaissance, are probably much better illustrated by the mosaics in the church of San Marco in Venice, where according to a tradition preserved in the cosmography of Julius Honorius, the pyramids have become the granaries of Joseph[7], and by the official conception of the obelisks of Rome, of which the Vaticanus right down until about fifteen hundred was considered the sepulchre of Caesar, whose ashes were supposed to rest in the gilt globe adorning its summit, just as the Capitoline obelisk was taken for a monument of Octavian[8]. (Pl. IX, 1 a–b).

From about the fifteenth century all this was changed, and as one of the results of the general evolution which transformed the Middle Ages into the Renaissance, grew an entirely new conception of Ancient Egypt and its relation to Western culture.

The transformation of one cultural epoch into another is always a complicated metaphysical process, in which it is dangerous to give prominence to individual agents and specific symptoms; but it is indisputable that the recovery of the classics, and the subsequent rediscovery of the classical past, more than anything else became responsible for the transmutation of scholastic culture into that of the Renaissance.

The authority of the church became challenged by that of the classics, and theology could no longer maintain its position as the sole begetter of knowledge. The sublimely and harmonious cosmological unity created by the inspired logic of scholastic thought was broken, and the subtle and unworldly speculations of scholastic theology were replaced by the burning humanistic problem of how to reconcile the doctrines of Christianity with the philosophy of the Ancients, above all Plato and the Neo-Platonists. Florence became the early centre of these efforts and studies, and the new ideas were to a great extent given form and shape by the members of its Platonic Academy. This famous society was founded by Cosimo de' Medici about 1439 with the explicit purpose to promote Platonic studies; and a new 'historical' approach to philosophic and scientific problems, the rediscovery of continuity in human existence, was one of the immediate results of its activities.

The increasing interest in Egyptian matters was at first merely a natural result of the increasing knowledge of the classical reports on the country. People became acquainted with the fact that many of the most prominent representatives of Greek genius, even Plato himself, had come to Egypt to learn and study, and had returned impressed by its culture and enriched by its learning. Works like Plutarch's book on Isis and Osiris awoke the interest in Osirianism and Egyptian religion, and Iamblichus' demonological elucidations concerning the so-called mysteries of Egypt, together with the Hermetic literature, purportedly written by Hermes or Thoth himself, and considered genuine Egyptian and true authentic evidence of the Egyptian way of thought, fascinated the humanists, and became responsible for their conceptions of what they considered Egyptian philosophy.

The general conception of the direct connections between Christianity, the Hermetic literature, and the philosophy of Plato was already formed by Marcilio Ficino (1433-1499), in his De Christiana Religione and his Theologia Platonica written in 1473-78. In 1471 he published a Latin translation of some of the Hermetic treatises, in 1483 a translation of Plato, in 1492 a Latin translation of Plotinus and in 1497 an edition of Iamblichus, and through his activity in the Platonic Academy he became one of the pioneers of the Neo-Platonic revival.

According to Ficino, Hermes Trismegistus was a sage of the Egyptians, a contemporary or maybe even a predecessor of Moses[9]. He had attained a knowledge of things surpassing even that which was revealed to the Hebrew prophets, and comparable only to that of the Evangelists. Pythagoras had become acquainted with his teachings in Egypt, and through his intermission they had been transmitted to Plato who was a student of Egyptian wisdom himself, and had eventually based his own philosophy on the doctrines of Hermes.

Egyptian wisdom, Neo-Platonic philosophy, and the humanistic studies, became in this way consecutive links in an unbroken chain of tradition, joined together and united with Christianity by their common aim: the knowledge and revelation of God.

It must always be remembered, however, that the basis of these grandiose reconciliatory efforts of the early humanists was their unwavering faith in the absolute universality of the Christian truth, which they considered a timeless cosmic force, incessantly emanating from the divine centre which was God, and constituting the very essence of the universe. Seen from this point of view the misfortune of the so-called heathen prophets, including Plato as well as Hermes, in having been born before the final revelation of this truth at the coming of Christ, was therefore merely 'historical', that is, dependent on time, and therefore inessential. 'Errors and mistakes' did not alter the fact that the pre-Christian revelations however imperfect and embryonic, were nevertheless anticipations of the final Christian message, and that the truth the pagan philosophers unwittingly had born witness to, was the cosmic truth of Christianity. By no means was the humanistic attitude, therefore, a display of religious tolerance in the conventional meaning of the word.

In the opinion of the humanists, there was quite simply no other possibility, as there was only one truth, and only one God who could, in fact, reveal Himself: the Christian God.

There was consequently no distinction between the aims of theology and philosophy. The former revealed God as love, and found its final expression in the Gospels, while the latter revealed him as truth. As such it had never found a more adequate and sublime expression than in the works of Plato and his Neo-Platonic expounders, and in the works of their common source and inspirator the Egyptian Hermes. But in drawing this distinction, in separating the manifestation of love from that of truth, the humanists became responsible for the subsequent separation of theology and science; and from their own preference for the philosophical truth, grew the dangerous modern conception of the finality and universality of scientific truth as such.

It is significant for the growing importance of the Egyptian tradition that Ficino's Hermetic translations appeared in eight editions before 1500, and saw no less than 22 editions between 1471 and 1641[10]. It is also characteristic that amongst the prophets and sibyls, since 1488 adorning the magnificent pavement in the Dome of Siena, the most conspicuous design is a picture of Hermes, placed in the middle of the floor at the western end of the nave, so as to be the first thing to meet the eye. In the accompanying inscription he is explicitly called 'Hermes Trismegistus, the contemporary of Moses', and he is seen in an oriental costume handing over an open book to two men, representing the Greek and the native population of Egypt, with the words: 'accept, oh Egyptians! the teachings and the laws'[11]. (Pl. IX, 2).

The same attitude, which has a remarkable parallel in the Mohammedan attitude towards the pre-Islamic religions, became responsible for the humanistic interest in Osiris. The myth about the suffering God, unjustly killed, his resurrection and position as 'King of the Dead' and 'Saviour', his relation to the great Mother-Goddess

Isis, who undoubtedly at an earlier period had contributed considerably to the development of the worship of the virgin[12], and his association with his loving son Horus, contained a profusion of elements which recalled the Christian passion, and by the humanists were considered an imperfect and anticipated, but nevertheless essentially true, reflection of it.

Osiris became consequently a recurrent topic in the literature of the period.

We know that Ficino's pupil, and Lorenzo de' Medici's friend, Angelo Poliziano (1437-1497), during his stay in Venice gave a series of lectures on Harpocrates and Osiris[13], and even in technical books such as Robertus Valturius' book on military matters[14], the author could not resist the temptation to boast of his erudition by using the Osirismyth for his explanations of the symbolic significance of the emblems represented on the Roman standards.

However, the most curious, and in many respects also one of the most typical illustrations of the capricious scientific spirit of the period, are undoubtedly the strange historical studies of the Dominican abbot Giovanni Nanni (1432-1502) from Viterbo[15]. Nanni – frequently known as Annius or Ennius – was a distinguished prelate acting as a confidential secretary to the Pope Alexander VI Borgia. He was a renowned preacher, published a treatise on the German empire, preached the crusade against the Turks, was well and professionally versed in the intrigues and the political affairs of the period, and was eventually, in true accordance with its spirit poisoned by Caesar Borgia, the unscrupulous son of his master.

His principal work, or at any rate the one from which most of his subsequent fame was derived, was an extensive commentary on chronological matters[16], in which he advanced some new and revolutionary theories concerning the early history of mankind from the deluge until the fall of Troy. It was his patriotic aim to discard the current ideas about the importance of Greek influence for the development of Italic culture, and to demonstrate the autochthonous origin of the latter. His basic allegation was that the wisdom of the Egyptians had been directly transferred to Italy by Osiris, and given rise to the Italian cultures without any interference of the Greeks, and he was utterly unscrupulous and absolutely ruthless in his efforts to substantiate these assertions.

Starting from the account of Diodorus, in accordance with which Osiris as a king had roamed the world as a conquering hero, Annius lets him appear in Italy, expel the giants, teach the Italians the elements of agriculture and wine-growing, and assign the subsequent dominion of land and sea to his Italian successors.

To prove this beautiful hypothesis, Annius had recourse to all his learning and knowledge, and quite a substantial amount of unscrupulous and dishonest cunning as well. He pretended to have rediscovered no less than 12 texts of ancient authors hitherto considered lost, among which the historical works of the Chaldean Berosus and the Egyptian Manetho were the most important, but the new texts were, in fact, very clever falsifications made by Annius himself.

All of them supported most cunningly his new Italic and Osirian theories, and they were constructed in the most ingenious way, so that they not only supported each other, but could be confirmed and illustrated by authentic passages from genuine authors, and their display of ability, and even of knowledge and erudition is indeed astounding.

It is in strictest conformity with the spirit of the period that his patriotic and heroic aims did not prevent Annius from pursuing minor and more personal ones at the same time; and he proved, as a side-line, the age-old nobility of the family Annius – gens Annia –, and provided a heroic genealogy for his papal patron by demonstrating that the Borgia family descended directly from the Egyptian Hercules, who was the son of Osiris, and that the bull of the family crest, was, in fact, the Osirian Apis.

Nothing illustrates better the transformative powers of the period, and its ability to turn sows' ears into silken purses, than the fact that these figments of an ambitious brain could inspire the delicate and tender pictures of Pinturicchio in the Borgia apartments of the Vatican, where the artist celebrated the heroic origin of the papal family by using motives from Annius' version of the Osirismyth[17]. (Pl. IX, 2). However, Annius' boundless ambition and insatiable avidity for sensation and effect demanded even more drastic proofs of his theories than those obtained from his historical 'reconstructions'; and to provide those, he had once more recourse to the history of Herodotus and its reports that Osiris in the course of his campaigns erected columns with hieroglyphic inscriptions to commemorate his victories all over the world. (Pl. XIV, 2). One of these columns was most conveniently 'rediscovered' in the church of San Lorenzo, a small sanctuary in Annius' hometown of Viterbo, and he was fortunately enough able to read and interpret its inscription, which undoubtedly had been made by himself and stated that it had been put up by Osiris during his stay in Italy, after he had liberated the Italian peoples, endowed them with wine and agriculture, and bequeathed his dominions to his Italian successors. The inscription, made with 'Egyptian hieroglyphic signs', was fabricated with cunning adaptation of information concerning the appearance and the function of the hieroglyphs obtained from classical sources, and as such it represents one of the earliest 'hieroglyphic' inscriptions of the period, and adds special interest to the whole of Annius' magnificent Egyptological fraud, by introducing us to what was to become the most spectacular result of Renaissance Egyptology: its hieroglyphic studies.

But to understand the importance of these, and the amazing influence they exerted upon art as well as literature throughout the fifteenth and sixteenth centuries, it will be necessary first to consider the period's theoretical conception of the hieroglyphs as such.

We have seen how the hieroglyphs in the later periods of antiquity became mono-polized by Neo-Platonic circles, and with the Neo-Platonic revival of the Renaissance, and its general dependence on Neo-Platonic ideas, it became quite naturally also dependent on the Neo-Platonic conception of the Egyptian writing.

It is characteristic that the final formulation of that which until the eighteenth century should remain the almost undisputed conception of the hieroglyphs, is founded on Ficino's translation of Plotinus[18], and represents an unconditional ac-ceptance of the latter's definition[19], according to which the script was a divinely in-spired Egyptian invention, a unique form of symbolic writing. It had nothing in com-mon with ordinary graphic systems operating with words and letters and, although they appeared as ordinary pictures of material objects, the individual signs were in reality symbolic entities, revealing their true meaning only to the initiated readers by means of a divinely inspired process of intellectual enlightenment. The true sig-nificance thus revealed was nothing less than an insight into the very essence of things, in fact their ideas, and the method involved, the ultimate understanding of the true nature of things made possible by an immediate contact between the human intellect and the divine ideas, was supposed to reflect and illustrate the dynamic process of divine thought.

The full scope of, and the stupendous importance attached to, the discovery of this 'sacred writing of ideas', can only be properly understood against the background of the general 'Platonization' of the mental activities of the period. Each individual ob-ject and each specific phenomenon were, from a theoretical point of view, considered an idea objectified, and consequently as so many symbolic entities; and to distinguish between matter and idea, to define the difference between appearance and signific-ance, in fact, to realize and interpret the symbolic qualities of things became the ul-timate ambition of philosophy and thought.

The result could be achieved in various ways, by pious contemplation, philoso-phical interpretation, and artistic creation, but the final aim was always the same: to manifest the idea, 'Gott zu verleiben'.

The Renaissance scholars found this symbolic conception of the hieroglyphs con-firmed by most classical writers on the subject, and they disregarded deliberately any other approach to their understanding, just as the ancients had done.

They collected conscientiously the examples with which the classical scholars had illustrated the use of the signs and used them for their own purposes, literary as well as artistic. Many of them became subsequently incorporated as popular motives in European emblematic and decorative art, and became such integral elements of it that their hieroglyphic origin was entirely forgotten. Such is undoubtedly the case with the common symbol of eternity, the snake biting its own tail, and the eye freq-uently used in ecclesiastic art to signify divine justice. (Pl. XXIII, 2a and Pl. X, 2b).

But the main source of the knowledge of the symbolic significance of Egyptian motifs was undoubtedly the Hieroglyphics of Horapollo, a manuscript of which was found on the Greek island of Andros about the year 1419 by the Florentine traveller Christoforo Buondelmonti, who brought it back to Florence about 1422. (Pl. X, 1).

It was a curious coincidence that a manuscript containing the remaining fragments of the history of Ammianus Marcellinus, with its excurse on the obelisks, should be found in a German monastery a few years earlier, in 1414, by the later chancellor of the Florentine republic Poggio Bracciolini (1380-1459). This manuscript was brought to Florence, where it was handed over to Poggio's friend Niccolo de' Niccoli (1363-1437), at that time the greatest living authority on classical bibliography, who immediately had it copied and made its existence known in humanistic circles.

The text was studied with avidity, and contributed essentially to the growth of interest in hieroglyphs, preparing the road for Horapollo who became the true sensation. As soon as it arrived in Florence, the manuscript of the Hieroglyphica was immediately copied and circulated, and in spite of the poor manner in which the text had been transmitted, and its late and obscure Greek, it was eagerly read and commented upon. Its erroneous and misleading conception of the script was not only generally accepted with uncritical confidence, but the book remained for centuries the unchallenged authority on hieroglyphic questions.

The Greek text was first printed and published by Aldus in Venice in 1505, and a Latin translation appeared already in 1515[20].

The book did not only stimulate the theoretical and literary studies of the hieroglyphs, but its elaborate descriptions of the signs induced a variety of artists to reconstruct them, and those efforts gave rise to the development of an artistic tradition of decorative hieroglyphic pictures.

Already Leone Battista Alberti (1404-1472) had undertaken such reconstructions, and used a hieroglyphic emblem for the decoration of the reverse of his medal, representing a winged eye with the motto 'Quid tum', indicating the swift retribution of divine justice[21], and he was also the first to encourage the use of hieroglyphs for architectural and monumental purposes. (Pl. X, 2 a–b).

In his famous and influential book on architecture, which spread his theories all over Europe in Italian, French, Spanish and English editions, it is pointed out how ordinary letters had an unfortunate tendency to fade into oblivion, and to become obsolete and unintelligible, as had been the case with the Etruscan ones.

It would, therefore, in Alberti's opinion, be better to discard the use of ordinary profane letters for inscriptions on architectural monuments made for posterity, and to replace them with 'sacred Egyptian letters'. These could always and under all circumstances be read and interpreted by initiate scholars[22]. But before these brilliant theories could be put into practice, there was first one practical problem to be solved: how these symbolic hieroglyphs were to appear in artistic representations.

To understand the way in which this problem was solved by the Renaissance artists, it must be remembered that they had practically no possibilities whatsoever to become acquainted with the appearance of original Egyptian hieroglyphs.

We know that the traveller and publicist Ciriaco de' Pizzicolli (1391 until some time after 1449) during his extensive travels came to Egypt where he copied hieroglyphic inscriptions, and that his material was brought to Florence[23], but it seems never to have been used by any of the contemporary artists. The Roman material consisted of a few fallen obelisks and other monuments such as the lions from the Capitol, which had hieroglyphic inscriptions at their bases[24], but also these were entirely disregarded. The Renaissance was not hampered with historical 'Stilgefühl' in our sense of the word, and preferred original creation to faithful copying. The problems concerning the reconstruction and representation of the hieroglyphs consequently presented no difficulties to the artists and craftsmen of the period. Their fertile imagination and dynamic creativeness told them how to make what they needed, in accordance with their own demands and requirements and conformant with their own taste and style, with supreme disregard of all traditional and historical facts.

Generally speaking the hieroglyphical representations of the period were, therefore, neither in style nor form distinguished from ordinary ornamental and decorative elements, and no efforts were made to stress their foreign or archaic origin. But from this general rule there is one notable exception which gave rise to special, pseudo-historical efforts to make 'historically' correct representations of the signs. These efforts had their origin in one of the peculiar historical misunderstandings, or rather misinterpretations, which not infrequently became happy sources of inspiration to the creative artists of the Renaissance, in giving rise to new trains of thought, and the development of new and fertile traditions of their own.

Modern opera was the result of the effort of the period to revive the classical tragedy in a misconceived form, its hieroglyphical studies were based on a false conception of the nature of the script, and the erroneous explanation of a classical Roman ornament gave rise to the development of a special type of 'historical' hieroglyphs which made their influence felt in the decorative arts of the period, right down until the eighteenth century.

In the Roman church called San Lorenzo in Campo Verano, or fuori le mura, the curious observer had from time immemorial been able to admire the remnants of an ancient temple-frieze representing a variety of cult-objects and ritual symbols[25]. It was undoubtedly considered a valuable and important relic, because not only was it removed for greater safety from San Lorenzo to the Capitol sometime during the sixteenth century, but it is found copied and reproduced again and again in the various sketchbooks of almost all important artists of the period[26], and there can be no doubt that it was considered one of the important tourist attractions of the city. (Pl.V,2).

In spite of the fact that similar friezes are by no means uncommon, and that their Roman origin should have been obvious from the fact that one – which was, in fact, reproduced somewhat later on one of the veduti of Piranesi – could be seen by any visitor to Rome in its original place adorning the Temple of Vespasianus[27], the signs of the fragments from San Lorenzo became nevertheless, for obscure reasons, considered 'sacred Egyptian hieroglyphs', and were generally and uncritically accepted as such. They had the practical advantages of being ancient, ornamental, and unintelligible at the same time, and were consequently open to any brilliant interpretation. The Venetian scholar Francesco Colonna was the first to make practical use of their artistic and literary possibilities.

Colonna belonged to a branch of the well-known Roman family, but was born in Venice in the year 1433. Very little is known about himself or his life, apart from the fact that he studied theology in Padua, entered the Dominican order, and died in his native town of Venice where he was buried in the church of San Giovanni e Paolo in the year 1527. He is supposed to have travelled quite extensively in his youth, and to have visited Sicily, Constantinople, and maybe even the Near East; but his fame and celebrity in literary circles is exclusively based on a remarkable specimen of literary fancy, written about the middle of the fifteenth century, and called 'Hypnerotomachia Poliphili', which means something like 'Poliphilo's dream-fight with Eros'.

The book was published by Aldus in Venice in the year 1499[28] and, although it was not an immediate success, it obtained eventually great celebrity and became increasingly popular in influential literary circles.

From a modern literary point of view it can hardly claim more than the interest of curiosity. It is written in a florid and pompous Italian, abounding in ornate and self-constructed words of Latin, Greek, and Hebrew origin, and obviously used as a display of the author's erudition. The story itself is no less complicated and tells how the hero Poliphilo through the innumerable vicissitudes of a dream, pursues his divine Polia, an allegorical personification of antiquity.

The scene is set in a fantastic sylvan landscape of fauns and nymphs, surrounded by forests and gardens, adorned with fancy monuments and ruins, all of which are profusely illustrated by exquisite wood-cuts, from a modern point of view forming the principal attraction of the book. They are made by an unknown artist, and display the same curious mixture of severe Gothic stylization and Renaissance luxuriance as the text itself. To stress the 'historical' correctness of the descriptions, the architectural monuments are frequently adorned with symbolic decorations, and with inscriptions which are elaborately translated and commented upon in the text to which they allude, subtly and allegorically. Many of them are written in what Colonna himself calls 'coelati hieroglyphi, ouero characteri aegyptici', and the signs used are in fact those of the above mentioned temple frieze supplemented when necessary with symbols of Colonna's own invention, carefully executed in the same style. (Pl. XI). The ambition and audacity with which Colonna undertook the redaction of his hieroglyphic texts is clearly illustrated from the inscription used for the decoration of his fanciful mausoleum, represented on folio b VII verso (Pl. XII, 2). Imitating a monument from Catania (Pl. XII, 1) it represents an elephant carrying an obelisk on its back, an idea which in 1667 was adopted by Bernini and used for his monument on the Piazza della Minerva in Rome. (Pl. XII, 3). The inscription consists of fourteen hieroglyphs, and signifies in Colonna's own Latin translation the following apophthegm: 'Sacrifice your toil generously to the God of nature. Little by little you will then subject your soul to God, and He will take you into His firm protection, mercifully govern your life and preserve it unharmed'[29]. (Pl. XI, 1).

A key is not always given to the understanding, and the disentangling of the symbolic meaning of the individual signs is generally left to the intelligence of the reader. It is by no means always an easy task. In some cases the signs are used merely in accordance with the pictures found in our rebus[30], as when the picture of a rudder stands for the verb 'to govern', or two fish-hooks for the verb 'to keep'. In other cases the sense is more farfetched and transferred, as when a tankard with a narrow spout is used to express the notion 'little by little'. The meaning of certain signs is arrived at only by subtle mythological expoundings. This is the case with the picture of a ball of yarn used to express the word 'conducting', which can only be understood with reference to the story about Ariadne, Theseus, and the labyrinth.

Some are even more involved, as when the picture of an eye – according to Horapollo the hieroglyph for God or divine justice – is drawn upon the sole of a sandal, with the meaning 'subject to God'. These examples will suffice to demonstrate the subtle method in the madness, which by no means was considered as such by Colonna's contemporaries and successors.

Strange as it might seem and difficult to understand, his inscriptions were in fact considered genuine and authentic by most of his contemporaries, and even a critical scholar like Erasmus was convinced that Colonna had had access to copies of the lost works of Chairemon in order to make them[31].

But the Hypnerotomachia was not the only place where the signs of the temple frieze were used as hieroglyphs. Maybe even on the direct instigation of Colonna they were also used by Mantegna (1431-1506), who characteristically enough has been suggested as one of the artists who might be responsible for the illustrations of Poliphilo. On his famous picture of Caesar's triumph, painted about 1490 and now at Hampton Court, they are used as hieroglyphic emblems adorning the front of the arch itself[32], and the whole picture abounds in hieroglyphical emblems taken from Hor-

PLATE IX

1 a-b. The pyramids represented as the granaries of Joseph. Mosaic from the church of San Mark's in Venice.

2. Hermes Trismegistus handing over the Tablets of the Law to the Egyptians. Pavement from the Siena Cathedral.

3. Osiris, Isis and the Apis, the heroic ancestors of the Borgia family. Painting by Pinturicchio from the Borgia Apartments in the Vatican.

PLATE X

1

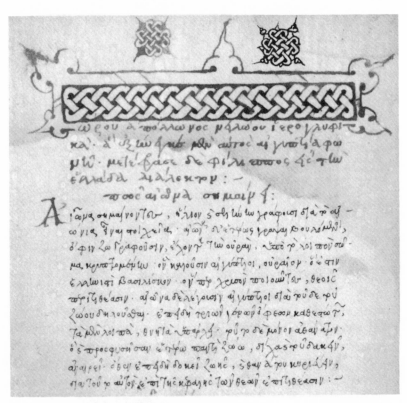

1. Frontispiece from a hitherto unpublished manuscript of Horapollo in the possession of the Royal Library, Copenhagen.

2 a

2 b

3

2 a-b. Matteo de Pasti's medal for Leone Battista Alberti. According to Macrobius and Diodorus the winged eye is used 'hieroglyphically' to represent the swift retribution of divine justice. For the Egyptian conception of the sign see the cover.

3. Roman obelisk with the signs from the temple frieze used as hieroglyphs by Jaques Androuët du Cerceau.

apollo and other hieroglyphical classics. The signs were also used as emblematic ornaments on the paintings in S. Augustino degli Eremitani in Padua from about 1459,
but nothing demonstrates the tenacity of the tradition better than the fact that their
hieroglyphic origin and nature were still uncontested and taken for absolutely granted as late as the end of the sixteenth century.

The renowned French architect Jacques Androuët du Cerceau published in the
year 1584 a collection of prints called 'Livre des Édifices Antiques Romains', containing reconstructions of the principal architectural monuments of Ancient Rome:
'telle qu'elle éstoit anciennement en sa plus grande splendeur'.

The reconstructions are made with supreme disregard of all archaeological and
historical facts, and they are monuments more to the fantasy of du Cerceau than to
ancient architecture; but amongst them are found reproductions of two Egyptian
obelisks, probably because these monuments had come very much into the limelight
just about this time, because of the competition arranged for the removal of one of
them from the Circus of the Vatican to the Piazza San Pietro. The competition was
won by the architect Domenico Fontana (1543-1607), who completed the difficult
task in 1586, an event which aroused astonishment and admiration all over Europe,
and even lefts its mark in the Sonnets of Shakespeare[33].

It is typical of the strange 'historical' ambitions of du Cerceau that he considered
it necessary that one of his obelisks should appear provided with its original hieroglyphical inscription, and it is equally characteristic that the problem of how original
Egyptian hieroglyphs should appear did not even arise.

During his stay in Rome he had apparently like the majority of contemporary artists seen and copied the signs of the temple-frieze, and had unhesitatingly accepted
the current explanation of them as Egyptian hieroglyphs. It was therefore only natural that he should consider himself perfectly justified in using them for an Egyptian
inscription, and the signs on the obelisk are consequently sign by sign copied from
the frieze[34]. (Pl. X, 3). It became obvious very soon, however, that these scanty signs
could not satisfy the growing demand for hieroglyphs, and that any amount of new
signs would be necessary if the ambitious projects of a universal system of symbolic
writing should become realized.

It became fashionable to create new hieroglyphic symbols expressing ideas and concepts not entertained by Horapollo, and also in this field Colonna was a pioneer.

The book abounds in hieroglyphic emblems, made in the exuberant style of the
period, and illustrating or rather expressing philosophical and moral maxims and
sentences. Some of them are very fanciful indeed, as the one representing a caduceus
– a wand with snakes – surrounded by four monsters, of which two are elephants,
the foreparts of which are crumbling into ants, and two are ants with elephant heads,
arranged around two vessels, one with flames issuing from it, and the other filled with

69

water[35]. The whole emblem is supposed to express the Sallustian maxim that peace and harmony (the caduceus) makes small things great (ants turning into elephants), while discord (the vessels with fire and water) makes great things small (elephants turning into ants). (Pl. XIV, 1).

In spite of their subtlety and the fact that they can hardly be said to be immediately or easily intelligible, some of the 'new hieroglyphs' became nevertheless greatly popular, and were frequently used for decorative purposes, above all on medals and as 'impresas'[36]. They were also used as architectural ornaments, and we know that the cloister garth of San Giustina in Padua was decorated with frescos representing the above-mentioned elephant emblems, the signs of the temple frieze, and several other motives from the Hypnerotomachia[37]. (Pl. XIX, 1).

The period following the first publication of Poliphilo and the first edition of Horapollo saw a rapid increase in the Italian hieroglyphic literature. Hieroglyphic questions were more or less thoroughly considered in such works as the Enneads of Marcantonio Sabellico (Venice 1504), the 'Antiquae lectiones' by Ludovico Ricchieri (Venice 1516, – the author's Latinized name is Coelius Rhodiginus –), and naturally enough also in the extensive introduction to Filippo Fasanini's Latin translation of Horapollo (Bologna 1517).

It is characteristic, however, for these as well as the subsequent authors on the subject that they accepted the current conventional conception of hieroglyphic writing unconditionally, and none of them had personal contributions of any importance to make, but their works became important for the propagation of the interest, and its expansion, outside Italy too. We find the same blind acceptance of Ficino's formulation of Plotinus' definition, also in the work which almost down until the beginning of the eighteenth century was to remain the unchallenged 'modern' authority on hieroglyphic questions, the 'Hieroglyphica' of Pierius Valerianus'[38]. The author, whose secular name was Giovan Pietro della Fosse, was born in Belluno in 1477, and died in Padua about 1558 or 1560. Already at the age of sixteen he was brought to Venice to live with his uncle Fra Urbano Valeriano Bolzanio (about 1443-1524), a distinguished hieroglyphical scholar and renowned traveller, who had visited Greece, Asia Minor, Palestine, and also Egypt, whence he had returned to become the tutor of Giovanni de' Medici, the later Pope Leo X[39].

He published a Greek grammar, and was a prominent member of the Aldinian Academy of Venice, and he is known to have lived for some years in Treviso at the time as the author of Poliphilo was also there. In comtemporary learned circles he was considered a distinguished and famous scholar. We know from Pierio's own words that his uncle furthered his hieroglyphic studies, and the 33rd book of the Hieroglyphica is dedicated to Fra Urbano. Pierio was introduced into the learned society of his uncle at an early age, and it was there that one of his tutors, the above-

PLATE XI

Hieroglyphic inscriptions from the Hypnerotomachia Polifili.

1. Fol. c I, recto. For the significance of the inscription see page 68.

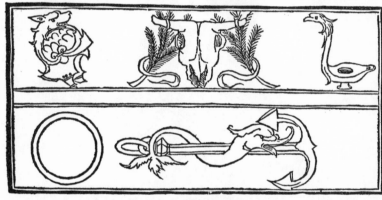

2. Fol. d VII, recto. The upper inscription translates: 'Patience is the ornament, protection and guardian of life'. The lower inscription expresses the motto of Augustus: 'Always hasten slowly'.

3. Fol. p VI, verso. Inscription from an imaginary obelisk attributed to Julius Caesar.

4. Fol. q VII verso. Inscription from sarcophagus stating that life's inveterate enemy death here has united two unhappy lovers.

PLATE XII

1. Fountain from the city of Catania with Roman elephant carrying an obelisk.

2. Mausoleum from the Hypnerotomachia inspired by the monument from Catania. For the hieroglyphic inscription on its base see plate XI,1.

3. Bernini's monument from the Piazza Minerva in Rome inspired by the Hypnerotomachia.

mentioned Sabellico, enchanted by the brilliance of his pupil, changed his name Pietro to that of Pierio, a derivation of 'pierides' one of the names of the Muses[40].

Through Fra Urbino the family was closely connected with the Medicis, and Pierio became the tutor of Ippolito and Alessandro Medici. He became the private secretary, or cameriere secreto, of Leo X, and was given the title of apostolic protonotary. In the year 1537 he took orders but refused the offer of the bishoprics of Capo-d'Istria and Avignon in order to be able to pursue his literary interests[41]. His production is neither extensive nor particularly interesting. It includes a major historical treatise on the antiquities of Belluno (Venice, 1620), a treatise on the significance of lightning (Rome, 1517), a defence of the right of priests to carry a beard (Rome, 1531), and the so-called Contarenus, or 'the misfortunes of men of letters' (Venice 1620). More important are his poems (Poemata, Basle, 1538, and Amorum libri quinque, Venice, 1549), like all his works distinguished by the purity and elegance of his style, and a certain charming grace which also characterizes his Hieroglyphica (Basle, 1556).

This enormous compilation which occupied him throughout his life, was the result of his consuming passion for hieroglyphic problems. The 58 books of the original collection were written at different periods, and each is dedicated to a different Maecenas or friend, but in the final redaction, such as it appeared in the first edition published in Basle only a few years before the death of the author, they form a strangely harmonious unity, at any rate seen from an aesthetic and literary point of view.

Each book deals with the symbolic significance of one or more hieroglyphs chosen in such a way that they always pay a special compliment to the dedicatee and refer to his personal relations with the author, a subtle artistic touch which adds to the intimate charm of the book. The first book is dedicated to Cosimo de Medici, Duke of Florence, and is consecrated to the allegorical significances of the lion. The following sections deal with the elephant, the rhinoceros, and a variety of other beasts, snakes, and monsters such as Gorgon, Hydra, and Medusa, proceeding to birds, fish, parts of the human body, numbers, geometrical figures, clothes, weapons, the celestial bodies, stones, plants, pagan Gods, etc. etc.[42].

The arrangement is undoubtedly based on Diodorus' remark that Egyptian hieroglyphs could be divided into distinctive categories according to the objects they represented, Gods, human beings, parts of the body, and ordinary objects and utensils being quoted as examples.

The same strict dependence on the classics is apparent everywhere in the work, and it has already been mentioned that its general conception of the script as such is based directly on the definitions of Ficino and the Neo-Platonists.

This becomes quite apparent from the preface of book XXVII[43], dedicated to Gio-

71

vanni Grimani, who was Patriarch of Aquileia, and member of a family famous for its classical interests and humanistic culture[44].

The dedication recalls in a very personal way 'questi giorni santi', when Valerianus and Grimani in Rome had conversed about antiquity, and had serene discussions about 'this mysterious knowledge, used in the paintings and the buildings of the ancients, who – undoubtedly on the authority of Egyptian priests – had invented a mute language, conceivable by means of the pictures of things alone, without any sound of the voice or combination of letters, a language which very soon by silent consent was adopted by other nations with pretence to cultural activities'. It was the grandiose aim of Valerianus to reconstruct this 'mute and symbolical language of ideas', so that each concept and each notion had its appropriate hieroglyphical expression, and so that the entire philosophical knowledge of the period could eventually be expressed in a universal system of hieroglyphical symbols.

The allegorical method used to explain the individual signs is copied from Horapollo and the other hieroglyphical classics. The elephant is the symbol of purity because it is supposed to bathe in the rivers at full moon, and when represented peacefully amidst young lambs it signifies 'gentleness'. The lion stands for 'nobleness of mind' and 'Majesty', and united in a yoke with a wild boar, for 'strength of mind and body'. Represented roaring it means 'bestial ferocity', and together with a cock 'pious timidity', because of its presumed awe of this animal[45].

The various expoundings are supported by quotations and references, brought together with an almost incredible diligence and learnedness from almost every single source available in the accessible literature of the period. A list containing the names of no less than about 200 authors used as references follows the introduction, and no less than about 1400 hieroglyphical categories, each with a variety of subdivisions, are mentioned in the index.

It is obvious that Christian elements could not be lacking in a book comprising the entire culture of the period, and there is also a substantial number of references to the Scriptures, just as special hieroglyphs are assigned to the expression of Christian ideas.

As God Christ himself is represented by the lion, and the night-raven or the owl signifies 'Christian humility'. The basic Christian attitude of Valerianus is clearly perceptible throughout the book by certain ethical and moralizing tendencies, closely related to those found in the Physiologus and the Bestiaries, but foreign to Horapollo and the classical hierogrammates.

There is no doubt that Pierio was convinced of the essential piousness of his work, and that its final aim was to manifest Christian ideas. This is clearly stated in the dedicatory remarks addressed to the reader on the title page of the edition from 1567, where the authority of Christ and the Apostles is invoked in defence of the use of al-

PLATE XIII

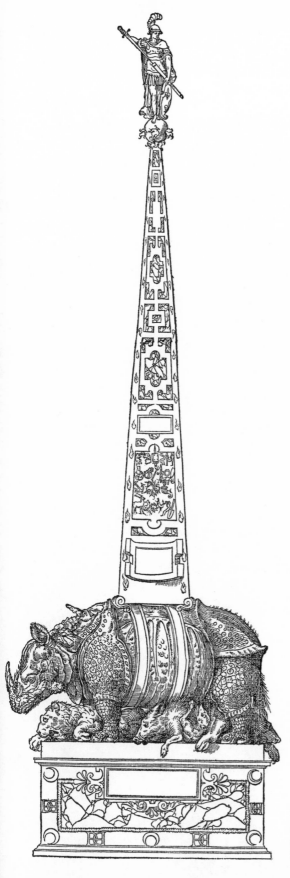

Rhinoceros with obelisk and hieroglyphic inscription
containing the homage of the city of Paris to Henry II
and Catherine de Medici. Monument erected at the
king's entry into Paris in 1549.

PLATE XIV

1. Hieroglyphic emblem from the Hypnerotomachia illustrating the Sallustian maxim that concord makes small things great, and discord great things small.

2. Valerianus' reconstruction of hieroglyphic inscription quoted by Herodotus (II,102): 'He—Sesostris—has subdued the brave by his arms, and the timid by his fame'.

3. Valerianus' reconstruction of hieroglyphic inscription from Sais recorded by Plutarch. It runs in Valerianus' expounding: 'We are born and grow old, we live and die as a result of nature's ambivalence'.

4. Pirckheimer's draft of his panegyric on the emperor Maximilian, with inserted hieroglyphs. The star is used for 'divus', as on plate XXXIII,2a.

legorical hieroglyphs, "because to speak hieroglyphically is nothing else but to disclose the (true) nature of things divine and humane".

From a prosaic modern point of view it is incontestable that the author 'a déployé plus d'érudition et d'imagination que de jugement'[46], but his learning, the ardour with which the enormous task is carried through, the inspired and inspiring love of his subject apparent on every page of the book, and above all the peculiar charm and grace of his style, endows the compilation with the unmistakable beauty of true qualities, artistic as well as human. In spite of its technical character, and its historical and methodical shortcomings, it carries the unmistakable stamp of genius, and of a noble and harmonious mind.

By his contemporaries, and right down until the seventeenth century, 'the divine' Pierio was considered the final authority on all hieroglyphic matters, and his book an immortal masterpiece. It was continually reprinted, re-edited, copied, and augmented[47], and it appeared in Italian, German, and French translations. Its careful descriptions of the hieroglyphs inspired – such as they were supposed to do – several illustrations, which together with the various illustrated editions of Horapollo became important for the creation of an ornamental and decorative hieroglyphic tradition. (Pl. XIV, 2–3). But in this respect it had already been preceded by another work, which became of unprecedented importance for the development of European iconography and allegory, the 'Emblemata' of Andrea Alciati.

Alciati was of Milanese descent. At an uncommonly early age he devoted himself to the pursuit of jurisprudence, which he studied in Bologna, where, in 1514, he was accorded the doctorate of law when only twenty-two years old. At this time he had already published his pandoxes of civil law, and acquired a wide-spread reputation as a jurisconsult and an inspired teacher. His commentaries on Roman law, based on new text critical and historical methods, were considered revolutionary, and also in this respect he was rightly celebrated as a reformer and, as his epitaph in the basilica of Pavia has it, 'the first to replace the studies of law in their ancient dignity[48].

But as a true humanist Alciati was primarily a man of letters, and already during his stay in Bologna he had become intensely interested in hieroglyphic questions, probably inspired by Fasanini and his translation of Horapollo[49].

He was not attracted by the theoretical or philosophical problems of the script, but wanted to make practical use of its allegorical possibilities in art as well as in literature.

The result of his efforts was the creation of a new literary genre of great charm and unprecedented popularity, the so-called emblematic literature.

The word emblem – derived from Greek 'emblema' – meant originally an ornament of inlaid work such as was used on shields and vessels. But Alciati used it as the terminological expression for his new literary invention, consisting of a combination

of a short fable or allegory written in Latin verse – the stanza –, an allegorical picture illustrating the fable – the device –, and a short motto expressing in proverbial
form the quintessence of the representation.

Each of the three elements was considered of equal importance, and the ensemble
– the emblem – was adjusted so as to form an indissoluble artistic unity. A single
example will suffice, taken from one of Alciati's English imitators, and directly borrowed from the master: The motto is 'ex bello pax', 'from war comes peace', and the
device represents a warrior's helmet surrounded by bees. The stanza runs in Witney's
translation[50]:

> 'A helmet stronge, that did the head defende,
> Beholde, for hyue, the bees in quiet seru'd,
> And when that warres, with bloodie bloes, had ende,
> They, honey wroughte, where soldiour was preseru'd;
> Which doth declare, the blessed fruites of peace,
> How sweete shee is, when mortal warres doe cease.'

It is obvious that these charming allegorical trifles are of quite a different nature
than Ficino's and Valerianus' heroic efforts to divulge the ideal nature of things. In
the words of Alciati's English editor the emblems are 'bagatelles to play with, trifles
to amuse...., but they are trifles which none but a scholar could gracefully sport
with, and none but a man of talent invent'[51].

Alciati says the same thing himself in the charming verses dedicating the first
edition (1531) to his friend Conrad Peutinger:

> 'While boys the nuts beguile, and youth the dice,
> And sluggish men the figured board detains;
> For festive hours each emblem and device
> We force, that artist's hand illustrious feigns.'[52]

But in spite of this seeming modesty Alciati was nevertheless convinced of his immediate connection with the true hieroglyphic traditions. Much of the raw material
used for his fables, mottoes, and devices was taken from the usual hieroglyphical
sources, and he considered the allegorical method by means of which the quintessence of each emblem was revealed as truly hieroglyphical in origin. This is explicitly
stated by himself in his characteristic concise and lapidary style: 'Words indicate,
things are indicated, but things can occasionally also indicate, as the Hieroglyphs of
Horus and Chairemon, in evidence of which we ourselves have also written a small
volume called Emblemata'[53].

The success of the collection was enormous, and until then unparalleled in the
history of books. The original print (Augsburg 1531) saw three editions by 1534,

PLATE XV

Dürer's 'Ehrenpforte' for the emperor Maximilian. One of the rare copies of the first imprint.

PLATE XVI

1. Dürer's conception of the hieroglyphic picture of the cynocephalus based on Horapollo's description. For the Egyptian rendering of the animal see the cover.

2. The same animal from a French edition of Horapollo.

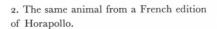

3. The cynocephalus as represented in an Italian edition of Horapollo from 1599.

4. The Austrian architect Fischer von Erlach's reconstruction of the tomb of Sothis. The hieroglyphic inscription is copied from the Hypnerotomachia. See plate XI,4

when an augmented edition appeared in Paris, provided with illustrations of a better artistic quality than those of the original. A third edition was published by the sons of Aldus in Venice in 1546[54], and the following years saw an almost innumerable sequence of French, Italian, Spanish, German, and English translations or imitations.

The illustrated editions competed for popularity with those of Horapollo of which the most famous were published by Jacques Kerver in Paris 1543 with woodcuts by Jean Cousin[55], and by Heinrich Petri in Basel 1554. The latter was a German translation made by the Swiss divine Johannes Herold, and characteristically enough published together with his translation of Diodorus[56]. The book is illustrated by various unknown artists, and each hieroglyph is represented separately in careful, if rather rude, cuts.

As a result of the intimate contact between most of the early humanists the abovementioned hieroglyphical publications were rapidly distributed all over Europe, and received with enthusiam as manifestations of the new spirit of the Renaissance; and in their wake we find everywhere local hieroglyphic traditions.

The widespread custom of dedicating books to patrons and friends makes it fairly easy to follow the general course of the tradition, and it was everywhere intimately connected with Neo-Platonism, and Christian mysticism.

Especially so in Germany, where the rapid and early diffusion of the hieroglyphical studies was greatly furthered by the personal taste and inclination of the emperor.

Maximilian, who ruled from 1493 until 1519, combined in a peculiar way the courtly manners and the chivalrous ideals of feudalism with the mental outlook and the personal taste of a humanist.

He had strong leanings towards mysticism, and his autobiographical poetry, 'Teuerdank', 'Weiskuning' and 'Freydal' – undoubtedly conceived and inspired, if not actually written by himself – bear illuminating evidence of a mystic, almost mythical conception of his office and his vocation, and of a pronounced predilection for the use of symbols and allegorical means of expression. Through his second marriage (1493) with Bianca Maria Sforza from Milan he became increasingly involved in Italian affairs, politically as well as culturally, and German humanists with close Italian relations belonged to his closest entourage, and were his personal friends.

His court became in an unprecedented way a humanistic centre and the emperor himself was a liberal protector and promotor of the arts. It is characteristic that he · should become attracted by the works of Annius, and typical that he should try to trace his descendance from Hercules Aegyptius[57], a genealogy which obviously furthered his interest in everything Egyptian, and consequently also in the hieroglyphs.

Already Erasmus (1466-1536), the acknowledged head of German humanism, had treated hieroglyphic questions in a small excourse dealing with Augustus' motto 'semper festina lente', supposedly expressed hieroglyphically in the picture of a ring, an anchor, and a dolphin, found on coins from the time of Titus, and used by Colonna in the Hypnerotomachia, and by Aldus Manucius for his printer's mark. (Pl. XI, 2).

The excourse is found in 'Chiliades adagiorum' (1508)[58], an annotated collection of proverbs and sayings, and it gives a short but concise account of Erasmus' conception of the hieroglyphic question, illustrated by examples from the classics, Horapollo, and the Hypnerotomachia.

The signs are explained as symbols or enigmatic letters, by means of which it was possible to express the innermost secrets and the true significance of things. As such they were heirlooms from the highest philosophy of the ancients and sacred tools for the initiates. But they were not for the vulgus, and only those who had learned to understand the true metaphysical nature of things could hope to understand them. The whole passage reflected the views generally accepted in Neo-Platonic circles, but the mere fact that Erasmus called attention to the hieroglyphic studies, sanctioned them, and treated them with respect and veneration, made them immediately fashionable and important among German humanists, and it was undoubtedly to a great extent due to this recommendation that they became generally accepted as worthy philosophic topics.

Also the works of Johan Reuchlin (1455-1522) 'De verbo mirifico' (1494) and 'De arte cabbalistica' (1517) became of great importance, if not so much for the hieroglyphic traditions as such, at any rate for the expansion of the ideas concerning the mystic wisdom of the ancients.

Reuchlin was together with Erasmus considered the leader of German humanism – together they were called its two eyes – and he occupied a distinguished position as a jurisconsult, and a teacher of 'the three languages' Latin, Greek, and Hebrew.

As far as the last-mentioned language is concerned he was a pioneer, and was justly considered one of the founders of modern Hebrew studies.

From frequent visits to Italy he had personal contact with most Italian humanists, especially the circle around Lorenzo de' Medici, whom he had met in Rome. He was a personal friend of Pico della Mirandola, by whom his interest in Hebrew was undoubtedly inspired, and Pico was also responsible for Reuchlin's rather fatal studies in the secret teachings and esoteric doctrines of late Judaism known as the 'cabbalah'.

We have seen how the majority of Renaissance scholars had come to consider the presumed author of the Egyptian Hermetic literature, the legendary Hermes Trismegistus, the most ancient and the greatest of ancient sages, but Reuchlin contested his priority, and emphasized the importance of Moses and the Hebrew traditions.

The mystical knowledge and the occult wisdom of the cabbalah represented in his opinion a tradition which was older, and surpassed that of the Egyptians, and the learning which Pythagoras and Plato had acquired in Egypt was Jewish and not Egyptian in its origin. But the indissoluble connection between cabbalah, Egyptian wisdom, and Neo-Platonic philosophy was nevertheless continually stressed, and Christ and his teachings were still considered the ultimate and final revelation of truth. He constructed a weird system of demonology, with 72 angels acting as mediators between God and man, and with mystical interpretations of numbers, strangely out of keeping with his sober philological methods. Nevertheless, it was as a mystic, and because of his efforts to establish magic as an ordinary philosophic or even theological discipline, that Reuchlin acquired his greatest fame. His teachings and doctrines exerted great influence on subsequent generations of German mystics, especially the theosophers of the seventeenth century. But it is strange to see how, contrary to his intentions and his thesis, his influence furthered the growing myth about an idealized Egypt, the original home of all mystic and occult knowledge, and it is a curious fact that the myth about the wisdom of Egypt flourished especially in those circles in which Reuchlin's influence was greatest: among the various occult sects and societies of the seventeenth and eighteenth centuries, among Freemasons and Rosicrucians, and among modern theosophists as well[59].

It is typical, however, for the hieroglyphical as well as the artistic traditions of the period that the work which should become the crowning hieroglyphical monument of the German Renaissance, was the result of an intimate coordination of literary, philosophic, and artistic efforts: Dürer's enormous triumphal arch made about 1517 in honour of no less than Maximilian himself. (Pl. XV).

Like the 'Teuerdank' and the 'Weiskuning' the arch was intended as an allegorical monument of Maximilian and his reign, and a symbolic representation of his virtues and ideals. Artistically seen it was the result of a collaboration between Hans Springinklee, Kölderer, and Dürer, but in its entity it bears the indelible stamp of the genius of the latter. The allegorical material was carefully prepared and adapted by Dürer's friend Willibald Pirckheimer in close collaboration with Stabius, Dürer himself, and probably also the Emperor. Pirckheimer, born in Eichstädt in 1470, was another outstanding German humanist, a competent classical scholar, a learned jurisconsult, a tasteful protector of the arts, and an ardent collector, mainly of books and coins. He was a personal friend of Conrad Peutinger to whom Alciati had dedicated his emblems, and during a seven-year stay in Italy he had become acquainted with most of the leading humanists, among others Pico della Mirandola, Erasmus, and Reuchlin.

His interest in hieroglyphical studies is explicitly emphasized by his contemporaries, and during a stay in Linz in 1514, he is known to have presented Maximilian with a Latin translation of Horapollo, made at the express demand of the Emperor. (Pl. XVI, 1).

It is therefore no wonder that the allegories of the arch became of a decided hieroglyphic character, and that the whole monument in its entity as well as in its details became something like a subtle and intricate hieroglyphic enigma.

77

Architecturally seen it represents a classical triumphal arch[60] provided with three gates, and it was adorned with pictures representing episodes from the life of the Emperor, and a variety of allegorical figures referring to his aspirations, virtues, and ideals.

The focal point of the representation is the so-called 'tabernaculum' inserted immediately above the main gate, called 'the gate of honour and authority'. It represents the Emperor enthroned, with all imperial regalia, and surrounded by animal figures and various ornamental objects of allegorical significance. Several of the pictures recurring elsewhere on the monument are here brought together and united in the tabernacle which, in accordance with the practice of the time, was intended to express the quintessence of the symbolism of the monument, and at the same time to provide the key to its understanding. In his contemporary commentary, Stabius, the historiographer of the Emperor, explicitly calls this panel 'a mystery in sacred Egyptian letters', but its true significance and meaning remained utterly obscure until the Austrian art historian Giehlow[61] demonstrated that all the figures were hieroglyphs, directly borrowed from Horapollo.

The original sketches for the various ornaments were originally made by Dürer as illustrations for Pirckheimer's above-mentioned translation of the Hieroglyphica, which was never printed, but the pictures were used for the decoration of the arch, to express its secret allegorical meaning. Read in accordance with Horapollo's indications the signs represent a pompous, and for our taste a rather long-winded panegyric on Maximilian, describing him among other things as 'a hero of undying and eternal fame (basilisk and star), a descendant of age-old nobility (the bundle of papyrus), a prince of exalted virtues (dog with stole), courageous, strong, and circumspects (lion, and heron with a stone in its claw), adorned with the gifts of nature and the arts (the dewing clouds), Roman emperor (the imperial eagle), who in a glorious victory (the falcon), almost impossible to obtain (the two feet in water), had vanquished the powerful king of France (the cock standing upon a snake) etc. That this interpretation of the monument is correct is proved by Giehlow beyond all possible doubt. The text corresponds to Stabius' rendering of what he calls the 'great title of Maximilian', and it is word by word identical with the subtitles of a small treatise made by Pirckheimer and called 'explanations of some Egyptian letters from Horapollo'. But the final proof is the fact that Pirckheimer's original draft for the whole text is still preserved, written in his own hand, and provided with his own rather clumsy drawings of the hieroglyphs themselves[62]. (Pl. XIV, 4).

To the modern mind the great importance attached to the allegorical significance of a work of art like this – its 'mystery' as Stabius calls it – may seem strange and difficult to understand, but it is well worth remembering that to the people of the Renaissance, form without content was craftsmanship, and an unphilosophic approach to art, vulgar.

78

In its philosophic conception any artistic representation was, in fact, in itself an example of 'sacred allegorical writing'. After theology and next to philosophy art was the highest and most sublime medium for the materialization of the divine realm of the soul and of the ideas themselves, and as such it was subject to the laws governing the relations between matter and idea. Mystical insight into the ideal nature of things was necessary for the artist to create it, and the same insight was necessary for the contemplative spectator in order to solve the enigma of the work, and read its secret message.

But this insight could in either case only be achieved by means of divine inspiration, and each true artistic experience, each true interpretation of the metaphysical message of art, became, therefore, necessarily a divine revelation.

The artist could point to the secret and indicate its nature by means of symbolic and allegorical details – it was in fact part of his artistic duty to do so – and by a devoted contemplation of these details the spectator could become as it were initiated, and prepare his mind for the allegorical revelation, the final miracle of understanding.

Only against this background can the allegorical art of the period be properly appreciated and understood, and its use of 'divine symbols and sacred hieroglyphic letters' explained.

It is obvious, on the other hand, that a true philosophical conception of allegories and hieroglyphs could only be maintained on the highest artistic level. The more these symbols became separated from their philosophical origin and became involved with the popular emblematic fancies, the more they became debased in nature as well as in use. Very soon the word allegory could be used for any pun or ordinary play on words, and any rebus or conundrum could be called hieroglyphic. Owing to the overwhelming popularity of emblems, 'livrées', and 'dévices' this vulgarization of the hieroglyphs is particularly easy to observe in France, but it is by no means a specific French phenomenon such as Volkmann would make us believe.

Neither in its origin nor in its nature was the French tradition different from that of other European countries. Its course was closely parallel to that of Italy, from whence its early and rapid introduction into France was furthered by the political development towards the end of the fifteenth century, which opened the country for a general influx of Italian culture. The ambitious policy of Charles VIII (1483-1498) aiming at the conquest of Constantinople, where it was his desire to be proclaimed emperor of the East, made the king renew his family-claims on the kingdom of Naples, and in 1494 he invaded Italy.

His advance was rapid and successful, but after an ostentatious entry into Naples in 1495, followed an inglorious retreat. Politically seen the expedition proved a failure, but culturally seen it became of the greatest importance by inaugurating the French Renaissance, and an increasing Italian influence on French manners, arts, and letters. This influence gained impetus under Charles' successor Louis XII (1498-1515), who in a renewed Italian campaign succeeded in conquering Milan, which remained in French hands for fourteen years, until shortly before the death of the king in 1515. It was during the reigns of Louis and his successor Francis I (1515-1547) that the hieroglyphic studies were introduced and developed in France.

Their harbingers were as usual Horapollo and Poliphilo. (Pl. XV, 2). The first French edition of the former did not appear until 1543, but we shall see that Geoffroy Tory had made a translation of the Latin text already before 1529 and the original Italian editions were obviously known as soon as they appeared[63]. A French translation of Poliphilo was published by Jacques Kerver in Paris 1546, under the title 'Discours du Songe de Poliphile'[64], but Francis' personal copy of the original edition is still extant[65], and its hieroglyphic emblems as well as its ordinary illustrations were already copied in an illuminated manuscript containing a 'Traité de la Grandeur et Excellence de la Vertu', made for his mother Louise of Savoy about 1515[66].

It is also more than a coincidence that Rhodiginus' above-mentioned 'Antiquae lectiones' – one of the fainter offshoots of the tradition – were dedicated to Jean Grolin, vicomte d'Aquisy, the hieroglyphical interests of this famous erudite and lover of books being well established, as hieroglyphical notes written in his own hand are found in the margin of his personal copy of the Adages of Erasmus[67].

But the true and most charming hierogrammate of the early French Renaissance was undoubtedly Geoffroy Tory, who was born in Bourges about 1480 and died in Paris in 1533 as the first 'imprimeur du Roy'.

Equally renowned and gifted as author, engraver, painter, and publisher, Tory was one of the typical, if one of the lesser, universal minds brought into existence by the spirit of the Renaissance. His publicistic activities include a series of translations and commentaries, but his main publication from our special view point was his 'Champfleury', published in 1529. The book contains certain calligraphic reflexions, based on strange theories concerning the natural proportions of letters; but in spite of its subject it is written with the most charming bonhomie, abounding in digressions and personal reminiscences, and displaying, almost on every page, evidence of the author's ardent interest in hieroglyphical matters.

Among other things the book contains an alphabet of 'lettres fantastiques' consisting of 'signs and pictures in the Egyptian manner' although not, as explicitly stated, based on 'philosophie naturelle'[68] as the Egyptian letters. Horapollo[69] and Poliphilo[70] whose hieroglyphic inscriptions were considered absolutely genuine, were quoted for Tory's conception of the hieroglyphs as such, and we are given the important information that he had undertaken a translation of Horapollo's Hieroglyphica: 'pour en auoir faict ung p̄sent a vng myen bon seigneur & amy'[71]. He provided an important list of the very few original hieroglyphical monuments to be seen in

Rome at his time including 'a porphyry' near the Pantheon – called 'Notre Dame la Ronde' – an obelisk – called 'une Ésquille et Pyramide' — at the Capitol (ara coeli), and another 'pres la Minerue'[72]. These were undoubtedly genuine Egyptian objects, while the hieroglyphs he describes as having seen on a painting in a house near the palace of Mount Jordan, and representing 'une teste de boeuf, une grenoille, ung oueil, une chaufferette pleine de feu, ung visage d'home, ung vaisseau de violettes en ung pot, ung oueil sus une sole de soulier' etc. were obviously contemporary copies of the hieroglyphic inscription found in the Hypnerotomachia fol. C I recto[73]. (Pl. XI, 1).

Outside the 'Champfleury' Tory used 'hieroglyphic methods' for the construction of ensigns and emblems, of which his own mark 'le Pot cassé' is a typical example[74]. It represents a broken vase with flowers, signifying the human body and the frail human virtues. The pot is pierced by an iron 'toret' – presumably an engraver's tool – representing fate, and placed on the closed book of life, sealed with iron chains and three locks or cadenas symbolizing the three goddesses of destiny.

The above-mentioned examples will show that Tory, in spite of his enthusiasm, was not a pioneer in hieroglyphics. He was inspired by his Italian predecessors and the currents of fashion more than by personal studies, and the practical possibilities of the art attracted him more than its theoretical and philosophic background, although he was undoubtedly fascinated by, and found great pleasure in, subtle interpretations of the signs.

Seen on the background of Tory's enthusiasm nothing demonstrates better the extent to which the hieroglyphs had become involved with the prevailing emblematic fashion, which from about the reign of Charles VIII swept all over France, than Rabelais' violent attack on the vulgarization of the literary allegory[75]. He anathematized relentlessly 'ces glorieux de cour et transporteurs de noms' and their 'devices', and called their allegorical efforts 'tout ineptes, tout fades, tout rustiques et barbares, que l'on doibvrait atacher une queue de renard au collet et faire un masque d'une bouze de vache a un chascun d'iceulx qui en vouldroit dorenavant user en France'.

On the other hand, it is equally significant that he made a definite distinction between this vulgar abuse and what he considered the genuine traditions. This is clear from the conciliatory remarks following the above mentioned invectives: 'bien oultrement foisoient en temps jadis les saigne de Égypte, quand ils éscripvoient par lettres qu'ilz appeloient hiéroglyphiques, lesquelles nul n'entendoit, qui n'entendist et un chascun, entendoit qui entendist la vertu, proprieté et nature des choses par icelles figures, desquelles Orus Apollon a en grec composé deux livres, et Polyphile au Songe d'Amours en a davantaigne exposé'.

A monumental example of the tradition is found among the monuments erected in 1549 to celebrate the solemn entry of King Henry the Scond of France and his Queen Catherine de Medici into the city of Paris. It represented 'un animal d'Éthiopie nommé Rhinocéros', carrying an obelisk on its back, and crushing lions, bears, wolves, foxes, and other 'bestes rauissantes' under its belly. Its symbolical significance was indicated by its Greek motto ἀλεξίκακος 'the suppressor or averter of evil'. The whole design is directly inspired by the obelisk-carrying elephant from the Hypnerotomachia, and like this the French monument is also provided with an extensive hieroglyphic inscription containing a respectful discourse presented to the King by his Parisian subjects, and expressing the wish: Force & vigilance puissent garder vostre Royaume ... que dominez à la mer ... & par ferme paix & concorde ... longement viuez, regissez & gouuernez'. As such it is a deliberate counterpart of Dürer's text, and it represents the longest neo-hieroglyphical inscription recorded. (Pl. XIII).

As a monument it has long ago disappeared, and we do not know who originally designed it, but we know that Philibert de Lorme was in charge of all the arrangements for the entry, and a picture of the animal is preserved in an exquisite woodcut by Jean Goujon in the charming publication commemorating the event[76].

Together with the various editions of Horapollo, Poliphilo, and Valerianus already mentioned, the more serious hieroglyphical traditions were in the subsequent French literature represented by 'Discours des Hiéroglyphes' and 'LIV Tableaux Hiéroglyphiques' both by Pierre L'Anglois, and first published in Paris in 1583[77], by Pierre Dinet's 'Cinq Livres des Hiéroglyphiques' (Paris 1614)[78], which is an annotated compilation of hieroglyphs, closely related to Valerianus' collection, and by 'De symbolica Aegyptortum sapientia' (Paris 1618) by Nicolas Caussin (1585-1651)[79], containing the Greek text of Horapollo together with a Latin translation and followed by various compilations of an emblematic and symbolic nature. (Pl. XVIII, 2b).

Examples of hieroglyphic material in the inexhaustible emblematic literature, the most monumental specimen of which is Menestrier's 'Art des emblèmes' (Lyon 1622), will be found in Volkmann[80], the emblematic tradition being too remote to occupy us seriously here.

It would seem, however, as if a latent interest in Egyptian matters was kept alive in French humanistic circles by the strong wave of Neo-Platonism which spread from Italy to France during the fifteenth century[81], and it was probably more than mere coincidence that the subsequent philological revival of Coptic was to a great extent furthered by French Neo-Platonic scholars.

In England the hieroglyphic material would seem to have been introduced mainly through the emblematic literature. We have already had opportunity to quote Geffrey Whitney (1548?-1601?) whose 'Choice of Emblemes' published by Plantin (Leyden 1586) was one of the first complete book of emblems in English[82]. It is to a great extent based on and directly translated from Alciati, but Whitney was apparently well versed in the hieroglyphic studies of his time.

In Green's facsimile reprint of the emblems, is found a reproduction of Whitney's

motto 'Victoria ex Labore Honesta, et utilis' – 'Victory achieved by labour is honourable and useful' –, illustrated by his badge which is a hieroglyphic rendering of
the motto. It represents a laurel-wreath (for victory), above a bucranium – an ornamental representation of an ox-skull, which stands for labour –, adorned with two
hoes and palm leaves, indicating what is honourable and useful. As such it is probably
the first example of an English 'hieroglyphical' inscription, but it is not an original
invention of Whitney's. The whole emblem, motto as well as device, is directly borrowed from a print made by Giulio Bonasone for an Italian emblem book by Achille
Bocchi, called 'Symbolicae quaestiones', and published in Bologna 1555[83]. But the
use of the bucranium with the two hoes as a hieroglyph for 'labour', was already introduced by Colonna for one of the inscriptions of his Hypnerotomachia (fol. C), and
there can be no possible doubt about the direct connection between this representation and Bocchi's symbol[84]. Whitney and his badge are consequently directly and
indissolubly connected with the very origin of the neo-hieroglyphic traditions.

Typical of the emblematic use of the hieroglyphic terminology are also the slightly
younger (1635) emblems of Francis Quarles (1592-1644), who states that: 'before letters God was known by Hieroglyphicks; and, indeed, what are the Heavens, the
Earth, nay every Creature, but Hieroglyphicks and Emblems of his Glory?' The
Christian allegories in Quarles' book have no connection with Horapollo, Colonna,
or Valerianus, and the word hieroglyph is used merely as a synonym of allegory, but
Quarles' later collection of emblems is nevertheless explicitly called 'Hieroglyphicks
of the life of Man' (published 1638), and the book is in its preface called 'an Aegyp-
tian dish, drest on the English fashion'.

Apart from the emblems the hieroglyphs are but rarely mentioned in the literary
and philosophical debate of Renaissance England. Its dynamic spirit of expansion
and national enterprise was apparently not attracted by hieroglyphical subtleties, and
although the literature of the period abounds in allegories and parables, it made little
or no use of the hieroglyphic material[85]. Neither could esoteric hieroglyphs be expected to appeal to the representatives of the austere protestantism prevailing in
learned and theological circles entirely dominated by the fanatic struggle against
Catholicism, and concentrating not only on the development of a new Protestant
theology, but on the creation of a new Protestant philosophy and science as well, uncontaminated by Catholic thought and based on the study of the Book.

However, sporadic traces of an influence from Egyptian material are found, characteristically enough in the works of the mystic philosophers of the period, its astro-
logers, and its alchemists, all of which were influenced by Hermetic literature and
Neo-Platonic thought.

The first English translation of 'The Divine Pymander of Hermes Trismegistus'
made by the mystic divine John Everard (1575?-1650?) was published in 1650[86];

but already Queen Elizabeth's renowned mathematician and astrologer John Dee (1527-1609) was a professed Hermetic scholar, who discussed the writings of Hermes with Dr. Hannibal during a stay in Cracow in 1585[87], and called his mystical expoundings of astrological symbols 'Monas Hieroglyphicas'[88]. Also Joseph Mead (1586-1638), another mystic divine of the period is said to have contributed to Egyptology[89], although a perusal of his 'Clavis Apophtegmata' (1627), in Richard More's translation from 1650, has not made the nature of these contributions clear[90].

Much more important for the subsequent development than these philosophical offshoots was the introduction of hieroglyphical studies into the archaeological and philological activities of the period.

The basic conceptions of the problem as well as the methods applied remained by our standards essentially unchanged, but the new 'scientific' approach became nevertheless of great importance as a healthy reaction against the allegorical extravaganzas which were frequently criticized. The main methodical improvement of these early scholars was to draw a clear distinction between the 'modern' reconstructed hieroglyphs and the original Egyptian ones, and this rediscovery of the real hieroglyphs, and the subsequent interest in genuine hieroglyphic inscriptions made as a matter of fact the Egyptological studies of the Baroque essentially different from those of the Renaissance.

The renowned Italian naturalist Michele Mercati (1541-1593) published already in the year 1589 an important archaeological treatise called 'De gli obelischi di Roma'[91], in which he devoted an extensive chapter to the study of the hieroglyphs[92]. His basic approach to the problems and his general attitude towards the script as such was not essentially different from those of his contemporaries, but the very fact that his account was based on a critical consideration of almost every single bit of accessible material, and that he made a careful distinction between the original Egyptian and the emblematic traditions made his book a significant progress.

It is also significant that he gave great prominence to Clement's account of the Egyptian writing[93], now known to be closer to the truth than any other, and that he considered Hermapion's obelisk translation genuine, and discussed it at length. His historical deductions, and his efforts to trace the history of writing through Palestine, Ethiopia, Egypt, and Greece, as well as his discussions about the relative importance of Noah, Moses, and Hermes for its development are only of historical interest; but it is typical of his alert mind that he should try to compare the Egyptian with the recently discovered Mexican hieroglyphs, and he made some rather shrewd observations, that the signs denoting abstract words such as 'glad', 'angry', and 'handsome', originally would have been derived from pictures of a glad, angry, or handsome man. His discussion of Clement occasioned some reflexions on the various categories of signs, and he distinguished between hieroglyphs directly used to express the objects they represent – our ideograms –,tropological hieroglyphs, expressing sentences and phrases, and as such considered the models of the Pythagorean maxims, and the 'ordinary hieroglyphs of Horapollo', which strangely enough, and for no obvious reason, seem to be considered as a group apart.

The actual results obtained may not seem important from an Egyptological point of view, but the very soberness of the book contributed to its popularity, and made it much read and frequently quoted in archaeological literature right down until the end of the eighteenth century. Its critical and analytic tendencies, rare for the period, show the author as an independent and observant scholar.

Even more independent and critical was Lorenzo Pignoria (1571-1631) in his scholarly edition of the famous Isiac table, or 'tabula Bembina'[94] as it was also called from the name of its first possessor, the Cardinal Bembo. It was discovered in Rome in 1525, and acquired almost immediately the reputation of being one of the most valuable and important antiquities ever found. Eneas Vico, the founder of numismatics, reproduced it on an engraving in 1559[95], and it became from then on a recurrent topic in the learned debate, gave rise to endless discussions and learned controversies, and the strangest theories and suggestions were thrown out as explanations of its origin and significance. To some of these we shall revert later, but Pignorius' commentary was in several respects a deliberate reaction against them. He declared from the very beginning that he was unable to give an explanation of the monument as such, and that he would not even attempt it. He was interested in the table as an archaeological object, and not as a symbolical manifestation, and all attempts to attribute a hidden allegorical meaning to the various pictures and ornaments were therefore deliberately excluded from his book. It was his avowed intention to consider each picture and each ornamental detail separately, and to base his explanations only on comparative material which could be obtained from, and corroborated with, classical sources. He did not even pretend to be able to date the object exactly, but contrary to many contemporaries, who considered it a mystic relic dating from the very beginnings of the history of mankind, he presumed that it was made sometime about the reign of Augustus, and he had even the courage to criticize its workmanship and its style.

He could hardly be expected to rise entirely above the prevalent prejudices of his time, and the allegorical expoundings of Horapollo and Valerianus are not infrequently found in his commentary, but his great methodical innovation and improvement consisted in his use of tangible archaeological material as evidence and material of comparison, such as gems, seals, amulets, and statuettes, which were not merely referred to, but engraved and reproduced as illustrations for everybody to judge and criticize. In this respect he was an almost unchallenged pioneer, and the question of

85

the scientific validity of his actual results becomes immaterial against the fact that he was the first to introduce archaeological evidence into a hieroglyphic and Egyptological treatise, thus anticipating the later archaeological and Egyptological efforts of the century[96].

In conclusion, another monumental publication, now unknown and forgotten, must be mentioned, which at the time of its appearance represented a significant step towards the development of methodical hieroglyphical studies, by providing for the first time an extensive collection of authentic hieroglyphical inscriptions; Herwarth von Hohenburg's 'Thesaurus Hieroglyphicorum'[97].

Herwarth (Hoerwarth) was a Bavarian diplomat and scholar born in 1553 († 1622), who combined a distinguished diplomatic career with learned studies in mathematics – he tried to construct a notation facilitating arithmetic calculations –, philology – his edition of the Bavarian collection of Greek manuscripts – and archaeology. His Thesaurus contains a complete engraved reproduction of the Isiac table, the decoration of which he strangely enough explains as a 'nautical description of the world', some sort of a celestial compass[98], and certain notes are in fact inserted on the first plate adjusting the various figures with respect to the cardinal points. (Pl. VI, 1). More important are his reproductions of the inscriptions of various Egyptian monuments, among which are the hieroglyphical texts of no less than 19 obelisks. Some of these, made by the Belgian engraver van Aalst[99], are entirely fictitious such as fig. 7; others are very clumsy and imperfect (figs. 1-4), but the rest (especially figs. 10-17, and figs. 32-34) are undoubtedly direct copies made from the original monuments. They are as a matter of fact, when everything is taken into consideration, remarkably accurate, and take obviously great pains to retain the 'style' of the original signs.

But not only obelisks were reproduced. Fig. 28 represents one of the famous lions, originally placed on the Capitol, and later removed to the fountain Acqua Felice[100], near the Baths of Diocletian, together with a fairly accurate copy of the inscription from its base. Figs. 51 and 54 represent two 'Würfelhocker' called 'hieroglyphic canopi', together with their inscriptions, and also ordinary archaeological material without texts is represented, such as vases and gems. The four pictures of one of the former, (figs. 62-65) – said to have come from the collection of Laelius Pasqualinus[101] – had rather a strange history of their own, as they were first appropriated by Athanasius Kircher, and later, from his publication, stolen by Fischer von Erlach, who made them into four separate objects[102].

It is characteristic, and could hardly be expected to be otherwise, that a considerable amount of non-Egyptian material was also included among the so-called hieroglyphs, either because it was supposed to have a secret allegorical – in the terminology of the period a 'hieroglyphic' – meaning, or quite simply because it represented objects of a weird and enigmatic appearance; and it is not surprising among this non-

Egyptian material to find an elaborate engraving of the temple-frieze from San Lorenzo[103] (fig. 37), explicitly called 'Hieroglyphicorum effigies'. (Pl. VI, 2).

Only a few of the representations are commented upon in short headings, but several of them are carefully numbered as if a more extensive commentary was planned[104]. But even as it is, as a mere catalogue, the book became a landmark in the history of early Egyptology, as the only book in which authentic Egyptian inscriptions could be found, and Egyptian hieroglyphs seen. As such it remained for a long time an important, though unfortunately very often unacknowledged, source of subsequent Egyptological publications.

IV. The Seventeenth and Eighteenth Centuries

The hieroglyphical theories of the Renaissance had been illusions based on Neo-Platonic speculations and an entirely erroneous conception of the script. But they had been fertile and fruitful, had inspired artists and thinkers, nourished their imagination, and left indelible marks on their work. (Pl. XVII).

During the seventeenth century this was changed. The hieroglyphs were taken out of their artistic and philosophic sphere and transferred to the realm of science, where, with some notable exceptions, they ceased to be considered as methaphysical, but merely as philological problems, henceforward inspiring nothing but learned quarrels generally unedifying and barren in themselves, but serving a purpose nevertheless by furthering the slow process of developing the methodical principles on which modern science has been based.

It was typical that these efforts should be based on the study of an archaeological object such as the Isiac table and not on Horapollo and his successors. The Flemish scholar Johannes Goropius Becanus (van Gorp. 1518-1572) seems to have been the first to introduce this object into the learned debate, where he used it, together with other hieroglyphical material, to support his weird theories about the Cimbrian origin of the Germanic races, and about Flemish as the colloquial language of our paradisian forefathers[1].

Furthered by nationalistic self-assertion – a not infrequent by-product of early Protestant culture – these discussions about the original race and language of mankind gave rise to ardent polemics, and the Swede Olaus Magnus, for instance, made efforts to prove that the ancient Scandinavians no less than the Egyptians could boast of a system of symbolic and hieroglyphic writing[2], a theory which was later elaborated upon by his countryman Buraeus, and later still, by Rudbeck[3]. The latter in his 'Atlantica' propounded the theory that the decorations of the Isiac table represented a runic calendar, and that its inscriptions were written in an original Nordic script, invented by the Laplanders. A different explanation was given by the German botanist Melchior Guilandinus (Wielandt. From about 1519 until 1589), who had made extensive travels in Asia and Africa[4]. His reflections on the table were included in his elaborate commentary on Pliny's account of the papyrus plant, and he came to the result that the inscriptions contained nothing less than the entire legal code of the

PLATE XVII

Hieroglyphic emblem by Th. de Bry expressing the motto: 'virtuti fortuna comes',
'fortune is the companion of valour'.

PLATE XVIII

2 a

2 b

I

6

1. So-called Canopus drawn by Th. de Bry in 1602. The inscription represents an honest if not entirely successful effort to copy the original.

2. Egyptian motives used for the decoration of seventeenth century books.
a. Michael Maier, Arcana Arcanissima. Oppenheim? 1614.
b. Nicolas Caussin, De Symbolica Aegyptiorum Sapientia. Paris 1618.

3. So-called bust of Isis the inscription of which Needham considered hieroglyphic and tried to explain from a comparison with Chinese writing.

3

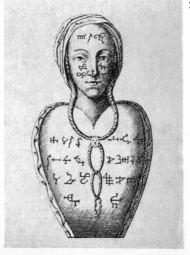

Egyptians, since copper tablets according to the Ancients generally were reserved for legal texts.

Also the Holsatian alchemist and Rosicrucian Michael Maier († 1622) devoted a separate volume to hieroglyphical problems, and called it 'Arcana Arcanissima hoc est Hieroglyphica Aegyptio-Graeca'[5]. (Pl. XVIII, 2 a). According to his interpretation the table contained chemical secrets of the greatest importance, and several other scholars tried, in the same way, to appropriate the monument for their own purposes, and to exploit it in accordance with their own theories and preconceived ideas.

This state of affairs was obviously only possible in a period which had not yet succeeded in formulating its scientific problems, or developed the principles of a methodical approach, and the results obtained were undoubtedly most often quaint and baroque in the original meaning of the word. Nothing is easier than to criticize and ridicule them, but it must not be forgotten in our slightly pedantic complacency 'wie unendlich weit wir's gebracht haben', that our own approach and our own methods are directly dependent on the struggles and quarrels, the mistakes and achievements, and above all on the ardent and untiring enthusiasm of these old scholars, and their often naive, but always inspiring, love of learning and knowledge.

It must not be forgotten either that when Egyptology emerged from this confusion as one of the first separate disciplines, it was due mainly to the erudition, the almost superhuman industry, and the unswerving dedication of Athanasius Kircher, who, in good as well as in bad, was a typical exponent of his time.

Kircher was born in 1601 in the small German town of Geisa in Hessen. He was educated at the local Jesuit college and received into the order at the age of sixteen. From about 1622 he was caught by the maelstrom of the Thirty Years' War, and the next ten years of his life were spent on an almost uninterrupted flight from the havoc of war, and the Protestant persecutions of his order.

The story of his peregrinations, during which he was frequently reduced to the state of an absolute pauper, and deprived of the barest necessities, recalls occasionally the tales of his younger contemporary Grimmelshausen, but he succeeded nevertheless in an almost miraculous way to increase his already remarkable learning and lay the foundations of that encyclopaedic knowledge which should make him one of the most productive scholars of his time. We are here only concerned with his Egyptological publications, but his interest in the natural sciences resulted among other things in an 'Ars Magnesia' (1631), the invention of the laterna magica, the first observations of sunspots[6], and a treatise on the plague, which is said to anticipate a 'théorie microbienne'[7].

His interest in Egyptology dates from a comparatively early period of his life, in fact already from 1628, when during a stay in Speier, he happened to pick up a book with pictures of Roman obelisks and their inscriptions in the local library, was caught by the fascination of the signs, and immediately inspired with an irresistible desire to decipher them.

It is significant that his interest should be aroused by genuine Egyptian inscriptions, but his first contributions to Egyptology were nevertheless, by a curious conflux of circumstances, made in Coptic, and not in the hieroglyphic field.

It is outside our present scope to trace the history of the Coptic tradition, but Kircher's efforts to combine his Coptic studies with hieroglyphical activities makes it inevitable to consider both, because both, in spite of their shortcomings, inaugurated a new epoch in Egyptology and heralded its establishment as a specific philological discipline.

As a living language, Coptic had shown a remarkable tenacity of life, and the Arabian historian Makrizi tells that in the fifteenth century it was still used colloquially by the Christian population all over Upper Egypt. It apparently lost much of its influence during the sixteenth and seventeenth centuries, but the report of the German traveller Vansleb, that during a stay in the town of Siut in 1673 he was introduced to a stone-deaf octogenarian, who was 'the man with whom the Coptic language will disappear'[8], is undoubtedly exaggerated, as we have evidence that the language remained alive in certain Upper Egyptian communities almost to the present day[9].

The existence of this 'lingua aegyptiaca' as distinct from Arabic, was occasionally mentioned in contemporary travel books[10], but generally speaking it was completely disregarded and ignored in the western world until about the sixteenth century. Some remarks on the language of Egypt are found in the 'Mithridates' (1555) of the Swiss polyhistor Konrad Gesner (1516-1575), who tried to give a condensed account of the characteristics of the various languages of the world, but his information concerning Egyptian was confined to some examples of Egyptian words such as quoted by the classics, and a list of the Coptic names of the months. His rendering of the latter is very imperfect, and he was obviously unaware that the variants he quotes from the 'Antidotes' of the Greek physician Nicolaus Myrepsis, who lived in Cairo in the thirteenth century, were better than his own[11]. It is obvious, therefore, that he had no real knowledge of Coptic; and for want of the necessary facilities, such a texts, grammars, and vocabularies, it would as a matter of fact have been virtually impossible for any western scholar to learn it. However, a certain amount of material began to sift in already during the sixteenth century, mainly as a result of the increased connections with the East.

The titular bishop of Sidon, the Maltese diplomat Leonard Abel († 1605), is generally considered one of the early promoters of the Coptic studies, but the evidence of his interest is very slight. He does not seem to have brought any Coptic manuscripts back from his extensive travels in the Levant[12] (from 1583-1586), and his Latin translation of a Coptic treatise dealing with liturgic matters, was apparently made from an Arabic manuscript[13]. The sole factual evidence of a more personal contact with Coptology are a few random words written in his own hand on a blank page in one of his manuscripts[14] and giving a list of the Coptic letters and some of the numerals. It is also very dubious whether his learned contemporary, the famous Arabist Giovanni Battista Raimondi (1540-1610?), had any personal knowledge of the language, although he did possess a beautiful, and for his time unique, collection of Coptic manuscripts[15], and had plans to include the Coptic version in his contemplated edition of a polyglot Bible, a project which was never carried through[16].

Men of action and initiative, such as the traveller Pietro della Valle and Peiresc, who were able to provide the material and organize its publication, became therefore at this critical stage more important for the development than scholars.

Pietro della Valle (1586-1652) was a Roman patrician of independent means, very well connected in influential Roman circles, and probably the first true traveller of leisure in the western world. It is characteristic that his famous oriental voyage should be undertaken as a diversion after a disappointing love affair, and that he had difficulties in deciding whether he should in fact travel, or commit suicide. Having decided in favour of the former, he seems to have enjoyed himself, and visited Egypt, the whole of the Near, and parts of the Far East. He married in Baghdad, and stayed away for no less than twelve years, from 1614 until 1626. Like most of his contemporaries Pietro was an ardent collector, and it was in this capacity that he made his contribution to Egyptology by returning with two mummies[17] and a collection of Coptic manuscripts, including no less than five grammars and two extensive vocabularies in the Bohairic – Lower Egyptian – dialect[18].

In Rome the importance of these manuscripts was immediately recognized, and steps were taken for their publication. The celebrated Arabic scholar Thomas Obicini (Thomaso da Novara † 1632), who had studied Coptic during a stay in the Near East[19], was entrusted with the task, and a fount of Coptic characters, necessary for the printing, was cast and ready for use already in 1629. Unfortunately all plans came to an abrupt end with the untimely death of Obicini in 1632, and the problem arose of how to find another competent Coptic scholar. For want of qualified candidates the problem seemed insoluble, and the discussions had entered into a deadlock, when the French erudite Nicolas-Claude Fabri de Peiresc (1580-1637) entered into the picture. As a member of the local 'parlement', Peiresc had settled in Aix en Provence after extensive travels at home and abroad, mainly in Italy, England and the Netherlands.

Eminently gifted, but with an intelligence which was probably more receptive than creative, he had to a remarkable extent absorbed the totality of the learning and knowledge of his period. As a scholar he was remarkably unproductive, but his energy and diligence made him one of the most prolific letter writers the world has ever seen[20]. He was in constant touch with almost all the outstanding personalities of his day, to such an extent that he is said to have contributed essentially to the diffusion of the discoveries of Harvey, Copernicus, and Kepler[21].

An ardent collector[22], he had correspondents and agents everywhere, in Egypt and in the Levant as well as on the coast of Barbary, whence he received an almost unintermittent stream of antiques, curios, books, and even animals – he was the first to import angora cats – and plants, the latter intended for his famous gardens, in which he, as the first, acclimatized the jasmin and the oleander. His general and dynamic interest in everything agitating the intellectual world drew him also towards Coptic, not as an active student, but as a promptor and mediator. He revived Raimondi's old idea, and proposed the inclusion of the Coptic text in the French polyglot Bible[23], only to realize that the time was not yet ripe and that much preliminary work would have to be done before the publication of any Coptic text could be thought of.

To promote the necessary studies, and probably also to make himself independent of della Valle's material, he began to collect Coptic manuscripts, and encouraged a small group of scholars to take up Coptic. Only one of these would seem to have mastered the language properly, the French philologist and historian Claude de Saumaise (1588-1653), and when the question arose as to who should succeed Father Obicini as the editor of della Valle's manuscripts, he was Peiresc's candidate for the task.

But before a final decision had been taken, Kircher had arrived in France, made the acquaintance of Peiresc about 1633[24], and was eventually entrusted with the publication, much to the disappointment and chagrin of Saumaise. The reasons for this decision are obscure, but they are probably connected with the fact that Saumaise was an ardent Protestant, and that Kircher now, mainly owing to Periresc's recommendations, was called to Rome (1633).

Here he was given the Chair of Mathematics at the Collegium Romanum, and in 1636 the first results of his Coptic studies appeared, his 'Prodromus coptus sive aegyptiacus', in which he professed to answer the question concerning the 'origin and age, as well as the fate and peculiarities of the Coptic or Egyptian language – which was formerly the Pharaonic language' –; and also to solve the problem of the hieroglyphs 'by means of a new and original method'[25].

Prodromus means herald or harbinger, and the book was obviously intended as what we should call an introduction into the study of Coptic, and as such it was in fact very well and methodically planned, and has undoubtedly served its purpose, in spite of its not always irreproachable methods and results. It treated in consecutive chapters the etymology of the word Coptic, Coptic institutions, the relationship between the Coptic and the Ethiopian Churches, and gave a survey of the activities of the early Christian missionaries in the East including an account of the famous Nestorian mission to China in the eighth century.

Then followed some reflections on the linguistic nature of the language as such, and its relations to Greek and Hebrew. These were mostly erroneous, but were used to support the basic and correct thesis of the book, that Coptic and the old Pharaonic language of Egypt were identical, and that the knowledge of Coptic was, therefore, essential for the understanding and interpretation of the hieroglyphs[26]. It is undoubtedly true that Kircher did not accept the logical consequence of this important and correct assertion, but the thesis about the identity of Coptic and Old Egyptian, as well as the short Coptic grammar, – the first ever written in a European language – with which Kircher ends his book, should always assure his Prodromus an honourable position among the books of early Egyptology.

Even more important from a practical point of view was his subsequent publication 'Lingua aegyptiaca restituta' (Rome 1644), containing the grammars and the great vocabulary (scala magna)[27] from della Valle's collection, together with a synopsis made by Kircher himself, and dealing with certain practical problems such as the nature of the language, the names of the months, the stars, and certain plants, some geographical information, and a digression on the organization of the Coptic church, with a list of its patriarchs. A very useful Latin index of the words contained in the scala was also included, and in spite of its inaccuracies and undeniable errors, the book remained for the rest of the century, the very foundation of all Coptic studies.

But, as far as Kircher himself was concerned, Coptic remained always a means and not an end[28]. His real ambition was from the very beginning to solve the problem of the hieroglyphs, and already the 'Prodromus' contained a detailed plan for that publication which should become his Egyptological life-work, his 'Oedipus Aegyptiacus'[29]. (Pl. XIX, 4). But in 1650 he was given an assignment which gave him an opportunity to propound almost all of his Egyptological theories and to display his famous hieroglyphical method in concentrated form, the publication of a description and explanation of the Pamphilian obelisk.

This monument, originally erected by Domitian, and probably executed in Rome, had already in antiquity been appropriated by Maxentius, who had used it for the decoration of his circus, where it was rediscovered during the pontificate of Innocent the Xth Pamphili. Under the supervision of Kircher the Pope had it repaired, and Bernini re-erected it at its present position in front of the Palazzo Pamphili on the Piazza Navona (1649-1651). (Pl. VII, 3). To celebrate this event, the Pope asked Kircher to publish an account of the obelisk, a publication which is of the greatest importance for our present purpose, because it gives, in concentrated form, a complete picture of the author's general attitude towards all hieroglyphical and Egyptological problems, and illustrates his aims as well as his method, that 'original hieroglyphical method', which he considered his great discovery and the very essence of his life-work. Nothing is easier than to ridicule his efforts. It has, in fact, been done often enough, and Kircher has for a long time been the whipping-boy of Egyptology. His devotion, his untiring enthusiasm, and his positive contributions have been disregarded by the science he sacrificed his life to further and serve. He has been derided and scoffed at, an easy prey to Egyptologists who have sacrificed his reputation for a witticism, mostly without having opened his books[30]. But books as well as human beings have a fundamental right to be appreciated for their good, and not only derided for their bad qualities[31]. To give an objective account of Kircher's life-work is therefore a simple act of justice and retribution. It is, however, no easy task, mainly because its scope went far beyond the limits of Egyptology, and represents one of the last efforts to combine the totality of human knowledge, in religion, philosophy, history, and science, into a theological system, a universal cosmology, based on the concepts and ideas of a Neo-Platonized Christianity.

From the Renaissance Kircher had inherited the conceptions of a God-centred universe, dominated by a timeless emanation of divine truth, pervading it as an elementary dynamic force. The supreme and final manifestation of this truth was in Kircher's opinion the revelations of Christianity, but it was immanent in all existing religions and philosophic systems as well, and the philosophy of the Egyptians, such as it had inspired a Plato and a Pythagoras, was its highest pre-Christian manifestation. As such this esoteric knowledge of the Egyptians was of eminent importance as part of the living tradition, and its study was in itself a Christian preparation and initiation. To prove the timeless universality of the underlying truth was Kircher's principal aim, and at the same time to demonstrate the basic religious conformity between the Egyptian, the Greek, and his own cosmological conceptions. The direct connections and the general theoretical conformity of the religious and philosophic ideas of Greece and Egypt were to Kircher proved beyond all discussion by Plato's self-avowed dependence on Egyptian wisdom, and by the fact that the classics were unanimous in their statements that Zeus *was* Osiris, that Horus *was* Apollo, and Isis Cybele. His accounts of Egyptian mythology were based on Plutarch, the Neo-Platonists, and the Hermetic literature, and they were consequently dominated by Osirian ideas. In Kircher's opinion the Egyptians had considered Osiris the principal emanation of that divine principle, the centre of the world, and the supreme source of all, called the soul of the world, or the King of Heaven, which astrologically seen was identified with the sun. Isis was the principal emanation of the corresponding female principle called the Queen of Heaven, and identified with the moon. All other Gods and Goddesses of the celestial hierarchy were considered corresponding emanations of lower orders, and each God, demon, and spirit had its own immutable position in the universe, corresponding to the fixed positions of the planets and the stars. As

94

manifestations of the same central force they were all united, but each had its particular cosmological functions and represented specific cosmic forces. Osiris was 'vis
penetrativa universi', the penetrative force of the universe, Isis was 'vis productiva
frugum', its productive, fructiferous force, and their son Horus was 'the combining
force', such as illustrated by the heat-transmitting qualities of the sunbeams. These
dynamic qualities corresponded to philosophic principles. As the penetrating force
Osiris was also the active principle. Isis was the productive force, and consequently
the passive principle, while Horus' combining qualities made him the compositive
principle.

A basic conformity was in this way established between the concepts of religion and
philosophy, and similar methods were applied to those of science.

In what Kircher called a right-angled Platonic triangle, the longest side, enclosing
the right angle, represented the active principle, and was, therefore, identified with
Osiris. The smaller side was the passive principle, or Isis, and the hypothenuse was
the compositive principle, or Horus. Geometry and mathematics were in this way
integrated in the system, and so was astronomy, because each God, and the forces
and principles with which he was associated, was identified with one of the planets
or one of the signs of the zodiac. According to Kircher's alchemistic principles the
natural substances were also cosmic elements, and iron, for instance, was identified
with the destructive principle of Seth or Typhon, and magnes or the loadstone, with
the bones of Horus. Each concept and idea, each substance and element, and each
phenomenon was, therefore, a divine manifestation of an ubiquitous God, the all-
pervading soul of the universe. But the true connection between the phenomena and
their divine originator, was the mystic secret of existence, and it could only be understood by divine inspiration, by means of an esoteric knowledge and understanding of
the symbolical nature of things.

The ideal nature of the phenomena made it impossible for our intellect to understand their true significance, and without the enlightenment of a symbolic interpretation we could only perceive the things as heterogeneous material objects. Only by
divine inspiration could they be made to reveal their true meaning, and the enlightened process which enabled us to see their ideal coherence, and conceive them as
symbolic entities in a harmonious cosmic unity, was what Kircher understood by his
universal and original hieroglyphic method. His interest in Egyptology was, therefore, based on the conviction that the Egyptians were the first to have understood
this fundamental truth, over which the whole of their religion and their philosophy
had been formed. The Greeks had also understood it, but the Egyptians were the only
people who had taken the final consequence and invented a system of symbolic writing to express it, and this writing was the hieroglyphs.

Consequently there was no doubt in Kircher's mind that he knew what the hieroglyphic inscriptions contained. The classics told us that they contained the esoteric knowledge of the Egyptians, and Kircher was convinced that his conception of this knowledge was correct. It was based on the best sources: the classics, the Neo-Platonists, the Hermetic literature, and the cabbalah, and the final proof of its indisputable truth was its absolute conformity with his own mystic conception of science and its aims, based on his own pious convictions, and his study of the Bible and the Fathers.

Against this background the actual interpretation of the hieroglyphs as such became of secondary importance. To read and decipher them was necessary to confirm his conception of Egyptian philosophy, and to demonstrate his method of symbolic interpretation, but the texts themselves could not tell him anything he did not know in advance. His problem was to consider the signs in the light of his inspired knowledge, and divine their true esoteric meaning. The actual results are obviously only of historical interest, but even so they represent one of the most illuminating examples of the mystic Hermetic science of the period.

As for the sign-forms with which Kircher operated, there is no doubt that they were generally based on genuine hieroglyphs, such as Kircher had seen them on the monuments, but they were frequently misunderstood, transformed, and adapted to suit his theories to such an extent that they became more or less free invention, but there was always a certain method in his reconstructions.

His explanation of their graphic functions was based on his general conception of the relations between matter and idea, which he found absolutely confirmed by the classical reports of the two different systems of Egyptian writing. He pointed out that the signs represented ordinary material objects, and maintained that in the vulgar script they retained this material nature. The picture of a human being performing an act, expressed the act performed, and the picture of a bird or an animal, signified the animal in question. But he was convinced that a script used for practical purposes would have to be essentially alphabetical, and that the signs, therefore, had alphabetical functions, and could be used as letters[32]. That this was in fact the case, was in Kircher's opinion obvious, because he thought that the signs had developed into the Coptic letters which he erroneously considered the prototype of the Greek alphabet. His general conceptions of the graphic development were based on entirely fictitious resemblances between the signs and the Coptic letters. A non-existing hieroglyph, supposed to represent an Ibis biting its left leg with its beak, was considered the prototype of the letter A. A picture of the same bird with its head turned upwards, was supposed to have developed into the letter Y, while the legs of the animal represented alone, had become a Λ. Generally speaking all this is nonsense, but in between there are strange glimpses of genius. On the monuments Kircher had apparently seen the sign 〰, and he explained its pictorial meaning quite rightly as water, an explanation which must have been based on a happy guess. But he went still further, and with a sudden reversion to a very sober and unmetaphysical method, he substantiated the phonetic value of the sign as *m*, with a brilliant reference to the Coptic word for water *mu*. This is indisputably correct, and the method employed corresponds in a remarkable way to that used by Champollion for his decipherment. It is, therefore, Kircher's incontestable merit as the first to have determined the phonetic value of an Egyptian hieroglyph. The other 21 signs which he considered the hieroglyphic prototypes of the Coptic and the Greek letters are fictitious, and he did not even make an effort to draw the natural consequences of his alphabetical theories, mainly because he was not interested in the vulgar writing at all, but only in the 'true' symbolic hieroglyphs and the esoteric knowledge they were supposed to transmit[33].

As far as the symbolical writing was concerned, it was Kircher's allegation that it operated with the same signs as the vulgar script. Superficially seen there was, therefore, no difference in the outward appearance of the two systems, which nevertheless represented two entirely different approaches to the graphic problem. The real hieroglyphs were true symbols and their symbolic meaning, their 'lectio idealis', could only be explained by initiated scholars by means of the allegorical hieroglyphical method. The above-mentioned picture of the Ibis, which in the vulgar texts represented the letter A, was in the sacred inscriptions the symbol of the agathodaemon, one of the beneficent spirits in Kircher's cosmological system. In accordance with some Pythagorean ideas concerning the letter Υ, Kircher explained its hieroglyphical meaning as 'the process of proceeding from an inferior sphere into a higher one', while the letter λ had the reverse sense, 'to proceed from a higher to a lower sphere'. The letter X was considered a combination of the two preceding signs, and its symbolic meaning was consequently 'the activity of the soul of the universe', the only force which could proceed in either direction.

By identifying each hieroglyph with a philosophic concept or a demonological manifestation, Kircher was able to make each hieroglyphic inscription a reflection of his own metaphysical system. The complex rules governing the period's conception of allegories and symbols, with their subtle distinctions between cyriologic, tropological metaphorical, anaglyphical, and enigmatical comparisons made such symbolic interpretations possible, and to consider Kircher's hieroglyphical expoundings as deliberate swindle, as is generally done, is equally unjust and unhistorical. As already pointed out they represent one of the last deliberate efforts to combine the total religious, philosophic, and scientific knowledge of a whole period into a grandiose vision of a living cosmology, still governed by the doctrines of Christianity. As such it is certainly no laughing matter, but represents an intellectual achievement which should command awe and respect. Even its theories about the inner connection between Egyptian wisdom and religion, and Greek, Neo-Platonic, and Hermetic philosophy have probably more truth in them than our philosophers dream about; and

97

although Kircher's conceptions of Egyptian religion and mythology are undoubtedly phantastic and unhistorical, one cannot help wondering, if they are very much further from the truth than the sterile and lifeless waxworks to which the more sober, unmetaphysical methods of modern Egyptology have reduced the Egyptian pantheon. From a humanistic as well as an intellectual point of view Egyptology may very well be proud of having Kircher as its founder.

It has already been pointed out that Kircher's ideas and theories were already fully developed and displayed in his edition of the Pamphilian obelisk, and they were merely repeated and elaborated upon in his subsequent publications, mainly in his enormous 'Oedipus aegyptiacus' (1652-1654), his 'Obeliscus Chigius' (1666), and in 'Sphynx mystagoga' (1676) which contained Kircher's reflexions on mummification, and its relation to the professed Egyptian belief in metempsychosis or transmigration of souls. It also contained various esoteric translations of inscriptions found on sarcophagi. Also other works of his, which were not primarily Egyptological, such as his 'Turris Babel' (Amsterdam 1679), contained a substantial amount of Egyptian material. This was also the case with the catalogue of his museum, published by his devoted friend and pupil Georg de Sepibus (Romani collegium musaeum 1678)[34], and including several plates of hieroglyphical inscriptions from obelisks, mainly reproductions from Kircher's earlier publications. Quite apart from their interpretations, all these books became of great importance as compilations of hieroglyphical material, and as such they remained useful right down until the end of the eighteenth century. Their results and their theories can only be evaluated in a historical coherence. Judged on their own premises they were consistent in their method, well and systematically planned and executed, and their display of knowledge, learning, and imagination was outstanding, and, even for the period, exceptional. (Pl. XIX, 4).

For the remaining part of the century the Egyptological studies were dominated by Kircher's achievements in good and bad. In certain circles Coptic studies became fashionable, and remained almost entirely based on his publications until new grammars were made, by Christian Gotthelf Blumberg (Fondamenta linguae copticae, 1766), Raphael Tuki (Rudimenta linguae coptae, 1778) and Christian Scholz (Grammatica aegyptiaca, 1778), and until a new dictionary was published by Mathurino Veyssiere la Croze (Lexicon aegyptiacum-latinum, 1775)[35]. New material for the study was provided by the manuscripts brought home from the travels of Petraeus, Huntington[36], Vansleb, and Aleman, but a systematic publication of texts did not begin until about 1715 with Tuki's and Wilkin's editions. But from then on Coptic developed steadily into a fairly well established philological discipline, with which we are here only concerned insofar as it influenced the decipherment of the hieroglyphs. (Pl. III, 3).

In this respect it was important that Kircher's untenable theory about the Coptic origin of Greek was abolished[37], while his correct identification of Coptic and the old Pharaonic language found general acceptance in almost all circles.

But the hieroglyphs were not forgotten, although the failure of Kircher's gigantic effort to decipher them discouraged other scholars from new attempts. This was also due to the fact that it proved difficult to find a new methodical approach to the problem, because the old metaphysical conception of the signs was inextricably connected with the Hermetic science of the seventeenth century, which was now rapidly deteriorating, and being supplanted by the new scientific and mental outlook created by the new scientific world picture.

It is significant at any rate, that hardly one single serious attempt to decipher the hieroglyphs was made in the time between Kircher's last publication and the finding of the Rosetta stone in 1799, although innumerable theories were propounded as to their nature, and endless discussions went on concerning their origin.

The growing philological activities gave rise to an increasing interest in Coptic etymologies, and various scholars began to make lists of the Egyptian words quoted by the classics. Irrespective of the fact that almost all of these words in the course of their tradition had become misunderstood, changed, and distorted, they were nevertheless accepted as correct and genuine, and quite uncritically subjected to the period's etymological Procrustes' bed. The etymological methods had hardly changed or improved since they were used by Plato and Plutarch and were still based on alliterations, and more or less fortuitous similarity between words, but they were nevertheless used to prove or disprove linguistic, historical, and religious theories of the greatest scope and importance. The whole procedure has now only historical interest, but numerous examples are already found in Bochart's 'Geographia sacra' (1646)[38]. Quatrèmere quotes similar attempts from the works of Guyot, and the distinguished author of 'Les origines de la langue Francaise' Gilles Menage (1650)[39]. Bonjour published a dissertation on the Pharaonic name of the patriarch Joseph, which became quite famous, and gave rise to many delightful controversies[40] after the manner of the period, but the short list of Hebrew words etymologically connected with Coptic provided by Blumberg in his above mentioned Coptic grammar, was quite scholarly and not entirely unsuccessful[41].

All of these scholars had unanimously accepted Kircher's identification of Coptic and Egyptian, but towards the end of the century it was violently contested by the German divine Andreas Acoluthus (1654-1704), who had studied Armenian and come to the conclusion that Armenian and not Coptic was the surviving language of Ancient Egypt, a theory which he professed himself able to prove by irrefutable etymological evidence. And not only was Armenian in his opinion the language of the hieroglyphic inscriptions, but the solution of the hieroglyphic problem itself was to be found in Armenian manuscripts, in which 'hieroglyphic' pictures of men and beasts were used as initials. Although this in itself not very probable thesis was immediately contested by one J. Hagen[42], it was, strange to say, resumed by no less than Leibniz himself. If is not surprising that this great scholar whose theocentric metaphysical system, with its emanative dynamics, was in many ways reminiscent of Neo-Platonic ideas, should display a keen interest in Egyptology, although mostly inofficially and in his private correspondence. He wrote the most flattering letters to Kircher, but criticized his Greek theories rather strongly to other Egyptologists, and strangely enough also his correct identification of Egyptian and Coptic. Although he does not mention his name, Leibniz had apparently heard of Acoluthus' theories, for we find him propounding exactly the same weird ideas about the Egyptian origin of Armenian, and prophesying the solution of the hieroglyphic riddle from a study of Armenian initials. He was more successful with his remarks on the inscriptions of the obelisks, and was convinced that they contained 'historical texts commemorating events and victories', rather than esoteric wisdom such as asserted by Kircher[43].

From the beginning of the eighteenth century the tradition once more entered into a new phase. Archaeology became the ruling fashion, and collecting the prevalent passion, although antiquity was not infrequently confused with antiques, a phenomenon not unheard of even in modern archaeological circles. Rome became the natural centre of the new science, which was furthered by the building activities of the period. As if drawn from an inexhaustible well, the monuments appeared, most of them obviously Roman, but many Egyptian.

A so-called table of basalt carrying a hieroglyphic inscription with the name of Nektanebos was dug up on the Aventine in 1709[44]. Two statues of Isis were found in 1714 near the Villa Verospi, which occupied the ancient site of Sallustius' gardens, and in 1719 when the foundations were being laid for a new public library dedicated by the late Cardinal Casanate, the remnants of the old Serapeum yielded several valuable monuments. They were later acquired by Benedict XIV, and together with the rich finds from the villa of Hadrian at Tivoli, brought together in the Egyptian cabinet on the Capitol[45].

Every day had its discoveries, and Montfaucon almost complains in the introduction to his publication of them, that 'new ones are found every day and several new pieces had to be included, which appeared while the printing was actually going on'[46]

In the history of the hieroglyphic tradition Montfaucon's compendious publication became of great importance, because as far as Egyptology was concerned, it terminated one epoch and inaugurated another at the same time. With great diligence he collected not only the Egyptian monuments of Rome and those reproduced by his predecessors, mainly Boissard and Bonnani, but included also objects from the otherwise inaccessible private collections, the Italian, – such as that of Maffei – as well as the French, – those of Rigord and Peiresc[47]. The reproductions are not always of a high quality, neither artistically nor technically, and the hieroglyphic inscriptions are even less conscientiously executed than Kircher's, but his collection contained most of the available material, and contributed therefore essentially to the spread of the knowledge of Egyptian art among the virtuosi and the dilettanti of the period.

Even a hieratic text is included, and it has not escaped the attention of Montfaucon that we were here faced with a form of Egyptian writing different from the ordinary hieroglyphs[48].

As a book of reference the book was nevertheless in spite of its indisputable merits, fairly soon outdated by other works. But its text is still useful, and important within its limitations. It is the first Egyptological book written in the spirit of the eighteenth century, and it is above all exquisitely well written. Its criticism of the earlier Egyptological literature is severe, but on the whole perfectly justified. With polite anonymity Montfaucon censured his predecessors for their insupportable and unnecessary long-windedness, their endless quotations, made necessary by their slavish dependence on the classics, and their lack of critical courage. Especially the etymologists had to bear the brunt, and their inconsistencies and the methodical deficiencies of these 'recherches rarement necessaires et plus souvent frivoles', were pointed out and ridiculed[49].

As far as the hieroglyphs were concerned the author showed a marked reticence, obviously because he did not want to become involved in what he considered a dangerous and indissoluble problem. His account was confined to a reference to 'the Egyptian Kosmos', an Alexandrinian geographer from the time of Justinian, whose works Montfaucon had published[50], and according to whom the hieroglyphs were not ordinary letters, but symbols of letters signifying a general conception of the ideas in question, but unfit for the rendering of consecutive statements[51].

No steps were taken even remotely approaching a decipherment, because 'most sensible persons concur that it is hardly possible to undertake the explanation of these enigmas, without running the risk of running wild', and this attitude towards the hieroglyphic problems was generally adopted until the end of the century.

Notwithstanding its critical attitude, Montfaucon's text became nevertheless a valuable handbook, comprising the entire field of contemporary Egyptology, and no modern student, who wants to understand the seventeenth century's attitude towards Egyptological problems, its strange terminology, and its intricate mythological conceptions, can possibly find a more profitable source.

As a true child of the eighteenth century, Montfaucon was no admirer of Egyptian wisdom himself, and he considered it very objectively indeed, and not without a slight disdain. Egyptian religion was 'monstrueuse', and the manifestations of Egyptian art were 'horrible', or at most 'bizarre'. As such he considered them of antiquarian interest as rarities and curious, but it is typical of his attitude that he refused to put the Egyptian material first in his book, such as demanded by chronology, quite simply because he considered it bad taste to put things as bizarre as Egyptian statues 'à la tête des Anquités'[52].

Much more personal in his genuine enthusiasm of things Egyptian was the Austrian architect Johann Fischer von Erlach, who in 1721 published his 'Entwurf einer historischen Architectur'[53] to demonstrate how the development of European architecture was dependent on an unbroken tradition of basic laws, which could be traced in Egyptian, Assyrian, and Hebrew, as well as in Chinese, Persian, and Arabic monuments, and how these laws from the ancients had been directly transmitted to the Renaissance and the Baroque, through the intervention of the Greeks and the Romans. This theory was illustrated by a series of magnificent reconstructions of some of the outstanding monuments of antiquity. They are undoubtedly better illustrations of Fischer's imagination and architectural genius than of the buildings they are supposed to represent; but they show the extent to which the old ideas about European culture, as the result of an unbroken esoteric tradition, were still alive.

From an aesthetic point of view it is remarkable to observe that it was not the grandeur of Egyptian architecture which impressed Johann Fischer, but its exquisite simplicity[54], and from our particular point of view it is interesting to see how hieroglyphical inscriptions and ornaments were used to add a touch of 'authenticity' to the pictures. The material was mostly copied from Kircher, or taken from vases and statuettes, but generally from what Fischer considered authentic and reliable sources. To find a 'genuine' inscription for his picture of the tomb of Sothis, he even took the trouble to consult one of the neo-hieroglyphical classics, as the text in question is directly copied from the tomb of the two unfortunate lovers in the Hypnerotomachia.[55]

That scientific and mathematical accomplishments on the highest plane were still compatible with esoteric philosophy and metaphysical speculations has already been pointed out in the case of Leibniz, and it is curious to observe to what extent even the most stringent minds of the period remained under the sway of theology in their attitude towards history and historical problems.

Even Sir Isaac Newton, the man who was to provide the mathematical proof of the discoveries of Copernicus and Kepler on which the period's new cosmology was founded based his chronological studies[56] on the theological argumentation of the preceding century, although his aim was to liberate the historical studies from the sway of the biblical tradition, as the preface cautiously has it: 'to make history suit with Nature, with Astronomy, with sacred History, with Herodotus the father of History, and with itself'[57]. As far as Egyptian chronology was concerned his investigations resulted in some genealogical reflexions by which he tried to prove that Osiris, Bacchus, Sesostris, and Sisac were in fact merely different names for one single person, and that it was he who had advanced Egypt from a state of barbarism to civilisation, a development which according to Newton had taken place about two generations before the Trojan war. In this way he succeeded in reducing the antiquity of Egyptian history considerably, but the new chronology was merely different, and not very much more correct than the old one. It was violently attacked by the theologists and is now only of historical interest, but it illustrates how the philosophical and historical problems of the period invariably developed into Egyptological speculations and theological controversies.

Even more characteristic in this respect is William Warburton's unfinished treatise 'The Divine Legation of Moses' (London 1741)[58]. The book was deeply rooted in the theology of the preceding century in approach as well as in argumentation although its style was perfect eighteenth century. It was an effort to prove in a rather sophistical way that the very absence of a doctrine concerning a future state of reward and punishment in the teachings of the Old Testament provided the ultimate proof of the divine legation of Moses.

No government could normally be maintained without a belief in a divine judgement and its absence from the Jewish teachings was therefore in Warburton's opinion in itself a definite proof that the Jewish people was under the immediate providence of God[59].

In order to support the thesis that 'the Jews were extremely fond of Egyptian manners and did frequently fall into Egyptian superstition, and that many of the Laws given to them by the Ministry of Moses were instituted, partly in compliance to their prejudices, and partly in opposition to those superstitions'[60], the whole of book IV contained reflections on Egyptological matters, including a very extensive digression on the hieroglyphs.

Although based on the traditional material the hieroglyphic section of the book is most unconventional as the result of an unprejudiced, intelligent and critical approach to the problems.

According to Warburton there were two ways by which the conceptions of the mind could be communicated to others: by sounds and by figures[61]. Sounds being momentary and confined, figures were very early invented to make the communications lasting and extensive. The figures used were originally simple images of things, and the idea of a man or a horse were expressed 'by delineations of these animals'. The first essay towards writing was consequently a mere picture. In Warburton's opinion this form of writing was illustrated by Mexican hieroglyphs, and represented 'the first and most simple way common to all mankind of recording the Conceptions' (p. 70).

But the Egyptians were supposed to have advanced one step further. They contrived methods to limit the necessary pictures by turning them into hieroglyphics; that is, making them both figures and characters (p. 71).

'This abridgement was made in three kinds of ways' (p. 71) by just degrees and at three successive periods. The first way was 'to make the principal circumstance of the subject stand for the whole', and it was illustrated by an example from Horapollo telling how the Egyptians 'described' a battle by painting 'two hands, one holding a shield, and the other a bow', a perfectly correct statement which could have been found in any Egyptian grammar. The second and more artful method of contraction, was by putting the instrument of the thing, whether real or metaphorical, for the thing itself. This was illustrated by a quotation from Clement of Alexandria (I,V.), stating that the Egyptians used the eye to represent God's omnipotence. The example is bad, but the formulation of the graphic rule itself is quite correct and could be illustrated for instance by the use of the sail for the verb 'to sail' or of the hieroglyph representing an arm with a stick for the verb 'to strike'. The third 'and still more artificial Method' (p. 72) was 'by making one thing stand for, or represent, another where any quaint Resemblance or Analogy in the Representative could be collected from their observations of Nature, or their traditional Superstitions'. This was illustrated by a variety of examples from Horapollo, for instance the snake biting its own tail for the Universe, and from Eusebius, all of which represented the usual allegorical misconceptions. But Warburton's own rule is again correct, and could be illustrated by the picture of the forbidden and unclean fish used as a determinative or an ideogram in the word 'abomination'.

His final conclusions about the origin of the script were no less astounding and for their time profoundly original, for he propounded that it was no sacred invention at all, 'made to conceal sacred secrets, as have been hitherto thought', but a practical device made for practical purposes. It had, in his own epigrammatical mode of expression, 'not been invented as a Device of Choice for Secrecy, but of Necessity for popular use' (p. 75). The remaining 200 pages of Warburton's Egyptological expoundings are of less interest. They contain his rather long-winded attempt to reconcile the various accounts of the Egyptian graphic systems and an effort to define the graphic terminology. He operated with four basic categories cyriologic, symbolic, hierogrammatic, and epistologic writings, of which the symbolic one had two subdivisions, tropical and allegorical (p. 97). Each category was supposed to represent a specific stage in the graphic evolution. They had so to speak become arrested in their development, and each had survived as a distinct graphic system with its own peculiarities and characteristics (p. 104). His distinctions were not always clear, and his definitions not always adequate, but in spite of the fact that most of his assertions were hypothetical to the extreme, some of them came almost deceptively close to truth. In his otherwise entirely speculative account of the relations between the hierogrammatic and epistological systems, of which he strangely enough considered the latter the highest and final stage in the graphic evolution and therefore reserved for sacred purposes (p. 132), we are for instance suddenly told that hierogrammatic

writing owed its origin to an abbreviation 'in the delineation of Hieroglyphic figures
.... which by degrees perfectioned another character, which we may call the running-
hand of Hieroglyphics' (p. 115), a pefectly correct definition of what we should call
hieratic. However, the speculative character of his results must not be forgotten. They
bear illuminating evidence of his intelligence and perspicacity, but even his most brilliant ideas were insofar deceptive, as no efforts were ever made to corroborate them
with factual evidence[62]. They remained lofty speculations and never any more and
it is characteristic that Warburton carefully avoided all contacts with original hieroglyphic inscriptions. Of the true system of hieroglyphic writing he had no more idea
than any other scholar before the actual decipherment. Firmly rooted in the XVIIth
century he was in many respects almost unwittingly also a true representative of
the XVIIIth[63], but it is curious to see him as Anglican Bishop of Gloucester and de-
fender of the faith deride Newton's chronological effort in the most scorching and
violent terms, because they infringed the historical authority of the Scriptures (Sect.
IV. p. 206), and also attack poor Kircher (p. 110) with equal vehemence because of
his Neo-Platonic sympathies: 'It is pleasant to see him labouring thro' half a dozen
Folios with Writings of late Greek Platonists, and forged Books of Hermes, which contain Philosophy, not Egyptian, to explain and illustrate old monuments not Philosophical. Here we leave him to course his Shadow of a Dream thro 'all the fantastic
Regions of Pythagoreic Platonism.' Little did Warburton understand that in dis-
missing Kircher to pursue his 'Neo-Platonic Shadows of Dreams', he heralded not
only the disappearance of Neo-Platonism from the hieroglyphical studies, but its total
disappearance as an active element in European culture as well. And even less did he
realize that this event closed one epoch in European intellectual history and inaugurated another[64].

For in abolishing the influence of Neo-Platonic thought, which until then had per-
meated its religion, its philosophy, and its science as an often hidden and disguised,
but always inspiring and dynamic force, European culture severed one of the stron-
gest traditions and one of the most immediate bonds connecting it with its origin and
classical past. If it be true, what has been said, not without a bitter appearance of
truth, that God died in the early XVIIIth century, the disappearance of Neo-Platonism was undoubtedly one of the symptoms of his demise. A new world with a new
mental and spiritual outlook was born. Revealed truth was replaced by scientific
truth, and the belief in the latter undermined the faith in the former. New problems,
new approaches and new values emerged, and as hitherto the hieroglyphic studies reflected the change. In the following period Archaeology again became the order of
the day. Everybody collected antiques, and everybody had become learned. Learned
letters on archaeological subjects were addressed to learned friends and influential
patrons. Countless, more or less learned, papers were presented to countless, more or

less learned, societies, and the general archaeological fancy became to a great extent an Egyptological fancy.

Claude-François Menestrier[65] had already in 1692 published his 'Lettres d'un Académicien à un Seigneur à la Cour à l'occasion d'une momie', and Huntington published his 'Letter from Dublin concerning the Porphyry pillars of Egypt' in 1684[66]. Rigord published his 'Lettres sur une ceinture de toile, trouvée en Égypte autour d'une Momie' in Journal de Trévoux in 1705, and received an anonymous answer in the same paper in 1740, thirteen years after his death. Johan Heinrich Schumacher published in 1754 his 'Versuch der dunklen und versteckten Geheimnisse in der hieroglyphischen Denkbildern zu erklären'[67]. Alexander Gordon published an 'Essay towards explaining the hieroglyphical figures on the coffin of the ancient Mummy belonging to Captain W. Lethieullier (1737), and another 'Essay towards explaining the Ancient Hieroglyphical figures on the Egyptian Mummy in the Museum of Dr. Mead.' (s. d.)[68], and Baron de Caylus (1692-1765) contributed several articles to the 'Recueil de l'Académie des Inscriptions et Belles Lettres', which since 1716 had been the name of the 'Petite Académie' founded in 1663 by Colbert as a subdivision of Richelieu's 'Académie Francaise' from 1634. The 'Académie des Inscriptions' and its official paper the 'Recueil' were right down until the XIXth century among the most important centres of archaeological studies.

De Caylus was also an ardent collector, but his most important contribution to Egyptology was his enormous 'Recueil d'Antiquités Égyptiennes Étrusques, Grecques, Romains, et Gauloises', which appeared from 1752 until 1764 in eight volumes.

As a mere collection of material this publication became of considerable importance, although its reproductions were not of a very high quality, and the speculations and the erudition of its author not very profound, although he had all the best qualities and the genuine enthusiasm of a dilettante. He was the first to show an aesthetic interest in Egyptian art, and although his effort to establish a 'demotic alphabet' proved a failure it contributed to turn the interest towards the inscriptions, especially those found on linen bandages and papyrus and presumably representing the vulgar script.

However, the topical problem of the learned debate was not so much the understanding of the hieroglyphs, but, strangely enough, the purely hypothetical and theoretical question of their relation to Chinese writing. Already Kircher had toyed with the idea of a direct historical connection between China and Egypt, and Pierre Benoît Huët (1630-1741) had in his 'Histoire du Commerce et de la Navigation des Anciens' (Paris 1716) described how the Egyptians during the campaigns of Osiris and Sesostris had roamed India and China, and given rise to the early development of Indian and Chinese cultures.

Needham tried to identify the letters on the so-called bust of Isis with Chinese let-

I   2

1. Etching by Mengardi of one of the frescos from S. Giustina in Padua with hieroglyphic emblem borrowed from the Hypnerotomachia.

2. Hieroglyphic inscription from the tomb of Herbert Mielemans in Liège from about 1558.

3

3. Egyptian caryatid by Raphael from the Sala del Incendio in the Vatican, inspired by Egyptianizing Roman sculpture. See plate V,2.

4. Obelisk with dedicatory inscription in honour of the emperor Ferdinand III made by Athanasius

4

ters (1761) (Pl. XVIII, 3), which involved him in a discussion with Stukeley[69], and the whole problem was also considered by the famous decipherer of the Phoenician alphabet, Abbé Barthélémy, in his reflections on the relationship between the Phoenician, the Greek and the Egyptian languages[70], in which he as the first guessed that the so-called 'cartouches' or royal rings frequently found in hieroglyphic inscriptions might contain royal names. (Pl. II, 1).

This guess was elaborated upon by de Guignes (1721-1800), first in a lecture given at the Académie des Inscriptions in 1785 and later in various articles and publications[71]. According to de Guignes, China was quite simply an Egyptian colony, and its culture in all essentials of Egyptian origin. Such was also the case with Chinese writing, its basic elements, the so-called radicals, being in their original forms identical with the presumed Egyptian 'letters', on which the Phoenician alphabets had also been based. The old Egyptian language had unfortunately become corrupted by its connection with Greek and its use of the Greek alphabet, and Coptic was consequently of no use as far as the decipherment of the hieroglyphs was concerned. All efforts in this direction should be based on Chinese and Chinese writing, an undertaking which de Guignes very sensibly left to posterity. The whole theory is obviously entirely erroneous and untenable, but it became enormously popular, although by no means generally accepted. It was immediately criticized by de Guignes' old teacher Deshautesrayes in his 'Doutes sur la dissertation de M. de Guignes', and the ardent discussion of the two scholars about the correct reading of the name of Menes in its relation to the Chinese name Yu occasioned some malicious remarks about etymologists and etymological methods in Voltaire's preface to his 'Histoire de'l'Empire Russe'. Quite apart from the Chinese theories, de Guignes' works contained several sensible remarks on hieroglyphic writing. In the second of the papers mentioned below he gave some ingenious comments on the abbreviated form of the script which he, probably influenced by Warburton, considered the origin of the vulgar system of writing (p. 8), and he had correctly observed that, although they invariably wrote from right to left, the Egyptians could apparently arrange the signs in vertical or horizontal lines ad libitum (p. 9-10). Like Barthélémy he had also made the observation that certain texts contained some strange ovals or rings circumscribing hieroglyphs which were not different from those found outside the rings, only in some cases somewhat smaller (p. 4). From his Chinese studies he was familiar with similar cartouches used in Chinese texts to give prominence to proper names, and he concluded that the Egyptian ovals served similar purposes and were probably used for the writing of royal names. We shall see that this observation was remembered and contributed essentially to facilitate the final decipherment.

Otherwise it must be admitted that all these highly theoretical speculations tended to obscure the hieroglyphical problems rather than further their solution, and even the well intended publications of Egyptian curios and rarities gave in most cases a misleading and false impression of Egyptian art, because of their poor workmanship, their lack of style, and their unmethodical collection of the material.

But towards the middle of the century, some excellent travel books began to appear which for the first time provided first-hand information concerning Egyptian art and architecture.

The first 'modern' description was de Maillet's 'Déscription de l'Égypte' (Paris 1735). It contained material collected during the years the author had served as French Consul in Cairo, was based on his journals, and primarily written with a practical purpose: to further the commercial and political intercourse between the western world and Egypt. It did contain some descriptions of ancient monuments, but Maillet tried deliberately to counteract the common conception of the country as a land of mummies, obelisks and pyramids, and criticized the conventional and the classical reports severely. Historically seen the importance of the book was therefore not so much dependent on its archaeological information, but on its records of the geography, the government and the institutions of modern Egypt which provided subsequent travellers with important information about the country and the ways and habits of its inhabitants. Among the first to make practical use of it was Frederik Ludvig Norden (1708-1742). Norden was a Danish naval officer, an efficient engineer and an uncommonly competent draughtsman, endowed with all the best qualities engendered by an old-fashioned naval education. He had studied geodesy and engineering all over Europe and in Italy, where he was introduced into learned and artistic circles by the distinguished German diplomat and collector Baron de Stosch. He was made an associate of the Academy of Drawing in Florence, and Stosch aroused his interest in Egypt to such an extent that Norden induced the Danish Government to send him on a journey of exploration to that country. In June 1737 he started from Alexandria, proceeding by boat to Derr in Nubia, further south than any other traveller before him. He visited most of the important sights and monuments on his way, and returned to Cairo in February 1738. From the very outset Norden made it quite clear that he considered the collection of geographical ethnographical and scientific material just as important as archaeology. Already in the introduction to his first publication he stressed that he did not consider himself an antiquarian: 'I lay claim myself to no erudition, and desire you will only look upon what I say, as a report of a faithful traveller, and of one who pretends no more than having seen with some care, and related honestly what he has seen'[72].

This basic attitude determined the final account of the journey, which owing to Norden's untimely death was not published until 1755[73]. It was directly based on his diaries and drawings and was in every respect an interesting travel book more than a scientific report. Twenty-nine of the hundred and ninety-five exquisite engravings were maps of the course of the Nile from Cairo to Derr[74]. The greater part of the remaining 130 were mainly of geographical and topographical interest. The archaeological material was confined to reproductions and plans of the major temples such as for instance Luxor, Karnak, Medinet Habu, Edfu, Esna, Kôm Ombo, Philae, and Elephantine, made with accuracy and architectural insight. Relatively few monuments, such as the Memnon colossi, the Sphinx, several obelisks, and a couple of reliefs, were also included, and it is obvious that Norden took great and special care to copy the hieroglyphic inscriptions as accurately as possible[75]. In his reproductions of Egyptian works of art, Norden was not able any more than other artists of his period to overcome the difficulties occasioned by the specific Egyptian style, but his very careful rendering of the various orders of columns and capitals from Luxor and Philae (pl. CVII and CXLIV) represented the first attempt to introduce elements of style into an evaluation of Egyptian archaeological material. Generally speaking the work was an honest and valuable achievement and one of the first attempts at an elaborate description of Egypt. (Pl. XXI, 2).

After his return Norden volunteered in 1740 to serve under the English flag, and it might be mentioned that together with the travellers Dr. Shaw and Dr. Pococke, whose book on Egypt published in 1743 should rival his own, he was one of the founders of the Egyptian Club, which held its meetings at the Lebeck's Head in Chandos Street[76].

Richard Pococke, the later Bishop of Meath, visited Egypt at the same time as Norden, to be exact from September 1737 until February 1738, and the two travellers actually passed one another on the Nile one night, Norden going up and Pococke down the river.

He returned to England in 1742, and the account of his Egyptian journey was already published in 1743 as the first volume of his 'Description of the East' under the title 'Observations on Egypt'. According to the introduction (p. III) it had originally been his intention 'to give the world the plans he had taken of the Egyptian buildings, together with some drawings of them, and to add an account and designs of all the different orders of Egyptian architecture.' Although this plan was considerably modified in the final publication most of its 76 plates still represent architectural plans and archaeological objects, but not all of them were based on original drawings, and they vary considerably in quality and value, from an artistic as well as an archaeological point of view[77].

An extensive collection of examples of 'the orders of Egyptian architecture' with their different pillars, capitals, and cornices were actually included, and tentative efforts were made to compare them with the Greek orders (p. LXVI-LXIX). Generally speaking they are not very carefully executed and made without any great architectural knowledge or insight. They are obviously not based on proper measurements, but like Norden, Pococke, was a pioneer, and his reproductions served their purpose by drawing the attention of subsequent scholars to architectural and stylistic problems. Also the geographical sections of the book proved useful, especially his description of the north-eastern borderland of Egypt, including Mount Sinai, where Pococke copied several inscriptions (pl. LIV-LV).

He also copied the extensive Greek and Roman inscriptions with which ancient tourists had covered the lower parts of the Memnon-Colossi, but the hieroglyphic texts were generally ignored or just vaguely indicated on his reproductions. Like most of his contemporaries Pococke apparently considered the decipherment a hopeless task, and although he was undoubtedly to a certain extent acquainted with the literature on the subject, his account of the hieroglyphs such as comprised in the fourth chapter of his book was directly based on Warburton, except for a few personal observations, such as the remark that, if the signs did stand for words, they would necessarily have to stand for fixed sound-values at the same time, viz. the sound-values of the Egyptian names of the objects or ideas they stood for.

That Carsten Niebuhr (1733-1815), the explorer of Arabia, alone amongst all his colleagues and contemporaries should not share this general pessimism with regard to the decipherment was another proof of his courageous and indomitable spirit. As a member of the tragic, but important Danish expedition to Arabia (1761-1767), from which he was to return as the only survivor, he was forced to remain inactive in Cairo for several months between 1761 and 1762, and 'for his own pleasure' he began to copy hieroglyphic inscriptions[78]. In his journal he gave a vivid picture of the practical difficulties facing a copyist in the Egypt of his day[79], but his stubborn energy made him persevere, and he succeeded in collecting about ten short inscriptions. Little by little his knowledge of the signs improved, and he was, at any rate in his own opinion, able to copy them 'like Greek or Cufic texts'. The results were not always remarkable, but the very effort was a progress. It was the first serious attempt to obtain a first-hand knowledge of the individual sign-forms, and Niebuhr had even the courage to compile a short, very preliminary sign-list (tab. XLI).

While collecting this material his constructive mind could not abstain from speculations concerning the functions of the signs and the nature of the script, and he was able to make some observations, which, for the period, were refreshingly unconventional and original. He was the first to draw a clear distinction between ordinary pictures and graphic hieroglyphs. Unlike Kircher, and most of his other predecessors, he was certain that the pictures – what he called the big representations –, had nothing to do with the script, but were just pictures of people or events. Only the smaller signs accompanying these pictures were in his opinion proper hieroglyphs, and he presumed that they explained the pictures[80].

He also made the observation that the signs could be written in either direction, and in his description of a sarcophagus from Cairo he made a clear distinction between the hieroglyphs and the ornamental signs of the frieze[81]. His final conclusions were that instead of attempting to explain the mythological significance of the pictures, the Egyptological scholars should stick to the inscriptions, make complete lists of them, compare the sign-forms of the various monuments, and then see if the script could not be deciphered by means of Coptic.

These sensible ideas were unfortunately never elaborated upon. They remained more or less causal remarks, but of an outstanding perspicacity; and in the history of Egyptology they preserve the memory of an original and penetrating mind, and of results obtained merely by assiduity, logical reasoning, and intelligent deductions.

There are no indications that they were ever used by the decipherers, but they remain of historical interest, also because they illustrate how hieroglyphical problems were everywhere fermenting and slowly ripening. But the time of their solution had not yet come, and for the remaining part of the century nobody made any significant contribution to their understanding, and the discussion stagnated. Generally speaking the Egyptian interest remained as great as ever, but it found other outlets and other forms of expression, mainly in artistic circles; and most of Europe was once more swept by another Egyptian fancy or fashion. Its influence became apparent in literature as well as in art, and in architecture as well as in interior decorating. One of the first examples of this characteristic interplay between art and archaeology, was Romeyn de Hooghe's (1645-1708) 'Hieroglyphica of Merkbeelden', published after his death in 1735. The book contained a collection of learned and subtle allegories together with their expoundings very much in the spirit of the seventeenth century, and propounded an interesting distinction between 'ars hieroglyphica', the art to make artistic allegories, and 'scientia hieroglyphica', the art to expound and understand them (p. 2). The author was obviously a devoted reader of Kircher, and all sorts of Egyptian elements, such as pyramids, sphinxes, obelisks and home-made allegorical hieroglyphs abounded in the pictures. But for the first time in a non-archaeological book original archaeological objects mostly copied from Kircher were also introduced, such as the statue which in the terminology of the period was called 'the sacrificial priest' (picture III. The statue is now in the Louvre), and the so-called 'water-canopus' (pict. X).

The same interplay between archaeology and imagination became apparent everywhere in the art of the period. Sphinxes and obelisks, pyramids and home-made hieroglyphical inscriptions appeared with increasing frequency in the picturesque landscapes of the period amidst ruins and heroic monuments. The pyramids were most often copied from that of Cestius' in Rome[82], (Pl.VII, 1) the sphinxes were generally in Greek style with female breasts and heads and the inscriptions free inventions, but original Egyptian statues and other antiquities were also used for the decoration of cabinets, galleries, and antiquity gardens. The whole of Baron de Caylus' collection was artfully arranged in his back garden such as illustrated on an etching in the Recueil, and the picturesque gardens of Italy, France, and England began to abound in Egyptian columns, temples, and monuments. In Rome Norden's representation of the main gate of the temple of Luxor was used by Aspucci as a model for a gatehouse in the gardens of the Villa Borghese[83], and the Villa itself had an Egyptian room, decorated with hieroglyphs and reproductions of Egyptian antiquities[84]. (Pl. XXI, 3).

The garden of the Venetian senator Angelo Querini near Padua was decorated with Egyptian statues, and called 'Canopus' after the Egyptian part of Hadrian's villa near Tivoli. All over Europe architects and interior decorators revelled in Egyptian designs[85].

The decorative arts became inspired by the Egyptianized wall-paintings from Pompeii and Herculaneum which directly influenced Piranesi's Egyptian decoration of the well-known 'Caffé Inglese' in the Piazza di Spagna in Rome (ca. 1760). (Pl. XX, 2). The actual paintings disappeared long ago, but are preserved as engravings in Piranesi's 'Cammini' (Divers Manners of ornamenting Chimneys), which appeared for the first time in 1769, with a preface containing the first 'modern' evaluation of Egyptian art.

Piranesi called his introduction 'an apologetical essay in defence of the Egyptian and Tuscan architecture', and its purpose was to demonstrate that those qualities of Egyptian art, which, in the common opinion, were held against it, – its purported lack of grace, and its 'unnatural stylization which to the vulgar observer made it appear bold, hard, and stiff' (p. 4), were the very elements of its nature and the foundation on which its specific character was based. It was essentially architectural and ornamental (p. 11), and as such essentially immobile and unemotional. It was not supposed to be graceful, but to remind us that the pathetic, the macabre, and the awe-inspiring had a beauty of its own and that 'pleasure can spring even from horror and fear' (p. 10). This important contribution to a theory of art which was undoubtedly responsible for much of what is best and most typical in Piranesi's own life work, was in the preface illustrated with a reference to a Roman monument, the fountain 'Acqua Felice', for the decoration of which 'naturalistic' as well as 'stylized' Egyptian ornaments had been used (p. 14). Piranesi's art-critical observations are important enough to be quoted in full: 'I have in view, among other works of theirs (the Egyptians) the two lions which serve to adorn the Felician aqueduct in Rome, together with two others studiously copied both as to action and design from nature, that is, worked after the Grecian manner. What mastery in the Egyptian ones, what gravity and wisdom! What union, and modification of parts! How artfully are those parts set off which are agreeable to architecture, while those are suppressed which are not advantageous to it! Those other lions on the contrary, which are exactly copied from nature, and to which the artist capriciously gave what attitude he pleased,

PLATE XX

1. Design for a chimney by Piranesi with the signs from the temple frieze.

2. Wall decorations in Egyptian style from the Caffé degl'Inglesi at the Piazza di Spagna in Rome.

PLATE XXI

1. Egyptian lion from the fountain Acqua Felice in Rome.

2. Norden's original drawing for plate CVI 'af Voyage d'Égypte'. The final etching made by Tuscher inspired Asprucchi's and Canina's Egyptian architecture in the gardens of Villa Borghese in Rome.

3. Reproduction by Canina of the Egyptian gate of the Villa Borghese.

what have they to do here? They only serve to diminish the great effect which the Egyptian ones give to the architecture of that fountain!' (Pl. XXI, 1).

Hardly ever was the cause of Egyptian art pleaded with greater clarity and more authority, and with more true insight, and an artistic understanding which makes Caylus' enthusiastic remarks about its 'magnitude' and 'immense grandeur' seem strangely banal and insignificant in comparison. Typical for the change of attitude of the period was the way in which Piranesi anathematized ornamental symbolism and professed himself an enemy of enigmatical art (p. 5); and the profusion of hieroglyphs, mummies, scarabs, crocodiles, and statues, which in his own inventions adorned his new Egyptian style served merely ornamental and never allegorical purposes. For the sake of curiosity and to demonstrate the tenacity of the tradition it should be mentioned that on one of the chimneys (pl. 38), we find once more, and probably for the last time in their history, the signs from the temple frieze of San Lorenzo used as ornamental Egyptian hieroglyphs (Pl. XX, 1). Against the grandeur of their theoretical background it is rather sad that Piranesi's own efforts in his new style, to put it mildly, were rather unfortunate, but his general artistic merits are sufficiently great to permit the undisguised avowal that the Egyptian chimneys and the other Egyptian decorations in the 'new' style were failures. They were uninspired and ugly and of rather dubious taste. They had very little relation to Egyptian art, or to Piranesi's own inspired conception of it.

It is fortunate, however, that his admiration of Egyptian art was based on a strong feeling of congeniality more than on theory, because the qualities lacking in the Egyptian pastiches abound for instance in his 'Carcere' and 'Veduti', and it was through these that his theories influenced the subsequent Egyptian tradition. Mauro Tesi's Egyptian sepulchre (1762), Raphael Mengs' awe-inspiring decorations, with their hieroglyphs and sphinxes, from the Camera dei Papiri in the Vatican (ca. 1770), and Desprez' sombre burial vaults from about 1780, – which were obviously influenced by pyramid structures –, as well as his Egyptian stage-settings[86], were all of them inspired by Piranesi's non-Egyptian engravings, and as far as Mengs and Desprez are concerned, probably also by the theories expressed in his apology.

It is unfortunate that his theories were almost entirely disregarded in the subsequent art-literature in favour of the much less inspired elucidations of Caylus, and, above all, of Winckelmann.

In his sometime exuberant and naive, but always genuine, enthusiasm Winckelmann had succeeded in framing a new conception of classical art, which not only evoked response from all susceptible parts of society, but also exerted a profound influence on the creative arts of the following period. It was therefore just that his supreme authority should be generally accepted whenever he expressed an opinion on the Greek and Roman antiquities he knew and loved, but it became rather fatal when it came to Egyptian art which was alien to his temperament, which he never understood, and where no enthusiasm could supply his want of knowledge and insight.

Nevertheless, and in spite of the fact that no satisfactory evaluation could possibly be based on the limited and heterogeneous material at Winckelmann's disposal[87], he felt it his duty as a conscientious historian of art to include a chapter on Egypt in his 'Geschichte der Kunst des Altertums' (1764). In Winckelmann's opinion there were three consecutive steps in the harmonious development of art[88]. At the first and most primitive the artist was forced to concentrate his creative energy on what was strictly essential. At the second he could aim at the manifestation of beauty, and at the third he could permit himself the extravagance of luxuriance, and even cultivate the super-fluous. According to Winckelmann the Egyptians had never proceeded beyond the first stage[89], but the reasons he advanced to explain the presumed stagnation of their art tell more about Winckelmann's sympathies and antipathies and about the limit-ations of his taste and understanding than about Egyptian art. It was his general idea that the artistic shortcomings of the Egyptians to a great extent were conditioned by their geographical, political and social environment, and that, generally speaking, they had not been favoured by fortune or the Gods as far as taste and aesthetics were concerned. First of all the Egyptians themselves were unfortunately not handsome in Winckelmann's conception of the word, an allegation which was proved with re-ference to Aristotle's remark that most of them were bandy-legged and snub-nosed. They were also monarchists, and did not foster tyrannicides. They were by nature conservative and conventional, and had never turned into liberty-loving revolution-aries. The artists were supposed to belong to the lowest strata of society and had no idea of anatomy. Their mental outlook was limited by religion and superstition, and they were also of a melancholy and unenthusiastic disposition, by nature adverse to joy and pleasure. To put it shortly, they neither shared Winckelmann's political con-victions, nor lived up to his ideals of manly beauty.

He admitted them to have a certain technical skill and acknowledged that their stylistic peculiarities were not entirely the result of incompetence, but also of their deliberate dependence on fixed traditional rules. He made a few interesting obser-vations of his own, for instance that the right foot such as represented on Egyptian reliefs and sculptures was generally longer than the left. He did acknowledge the skill of the animal representations, but generally speaking Egyptian art was in Winckel-mann's conception awkward, stiff and unelegant, devoid of grace and charm. It is obvious that this criticism was merely a negative profession of Winckelmann's per-sonal aesthetic creed and nothing less than an objective evaluation of Egyptian art. But even so it found universal response and was generally accepted; and with few exceptions Egyptian art was for nearly a century measured by Greek standards and considered barbaric and imperfect, at most a sombre background against which the Greek perfection could shine the more.

However, his history of art was not the only work in which Winckelmann embarked upon Egyptological problems, and in 'Versuch einer Allegorie' (1766) he settled with the hieroglyphic tradition.

Compared with the art of earlier periods that of the eighteenth century maintained generally a marked reserve in its use of allegorical elements. We have seen Piranesi inveigh against them and already Caylus had noticed their disappearance, and explained it as a result of the new demand for clarity and preciseness[90]. On the same lines it was Winckelmann's intention to provide a 'modern' handbook in allegory made for the use of contemporary artists, but it proved no easy task to make artistic symbolism comply with enlightenment and reason. As we have already seen, previous studies in the theoretical nature of symbolism had already during the Renaissance resulted in the establishment of a fully developed 'theory', with subtle distinctions of categories and an elaborate terminology. To a certain extent these studies had actually developed into a philosophic discipline of their own, still commanded by Kircher and Warburton.

Against this philosophical background Winckelmann's efforts appear strangely dilettantish, and his definition of the word allegory: 'An indication of ideas by means of pictures' (p. 2) seems banal and unoriginal, especially because the word 'idea' in Winckelmann's terminology had become debased, and could be used without any philosophical implications for any abstract concept. This becomes obvious from his subsequent extension of the definition in which we are told that generally speaking an allegory meant 'everything indicated by signs and images, and corresponded to the word Iconology'[91].

But in depriving the allegories of their religious and metaphysical significance and reducing them to mere ornaments and decorations, Winckelmann deprived them of their very essence and raison d'être. His book became therefore a dreary enumeration of mythological attributes, enigmatic ornaments, and numismatic decorations, provided with remarkably uninspired, rationalistic, and very pedestrian explanations. But even worse than his expoundings of the old were his proposals for new allegories. Antipathy should be indicated by the pictures of a lion and a hare, or, an elephant and a pig (p. 139), a fish should indicate deaf-muteness! (p. 141) and timidity should be expressed by a warrior hiding his face behind his shield. With a strange relapse into the old hieroglyphical tradition, a righteous judge should be represented as a man without hands, an idea based on a quotation from Plutarch.[92]

It is obvious that these failures do not in any way detract from Winckelmann's indisputable merit in other fields. He will always be remembered as the man who by introducing new aesthetic values and principles contributed more than anybody else to a new evaluation of classical art. Even his otherwise rather unfortunate Egyptological and allegorical efforts are interesting and symptomatic insofar as they heralded a new intellectual climate unfavourable to artistic mysticism. The old allegorical traditions were obviously dying. Even in their Christian manifestations they had been based on Neo-Platonic ideas and Neo-Platonic conceptions of the nature of art, and they had always been inextricably connected with the hieroglyphical traditions. It was therefore natural that these should fade away at the same time. Winckelmann had apparently a vague feeling of this connection because his attacks on the representatives of the old allegorical methods were accompanied by an attack on the hieroglyphs themselves, an attack which in his rather unkind and arrogant formulation became the eighteenth century's epitaph on the tradition, although a false prophecy: 'Die Erklärung der Hieroglyphen ist zu unsern Zeiten ein vergebener Versuch, und ein Mittel lächerlich zu werden'[93].

It is therefore natural that the Egyptianizing tendencies in the arts after Piranesi and Winckelmann should manifest themselves as copies and reconstructions of original Egyptian material and no longer as original inventions. Undoubtedly stimulated by the travel books a new interest in Egyptian architecture began to make itself felt, first in a rapidly growing literature on the pyramids, and, somewhat later as a continuation of Norden's and Pococke's efforts to trace its various orders and to establish their connection with Greece. It was a symptom of this architectural interest that the Académie des Inscriptions in 1785 set a prize-question on the origin of Egyptian architecture considered against the background of its technical and aesthetical principles and compared with Greek architecture[94].

The question was answered, and the prize won, by the already mentioned Quatremère de Quincy in a critical dissertation called 'De l'état de l'architecture Égyptienne'[95], which was strongly influenced by Winckelmann. From an Egyptological point of view the book is only of interest insofar as it illustrates the extent to which Quatremère like most of the archaeologists of his period was prejudiced against his subject and unable to arrive at an objective historical evaluation. With reference to Vitruvius he considered architecture as well as art essentially imitative in origin as well as in nature. The architecture of Greece had developed from an imitation of the primitive wooden abodes of its original inhabitants, and Egyptian architecture had in Quatremère's opinion a similar origin, imitating the primitive dwellings of the original Egyptians, supposedly excavated as subterraneous caves in the cliffs of the Nile Valley. Following Winckelmann's ideas Quatremère contended that the lack of development in Egyptian architecture was a direct result of this origin. 'In the eyes of men of taste it would always remain sculptured quarries', and it had never developed beyond the most primitive stage of art, the one, concerned only with elementary technical problems, with what was absolutely necessary. It had no aesthetic qualities, no *goût*. It was monotonous, exaggerated, graceless and unpleasing to the eye, and its one quality, force and solidity, was only an apparent quality and in reality the result of technical and artistic incompetence. It had never developed any governing principle of reason, never any system of proportion, nor any distinctive styles, and although it had made use of a profusion of ornamental and decorative elements, above all the hieroglyphs, these were by their nature enigmatical and confused (p. 209) and from an architectural point of view therefore merely disturbing. With this attitude it was natural that Quatremère should come to the conclusion that it would be a profanation, and almost a sacrilege, to speak of an Egyptian origin of Greek architecture and art. The Greeks might have borrowed certain technical elements, as for instance certain forms of capitals, sphinxes, and decorative symbols, but they had never permitted themselves to become influenced or inspired by a barbaric and uncouth culture in every way inferior to their own.

It is undoubtedly true that with the limited and imperfect material at their disposal, Winckelmann and Quatremère could hardly be expected to pass a satisfactory and adequate judgment on Egyptian art, but that their prejudices were more fatal to their judgment than their lack of material, and that a different approach could give entirely different results, was demonstrated with remarkable clarity in the works of Georg Zoëga (1755-1809).

Zoëga was born in the small town of Daler in Schleswig, but inspired with an ardent interest in antiquity by his teacher at the University of Göttingen, the noble classical philologist Heyne, he settled permanently in Rome in 1783 after a couple of previous visits, and became generally acknowledged as one of the most distinguished and outstanding authorities on antiquity.

Greatly influenced by his genious, Zoëga's lifework became in certain respects a continuation of Winckelmann's, whose unbridled enthusiasm for what was to a certain extent a poetic illusion about classical art he transformed into a no less ardent, but more dignified and methodical and, above all, a less dogmatic and prejudiced love of antiquity.

To a remarkable extent their activities followed parallel courses. Winckelmann's publication of Baron de Stosch's gems[96] corresponded to Zoëga's publication of the Egyptian coins belonging to Cardinal Borgia[97], in whom he had found a constant protector and friend, just as his unfinished publication 'Li Bassirilievi Antichi di Roma,[98] containing the monuments from the Villa and the Palazzo Albani, became a revision of Winckelmann's 'Monumenti inediti'[99]; but Winckelmann's predomiantly artistic and aesthetic approach was in Zoëga's work modified in favour of a more sober archaeological method, based on his profound learning and erudition, his cultivated taste, and his practised 'Stilgefühl'.

His principal work, and the one with which we are here primarily concerned, was

'De origine et usu obeliscorum' (Rome 1797). It has no direct counterpart in Winckelmann's production, but it was intimately connected with his lifework, and without ever turning unduly polemic it became an authoritative refutation of some of his most fundamental Egyptological mistakes. Historically seen the book was just another manifestation of the all-pervading archaeological passion of its time, but it made history itself by inaugurating a new era in the history of archaeology.

The pontificate of Pius VI, which was to end with the occupation of Rome by French troops and the proclamation of the Roman Republic, while the octogenarian Pope was dragged as a prisoner to France to die, was before the catastrophe characterized by a revival of arts and letters and of ancient pomp which went very well with the magnificent appearance of the Supreme Pontiff himself. His grandiose plans and designs for the embellishment of Rome and the draining and cultivation of the Campagna were unfortunately left unfinished, but his pontificate recalls for the last time in papal history the Renaissance; and the Pope's interest in the monumental possibilities of the obelisks was only one of the symptoms.

Already in 1711 Clement IX had resumed the activities of his predecessors, and re-erected a broken obelisk, found in the Campus Martius, in front of the Pantheon, and in 1787 Pius VI ordered his architect Antinori to re-erect in front of the Quirinal Palace an obelisk found near the mausoleum of Augustus. Antinori combined it with the two antique colossi known as the 'Horse-Tamers' and an ancient fountain into a magnificent monument which was undoubtedly inspired by Fischer von Erlach's reconstruction of the obelisk of Marcus Aurelius and Lucius Verus at Corinth[100].

In 1789 the same architect removed the so-called Sallustian obelisk to its present position opposite the church of La Trinitá dei Monti, and in 1792 he restored at the Monte Citorio the gnomon obelisk which had formerly been one of the sights of ancient Rome, where Augustus had used it as the pointer of a gigantic sun-dial at the Campus Martius. It was the Pope's desire that these efforts to let the obelisks reappear as characteristic elements in the architectural physiognomy of Rome should be accompanied by a literary record of their history, to replace the old publications of Mercati and Bandini[101], and in 1797 Zoëga, now also acknowledged as the outstanding authority on Egyptological matters, was entrusted with the task. The result was an enormous volume of nearly 700 pages in folio containing a critical evaluation of all results until then obtained by Egyptological studies. The first two chapters, in Zoëga's own words, placed at the beginning of the book like the two obelisks flanking the entrance to Egyptian temples, contained the material from the classical authors on which almost all knowledge of Egypt still had to be based. They were followed by archaeological and historical descriptions of all known obelisks, in Europe as well as in Egypt, which quite naturally occasioned a digression on the literature of travels, and a chapter on technical problems, including an excursus on the pyramids, in

118

which Zoëga came to the conclusion that there were no esoteric or symbolic secrets involved in the shape of these monuments.

The chapter on the aim and significance of the obelisks gave rise to another digression on the religious and philosophical doctrines of the Egyptians, their burial customs, and general religious ideas, which, although devoid of his demonological speculations, came fairly close to Kircher's account, and was based on the same Neo-Platonic and Hermetic sources; but Zoëga warned explicitly against the dangers of method, arising from confounding the problems of the symbolical philosophy of the Egyptians, with the problem of the hieroglyphs (p. 461). The latter problem was treated at great length, and nowhere were Zoëga's critical faculties, and his outstanding sense of essentials as well as his deductive powers more apparent.

His reflexions were based on an exhaustive presentation of the classical material concerning the hieroglyphs, but were combined with a critical review of the entire Egyptological literature, from which Zoëga drew his own, often striking, conclusions[102].

His general attitude towards the basic problem of decipherment was conventional insofar as he considered it insoluble (p. 179)[103], and he refused to acknowledge the previous attempts as serious scientific efforts (p. 461). Renouncing any attempt of decipherment himself, his account was confined to a very personal and critical exposition of what he considered the theoretical nature of the script illustrated by the most extensive and carefully reproduced collection of original hieroglyphical inscriptions hitherto published.

His conception of the hieroglyphs was undoubtedly influenced by d'Origny who had criticized Warburton and come to the conclusion that, basically seen, only two different elements were involved in the system: symbolical and alphabetical ones.

To explain their mutual relations Zoëga described the hieroglyphs as pictures of material objects, which, as far as their meaning and significance were concerned, always retained a connection with the objects they represented even if this relation was of an allegorical or symbolical nature (p. 438), a characteristic which in his opinion made them essentially different from Chinese as well as Mexican letters[104] (ib.). In accordance with the current distinctions and the established terminology he divided them into various groups according to the nature of their symbolic significance; and the difference between the various categories was illustrated by examples from the classics. He proved that what had hitherto been considered cursive hieroglyphs were in most cases just ordinary hieroglyphs carelessly executed, which made him exclude them from his graphic system. The symbolic signs were according to Zoëga used in all official and lapidary inscriptions, not only for religious purposes but also, as for instance on the obelisks, for ordinary historical texts and records. It is characteristic that although he refrained from any attempt at decipherment himself, he had quite

119

definite ideas how the problem should be approached methodically. It would be advisable to begin with the texts accompanying the pictorial representations, because the pictures would in those cases give a clue to the content of the texts, and he made the correct observation that inscriptions accompanying pictures facing left, appeared to be written from the left, but from the right if the picture faced that direction. He also called attention to the cartouches. He was convinced that no results could be obtained until a reliable collection of all available hieroglyphical signs had been made. We have seen that Niebuhr had made some preliminary efforts in this direction, but Zoëga was the first to make an exhaustive revision of the available material from which he derived a list of 958 different signs which he arranged in groups according to the objects they represented[105].

He was convinced that they were essentially allegorical by nature, but tried to explain how the individual signs by slow and gradual evolution had acquired alphabetical functions, first by being used for homonymous words and afterward by being split up in such a way that the various characteristic features of each sign could be used independently for various words with related sound-values (p. 552-53). He did not believe that a proper alphabet had been invented, such as stated for instance by Plato and Plutarch (p. 552), but he was convinced that phonetical writing had nevertheless developed in Egypt. He was uncertain about the relations between the Greek and the Egyptian alphabets, but demonstrated against Kircher that Coptic letters did not appear until late, probably not until the third century A.D., and he contested an allegation still defended by Winckelmann that the hieroglyphical traditions had become extinct after the Persian conquest of Egypt, by demonstrating inscribed monuments undoubtedly dating from Roman times.

But Zoëga's critical revision of current misconceptions was not confined to the hieroglyphic field, and he was the first to refute Winckelmann's thesis about the stagnant immutability of Egyptian art, by demonstrating how obelisks, statues, and hieroglyphic inscriptions could be divided up into distinct periods according to their style and the quality of their workmanship. His efforts to define these periods were not entirely successful and could hardly be expected to be so with the very limited material at his disposal, but it is characteristic of his 'Stilgefühl' that he considered what we should call the twelfth dynasty the culmination of Egyptian art, demonstrated the subsequent decline, and was the first to point out the Saïte revival.

He had much more instictive feeling for Egyptian art than Winckelmann, and he understood that most of the Graecizing Egyptian sculptures of the Hellenistic and the Roman periods were barbaric imitations and rude caricatures of Egyptian style, and represented the final decline and deterioration of its ideals.

In spite of the fact that he very wisely evaded the decipherment his book represents nevertheless a culmination in the hieroglyphic and Egyptological studies, and even the problems which were left unsolved received frequently their final formulation in Zoëga's exposition. But we have already seen that the scientific interest was only part of the hieroglyphic tradition, and that there was often no small discrepancy between the scholarly doctrines, the artistic taste, and the popular beliefs. Winckelmann's condemnation of the Egyptian style did not prevent it from inspiring contemporary artists, and the myth about the wisdom of Egypt, the original source of all true occult and mystic knowledge, remained alive as a strong undercurrent below the archaeological and scientific demands for what was called reason and enlightenment.

The extent of the belief in magic, demonology, and occultism, together with an uncanny urge for mystic experience and occult revelations, is demonstrated by the rather frightening reports of the case against the poisoners in Paris and at the court of Louis XIV about 1700, and the memoirs of the period bear illuminating evidence of how astrology, alchemy, and magical experiments were fashionable occupations for the idle rich as well as the ambitious poor.

The ardent adherents of true mystics, as for instance Boehme, Swedenborg, and Gessner, formed influential congregations round the mystic doctrines of their leaders, and adventurers and rogues such as Schrepfer, Saint Germain and Cagliostro could live on the fat of the land, be accepted in high society, and become almost religiously revered by means of a mystic oratory, simple conjuring tricks, and demonological thimbleriggings. Semi-religious and secret societies of every denomination abounded, and common to most of them was their dependence on esoteric doctrines, cosmological conceptions, and a mystic terminology based on a weird conglomeration of debased Neo-Platonic, Gnostic, Hermetic and Cabbalistic ideas. The theoretical aim of most of them was a vague ethical desire to obtain perfection by means of a secret knowledge of an esoteric truth, manifest in allegorical symbols, the true meaning of which was gradually revealed to the initiate as he passed through the rites of the various degrees of the societies among which the Rosicrucians and the Freemasons were the most influential and respectable.

How the essential mystery which in the old Neo-Platonic manner would seem to have been considered a secret mystic experience more than an actual secret, was considered an Egyptian heritage is well established in Masonic literature and was a natural consequence of the tendency to ascribe an Egyptian origin to any mystical creed and doctrine.

In more or less direct connection with the interest for secret rites and allegorical ceremonies engendered by the Masonic activities grew an extensive literature with Egyptian subjects, almost invariably centred round cultic mysteries and secret, symbolical initiations. Typical is Jean Terrasson's moralizing novel 'Sethos' (1731) which in the author's own words was strongly influenced by 'Télémaque'.

By far the most important parts of the voluminous book are the elaborate descriptions of the various trials, rituals and mysteries to which the hero, the young Sethos, was submitted by his fatherly tutor, in order to ennoble and fortify his character, and develop the lofty virtues of an enlightened monarch. The book is not without a certain historical colouring, obviously based on extensive studies of classical authorities as Apuleius, Plutarch, Iamblichus and Eusebius. It was widely read, and not infrequently considered an authoritative source of information concerning Egyptian cult and mythology, with unjust disregard of Jablonski's compendious and scholarly 'Pantheon Aegypthiorum', which appeared in the years 1750-52. In Masonic circles 'Sethos' became of almost historical importance, because it became the basis on which the French reformers framed their so-called Egyptian ritual[106].

Seen from a literary point of view it gave rise to countless imitations, a true literary Egyptomania. Already in 1739 it was dramatized by Tannevot into a five-act tragedy in verse[107], and in 1751 Rameau wrote an opera ballet 'La naissance d'Osiris', the text of which – by Cahusac – is said to be reminiscent of Sethos. Von Köppen published in 1770 his 'Crata Repoa', or 'Initiations into the ancient society of Egyptian priests', much read in Masonic circles and frequently reprinted[108]. The first German translation of 'Sethos' appeared in Hamburg already in 1732, and no less a person than Matthias Claudius made a new and better one in 1777. An opera by Naumann 'Osiris', with libretto by Mazzola, was produced in Dresden 1781, and the renowned geologist and Mason, Ignatz v. Born inaugurated his 'Journal für Freimauer' with a great article on the mysteries of the Egyptians based on Terrasson and v. Köppen.

Born was Master of the Lodge 'Zur Wahren Eintracht' in Vienna, into which Mozart was originally introduced; and the dependence of Schikaneder's text to 'The Magic Flute' (1791) on the above-mentioned material was long ago indisputably established and acknowledged. It must not be forgotten either that Goethe, who during his Italian journey had shown a keen interest in Egyptian antiquities, and even taken casts of hieroglyphs and smaller monuments[109], wrote a continuation of 'The Magic Flute' (1795)[110], and that Spiess, the very popular author of novels of horror, wrote a 'Geheimnisse der Alten Egypzier', which I have not seen, but in which 'the irresistible longing for Egypt' is said to be the leitmotiv[111].

As the very last and remotest offshoot of the tradition must be mentioned the extensive polemic literature provoked by the extraordinary activities of the so-called Count Cagliostro (1743-95) who, after an adventurous and dubious career during which he probably paid a visit to some parts of the Near East and maybe to Egypt, appeared in Paris and London about 1771 as an international swindler on the highest plane. He specialized in love-philtres, beauty preparations, alchemistic powders, and arranged demonological and spiritualistic seances. It was his ambitious and cunning scheme to use the Masonic organizations to gain an international position of power

122

and influence, and in order to establish a universal jurisdiction over the lodges under his own supremacy he proclaimed that his tutelary spirit, the so-called Grand-
Copht, had ordered him to reorganize the Masonic organizations by introducing a
new Egyptian rite. He succeeded to a certain extent, if only for a time, and founded
in 1782 a lodge in the Rue de la Soudière in Paris, called 'Mère Loge d'Adoption de
la Haute Maconnérie Égyptienne'[112], combined with a private temple of Isis at which
Cagliostro himself acted as the High-Priest. With unparalleled impudence and utter
unscrupulousness, the 'divine Cagliostro' kept things going until 1789, when he was
arrested in Rome and condemned to death as a heretic.

The sentence was commuted to imprisonment for life, and he died in prison in
1795. But the enormity of the imposture had stirred Europe long before the final
catastrophe. Already in 1787 appeared the dignified but pathetic confessions of a
former faithful follower, the Courlandic Lady v. d. Recke, which unmasked Cagliostro completely[113]. Schiller gave in his novel 'Der Geisterseher' (1788-89) a picture
of the swindler's career and his methods, and the Empress Catherine the Second of
Russia, who refused to receive him during his stay in Russia, and finally expelled
him, wrote no less than three comedies, in which she ridiculed him and his followers[114].

Goethe, who already during his visit to Sicily had tried to trace the background
of Cagliostro, wrote with biting wit and profound psychological insight, a scathing
satire called 'Der Gross-Copta' in which he describes his connection with the fatal
affair of the necklace at the court of Louis XVI, and two 'Coptic songs', one of them
with the significant refrain: 'töricht auf Bessrung der Toren zu warten'.

It is obvious that these works were only indirectly and very remotely connected
with the Egyptian traditions, but the stupendous fraud responsible for their appearance was based on a cunning understanding of the fact that a mystic belief in the
occult science of ancient Egypt was still alive and strong enough to be used in dangerous efforts to dominate the imagination and the minds of men.

v. The Decipherment

The uncanny Heraclitean maxim that the father of all things is war was also in the hieroglyphic field to prove its sombrous validity. Since the ascent of the powerful and gifted Osmanic Sultans, their destruction of the frail remnants of the Eastern empire, and their conquest of Constantinople in 1453, the Western powers had been forced into a precarious attitude of defence; and a permanent state of unrelaxed tension intermittent with ferocious fighting governed for centuries the relations between the continents.

But strong internal forces of disintegration had already begun towards the end of the sixteenth century to drain the expansive forces of the Turkish empire, in which domestic strife, dynastic rivalries, and inordinate luxuriousness exhausted the strength of its rulers and made them still formidable, but much less ferocious adversaries.

Soliman's efforts to conquer Vienna had come to nought in 1521 and 1532. The Christian league succeeded, under the supreme command of John of Austria, in destroying the Turkish fleet at Lepanto (1571), and the imperial Field Marshal Montecucculi inflicted a decisive defeat on the Turkish army near the Abbey of St. Gotthard on the Raab in 1664, followed by the no less important victory won by John Sobieski of Poland at the gates of Vienna in 1683.

But even while these life and death struggles were going on, on which the very fate of Europe and Christianity depended, few European rulers and monarchs had resisted the temptation to make secret and humiliating advances to the universal enemy in order to further their political schemes and ambitions and counteract those of their adversaries. But the advantages of a Turkish alliance diminished with the decline of Turkish power, and with the unerring instinct for weakness, common to beasts of prey, the European nations began cautiously to draw together in a universal hope of easy spoil. The admonitions and exhortations of the Church, which had hitherto been preached to deaf ears, began to resound, mainly because a pious crusade against the infidels was now a welcome pretext for the expansive aspirations of the Great Powers.

In 1661 serious efforts were made to form an anti-Turkish league including the Pope, the Emperor, and the King of France, but the negotiations were interrupted by the last-mentioned, who at home went so far as to call the Turks 'l'énnemi commun, l'énnémi de toute la chrétienté', but at the same time suffered his ambassador to be maltreated at the Sultan's court.

The political situation, with its continual internal strife and war in Europe, while a still powerful enemy was at its gates, caused universal anxiety, and among those who seriously considered what might be done about it was the young Leibniz.

In 1670 he submitted an important report on the establishment of a federal system of defence among the German states, and from the political reflections here involved arose a gigantic political vision, his secret plan for a French occupation of Egypt[1].

The ultimate background of this remarkable scheme was Leibniz' ardent desire to secure European peace in order to prevent Germany from becoming the constant battle-ground of the Hapsburgs and the Bourbons. In Leibniz' opinion France represented the active dynamic principle in contemporaneous Europe, and only if its dynamic and aggressive energy could be diverted, would a European peace be possible; and how could French energy possibly be employed with greater 'gloire' and with more profitable results than against 'l'énnémi commun', against the Turks? But unlike most politicizing philosophers he did not merely throw out his plan as a brilliant scheme, but took it upon himself to work it out in all details and to outline the strategy as well as the political complications involved. Theoretically seen his plan was based on irrefutable logical reasoning.

Any attack on Turkish soil in Europe would have to be carried out on German territory and was therefore against the very background of Leibniz' plan. An attack on the Near East was out of the question, because such attacks had proved failures ever since the crusades. But Egypt was vulnerable. It was the very backbone of the Turkish empire, and its granary, just as it had been the granary of Rome. It was easy to attack and had always fallen an easy prey to any determined assailant. Cut off from the resources of Egypt the Turkish power would become negligible. France had a fleet, and the martial spirit necessary for such an enterprise, and it would gain immeasurable advantages from the possession of Egypt. The country's climate was healthy, and occupied by an energetic power it would command the Red Sea, the Mediterranean, and could be used to support the mastery of the sea. With Egypt at its back France would control the access to Asia and Africa and dominate the trade of the world. The martial youth of Europe would flock around the French standards, and the whole undertaking would surround the name of France and its King with undying glory and fame. From the time of St. Louis and the Crusaders, France had a direct tradition of oriental warface, and it was desirous of developing its naval power. In Europe itself the plan would not create internal complications of serious importance. It would suit the Emperor's policy, because it would relieve his eastern frontier, and open possibilities for an expansion towards the east. Spain, Portugal, and Rome would probably support the plan as a crusade. Denmark was only concerned about its own security which was linked up with that of Germany. Sweden would probably stick to its traditional pro-French policy, and could be asked to join Poland in an anti-Turkish campaign to prevent any future aggressions towards Germany.

Only England and Holland would be in opposition, Holland especially, because its Indian trade would go to France, but neither would be able to interfere beforehand provided everything was kept secret, and afterwards nobody would be able to resist the combined and reconciled forces of Emperor and King.

The European countries would enter into a new era, and could envisage a prolonged period of peaceful coexistence with the irresistible arms of Hapsburg and Bourbon.

For sheer grandeur of vision, razor-sharp logic and psychological insight, the plan was almost staggering and characteristic of the cool-headed, almost cynical, reasoning of a period which could still regard political problems unemotionally, without sentimentality and hypocrisy.

The scheme was submitted to Pomponne and the King in preliminary outlines, and they were not unwilling to consider it. But an ambassador Nointel had already been sent to Constantinople to negotiate a treaty which after much trouble and indignity was suddenly and unexpectedly signed by the Turks in 1673, and Louis' remarkable lack of imagination and foresight made him also on this occasion prefer an immediate illusory advantage to the demands of patience and reason. He ratified the treaty, and embarked on the fatal policy which was to plunge Europe into an almost continuous state of war until the peace of Utrecht (1713), exhaust and ruin the empire as well as France, and secure for the Turks the uncontested possession of their dominions. Leibniz left Paris without submitting the details of the plan, and the project was discarded and forgotten, but the Egyptian problem was in the air, and it is curious to find a parallel to Leibniz' scheme in Dominique Jauna's 'Histoire Générale des Royaumes de Chypre, de Jérusalem etc.' (Leyden 1747), which contains a chapter called 'Réflexion sur les moyens de conquérir l'Égypte et le Chypre'[2].

During the wars of the eighteenth century between England and France the position of Egypt was not forgotten. As far as the East was concerned the political situation remained essentially unchanged and in 1798 the French invaded Egypt according to plans made by the Directors of the French Republic and carried out by Napoleon, who at that time had probably no direct knowledge of Leibniz' memorandum[3]. His aim was not to assure the peace of Europe, but to establish a base for his struggle against England.

As a military operation the campaign was brilliant and glorious. The whole country was entirely subdued in less than three weeks, but strategically and politically seen, the expedition was an utter failure. Nelson destroyed the French fleet at Aboukir (1798), Napoleon escaped to France (1799) after a vain effort to conquer Syria, and General Abercrombie landed an army at Aboukir Bay in 1801, which eventually forced the French to capitulate.

Seen from a cultural and scientific standpoint, however, Napoleon's Egyptian venture became of great and long-lasting importance.

Already before his departure Napoleon had determined that the expedition should be scientific as well as military, and a committee of about 150 scientists and artists, mostly recruited from the 'Académie des Inscriptions', accompanied the army to collect scientific and archaeological material for the planned publication 'Déscription de l'Égypte'. Cairo became the headquarters of these activities centred around the newly-founded 'Institut d'Égypte'. However, the expedition's most spectacular and sensational find, the discovery of the bilingual Rosetta stone, which by one stroke was to revolutionize Egyptology and archaeology, was not the result of deliberate archaeological investigations, but was made fortuitously, and in the field. (Pl. XXII, 1).

The exact circumstances of its discovery are obscure, but according to the report published in the 'Courier d'Égypte', a detachment of the French army was working on some fortifications near the small village of Rashid-Rosetta in the Western Delta, some thirty miles from Alexandria on the left bank of an arm of the Nile in antiquity known as the Bolbitinic[4]. During the work the pick of one of the men struck an irregular slab of black granite, and by some sort of a miracle, the finder was conscientious enough to notice that its front was covered by inscriptions in three different characters, one which was probably hieroglyphs, another which was in fact demotic, but was at first considered Syriac, and one which was undoubtedly Greek. The stone was cleaned and sent to the commanding officer in Alexandria, General Menoce, who immediately had it transported to Cairo, and committed to the care of the Institute. It became immediately the object of the most vivid interest, and it was Napoleon himself who ordered the inscription copied and reproduced.

The orientalist Jean Joseph Marcel (1776-1854), who took part in the expedition as director of its printing works made some primitive copies by inking the surface of the stone and rolling sheets of paper over it, and Raffeneau Delile[5] made sulphur casts of the inscription, which were brought to France by General Dugua, who handed them over to the 'Institut National', which requested a translation of the Greek text from the old Hubert Pascal Ameilhon (1730-1811), the author of a 'Histoire du Commerce et de la Navigation des Égyptiens sous le Règne des Ptolémées (1766), and a 'Notice des Inscriptions rapportées d'Égypte par les officiers de l'armée commandée par le Général Bonaparte' (1802). However, the 'Gentleman's Magazine' for 1801[6] could already accompany its announcement of General Dugua's return to France with the copies with the remark 'that the rare and valuable collection .... made by the French scavans with so much toil and care in Egypt, having been captured by the English army will, no doubt, be brought to this country by General Hutchinson'.

The paper concluded its article maliciously: 'This is what Virgil would have said: 'sic vos non vobis''.

The successful landing of General Abercromby's forces and the subsequent capitulation of the French (1801), surrendered to the British army all antiquities collected by the committee and among them also the Rosetta stone, which arrived at Portsmouth in February 1802[7]. From here it was taken to London, where it remained for some time in the apartments of the Society of Antiquaries, previous to its deposit in the British Museum[8].

In Paris the monument was described by Duteil, and in London a preliminary translation of the Greek text was submitted to the Society of Antiquaries by the Rev. Stephen Watson in 1802[9]. Copies of the stone were made and engravings of the Greek inscription were presented to various learned societies all over Europe. A full translation of the Greek text, by Mr. Weston, was read to the Society in November 1802, and another was at the same time submitted by Zoëga's teacher, Professor Heyne from Goettingen[10]. A final and correct translation proved no easy matter, because the official curial idiom of the Ptolemaic administration in which the text was written was relatively unknown at the time; but the general content of the text was quite clear.

It contained a copy of a decree issued in 196 B.C. in Memphis by an assembly of Egyptian priests in honour of King Ptolemy V Epiphanes (203-181 B.C.), to commemorate his benefactions towards the indigenous priesthood. As a historical document the text was of minor importance, but it contained a colophon which decreed that it should be engraved on stone in three different characters: hieroglyphs, native letters, and Greek, and erected in all the principal temples of Egypt. There was, therefore, no doubt that the stone contained three versions of the same text and that the Greek text might prove the key to the reading of the two others. The old ideas about the symbolic nature of the hieroglyphs and the alphabetical character of the vulgar script, made it natural to start all efforts at deciphering with the demotic text.

The first attempt was made by Sylvestre de Sacy, at the time Europe's leading orientalist, and professor of Arabic at the famous school of living oriental languages in Paris. His efforts were based on a copy provided by Citoyen Chaptal, now Minister of the Interior.

The result of de Sacy's investigations were published in his 'Lettre au Citoyen Chaptal' (1802), and based on an irreproachable methodical approach. Starting from the proper-names mentioned in the Greek text he tried to locate their position in the Demotic inscription. It was his intention to submit them to a graphic analysis, and to reduce them into their graphic elements, in order to establish an alphabet which could be used for the other words of the text. He succeeded in establishing the approximate groups representing the names of Alexander and Ptolemy, but his ef-

PLATE XXII

1. The Rosetta stone.

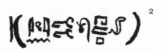

2. Champollion's signature written by himself in hieroglyphs in his 'Lettre à Mons.
Dacier'.

PLATE XXIII

1. The hieroglyphic sign of the bee used for the writing of the official title: 'King of Lower Egypt'. Ammianus Marcellinus' information that the bee was the hieroglyphic symbol of Royalty is based on this use of the sign.

2 a-b. Monogram and cartouche from the frontispiece of 'Déscription de l'Égypte'. The snake biting its tail as a symbol of eternity is taken from Horapollo, and the star and the bee inscribed in the cartouche have the 'hieroglyphic' significance: 'divus Rex', 'divine King'. For a corresponding use of the star see plate XIV,4.

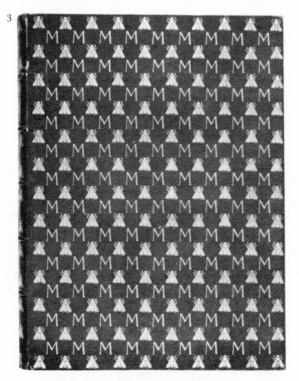

3. Bookbinding with bees used instead of crowns in the monogram of the Princess Mathilde Bonaparte.

forts to decompose them failed. The fifteen letters, which he tentatively thought he had been able to isolate, were mostly erroneous, and it proved impossible to corroborate their phonetic values with other words. He had hoped to be able to find such words as 'God', 'King', and 'Son', the vocalization of which he knew from Coptic, but as he did not succeed, he admitted his failure with admirable frankness and dignity and handed his material over to a fellow orientalist, the Swedish diplomat and scholar Johan David Åkerblad (1763-1819), with a beau geste.

After an education at the University of Upsala, where he had studied the classic and oriental languages, Åkerblad had in 1788 entered the diplomatic service, spent several years in Constantinople, and travelled extensively in the Near East and in Egypt. He combined a remarkable linguistic talent with a keen interest in graphic problems, and his first important publication was a brilliant interpretation of one of Pococke's Phoenician inscriptions[11], which had previously been studied by Barthélémy. He was also a very competent Coptic scholar, and had about 1801 been the first to draw attention to the existence of a cursive hand in Coptic writing[12].

The results of his studies of the Rosetta stone were equally remarkable, and after less than two months he was able to solve most of the problems which had baffled de Sacy, and to publish them in a letter addressed to the latter: 'Lettre sur l'inscription Égyptienne de Rosette'. (Paris 1802).

His general approach was not different from that of de Sacy. Starting with an analysis of the name of 'Ptolemy' he was able to prove, what his predecessor had come to doubt, that the proper names of the demotic text were in fact written with alphabetic letters. He identified with a fair amount of certainty the greater part of the proper-names of the inscription such as Alexander, Arsinoë, Berenice, and Aëtos, and by comparison he was able to establish a demotic alphabet of 29 letters of which about half were correct. Some signs, f for instance, proved direct prototypes of the auxiliary letters by which the Copts had augmented the Greek alphabet, in order to express specific Egyptian sounds, an observation which in itself was a striking proof of the validity of Åkerblad's theories.

But he went still further. From his Coptic studies he knew that f represented the personal pronoun of the third person masculine, and he observed that it had the same functions in demotic (p. 45), and when he analysed the graphic compounds presumably representing such words as 'Greek', 'Egyptian', 'temple', 'love', and 'abundance' he found that these too contained alphabetical elements, and that the demotic words arrived at were more or less identical with the Coptic words for the same concepts.

All this was of eminent importance, because the discovery that alphabetic letters were not only used for the writing of foreign words and proper names but also for the spelling of ordinary words demonstrated the general alphabetical character of the script as such. The identity of the demotic and the Coptic words proved not only that the language of the inscription was closely related to Coptic but also that Coptic was in fact the language of the ancient Egyptians.

It is difficult for us, who are to a certain extent dazzled by the subsequent achievements of Champollion, to judge Åkerblad's discoveries justly and to understand their full scope, but it was his unfailing merit to have turned what had hitherto been play with hypotheses and theories into methodical investigations. In the end he was unfortunately to a certain extent caught by his own success. He became convinced that the script was exclusively alphabetic and barred his own way by vain efforts to find phonetical values, also for the unphonetical elements. Apart from a few casual remarks on the first three numerals, he disregarded deliberately the hieroglyphic inscription, being convinced of the symbolical nature of its notation. It is characteristic that he was not unimpressed by the hieroglyphical extravaganzas of his countryman and fellow-diplomat, Count N. G. Palin (1765-1842). The latter's efforts to solve the hieroglyphic problem were published in his 'Lettres sur les Hiéroglyphes' (s. l. 1802)[13], his 'Éssays sur les Hiéroglyphes' (Weimar 1804) and in 'Analyse de l'inscription Hiéroglyphique du Monument trouvé a Rosetta' (Dresden 1804), but these publications can hardly claim even a historical interest[14]. They were based on signs, which in most cases had very little connection with Egyptian hieroglyphs, as he worked with a very bad copy of the Rosetta inscription. He had recourse to the old parallels with Chinese writing, and the concord between the Greek and the hieroglyphic texts was established by allegorical expoundings[15]. As a side-line he made efforts to prove that the Psalms of David were Hebrew translations of Egyptian texts which could be reconstructed by translating the Hebrew text into Chinese. By rewriting them with Chinese letters, they could be made into a key for the decipherment of the hieroglyphs. It will be seen that it would be unkind and superfluous to submit his production to any serious criticism or comment. More important were his activities as a collector, and he possessed an important collection of more than 1700 scarabs[16].

Count Palin was not the only scholar who was inextricably caught in the traditional allegorical prejudices, and their lack of success did not prevent innumerable scholars from undertaking new attempts. The Austrian orientalist Joseph v. Hammer Purgstall (1774-1856), who was editor of an important journal called 'Fundgruben des Orients' or 'Mines de l'Orient' (Vienna 1809-18), published in 1806 an English translation of an Arabic manuscript purportedly written by an Arab scholar Achmed ben Abu-Bekr[17]. It contained examples of various mystic and enigmatic alphabets, and a fanciful account of the initiations and the duties of Egyptian priests. As already pointed out by de Sacy in his critical review of the book[18], the signs supposed to be Egyptian had nothing whatsoever to do with hieroglyphs, which did not prevent v. Hammer from explaining them as such, in accordance with the well-known symbolical methods. The text itself is not without interest, in so far as it proves the exist-ence of an original Arabic literature dealing with hieroglyphic questions, and ob-viously influenced by Neo-Platonic ideas[19]. We have already seen that Kircher pos-sessed a similar manuscript, and von Hammer's assertion that it was a copy of the same text is by no means improbable. But even if his personal attempts were failures, he was nevertheless able to make an indirect contribution to Egyptology by his im-mediate enthusiastic acceptance of Champollion's results and by defending them against the attacks of the philhellenes whom he accused of 'only acknowledging as truth what they find in their classics'[20].

Also Alexandre Lenoir (1762-1839), who during the revolution courageously saved the antiquities of Paris and published a series of useful works on various archaeological and antiquarian subjects[21], made some rather unfortunate attempts at deciphering in his voluminous 'Nouvelle Explication des Hiéroglyphes, ou des anciennes Allé-gories sacrées des Égyptiens', I-IV (Paris 1809-22)[22]. It was his aim 'de faire con-naitre par la sphère céleste, que les mystères et les anciennes allégories sacrées ne sont qu'une traduction fidèle dès phénomenes de la nature' as a contribution to what he called 'the hiero-astronomic science'. The results need hardly occupy us here.

What Miss Hartleben has very appropriately called the 'Devil of hieroglyphics' was at large, and an incessant stream of explications and hieroglyphical expoundings spread confusion amongst the unwary and contempt of Egyptology amongst the learned[23].

Lacour's 'Éssay sur les Hiéroglyphes' (Bordeaux 1821) propound the theory that the language spoken in Egypt at the time of Moses was in fact Hebrew, and that the hieroglyphs could be identified with Hebrew letters, which in many cases were also the prototypes of the letters of the Greek alphabet. But apart from the almost re-freshing assertion by Tandeau de St. Nicholas that the hieroglyphs were not letters at all and nothing but ornamental and decorative patterns[24], we are not going to enu-merate more failures, but proceed to the more profitable achievements of the period. One of the most important and epoch-making events was the publication of the sci-entific and archaeological results of the Egyptian expedition, the gigantic 'Déscrip-tion de l'Égypte' (1809-28). The secretary of the editorial committee was Edme Jomard (1777-1862), and to his unswerving care and dedication were due, not only the imposing appearance of the publication, the scientific quality of its various topo-graphical, zoological, and scientific sections, but above all its magnificent and hi-therto unequalled reproductions of antiques and architectural monuments, made by a variety of artists under his personal supervision. Its careful and relatively correct reproductions of hieroglyphs and inscriptions, including a copy of the demotic text from the Rosetta stone, provided for the first time adequate material for methodical studies, and contributed essentially to the final results. But no account was included of the hieroglyphic problems, and the decipherment was hardly mentioned. Jomard was possessed by an ardent ambition to solve the problem himself, but as he was not yet able to submit any positive result, he guarded jealously the inscriptional material from all other Egyptologists, and announced the publication of some 'Observations et Recherches sur les Hiéroglyphes' but all that ever appeared was his important article on the Egyptian numerals, their system of notation, and their hieroglyphic forms[25]. Jomard contributed several other articles and memoirs on Egyptological subjects[26], but his account of the numerals was undoubtedly his masterpiece. He gave a brilliant review of the problems involved and a scholarly solution of them, which so far as it went was correct in all essentials. The merit of having cleared this limited but important section of the hieroglyphic jungle is incontestably due to Jomard.

The extent to which the new Egyptian fancy in architecture and the decorative arts became stimulated by the Egyptian expedition has been lavishly illustrated by Pevsner[27] and Lang. Pylons and temples, pyramids, obelisks, and sphinxes, became once more recurrent, if not always tasteful, features of European art, and appeared together with Egyptian ornamentation and decorative hieroglyphic inscriptions at the strangest and most unexpected places. It is not surprising, therefore, to find that even the strange heraldic reform introduced by Napoleon when he replaced the old monarchical symbol, the 'Fleur de Lys', with a new heraldic emblem, the bee, has a direct hieroglyphical background, and was probably devised by Jomard. Regarded as an isolated phenomenon, and by itself, the choice of this particular animal for this particular purpose has always appeared rather strange, rather banal and unheroic, and above everything utterly out of keeping with the solemn rules of heraldry. Seen from a hieroglyphic point of view, however, its employment becomes most appropriate, and acquires a new and illuminating significance.

It is obvious that the Emperor took the reform seriously, and it was his desire that the new emblem should in fact be regarded as a new national symbol. His coronation robe was spangled with it – and so was that of the Empress –, it was used as a pattern on the fabric of his throne and the furniture of the state-apartments, and occasionally as the empire's official coat of arms instead of the eagle. (Pl. XXXIII, 3). Its true significance can only be understood from its hieroglyphical origin, and the key to its explanation is found on the frontispiece of the first volume of the 'Déscription de l'Égypte', a magnificent eau-forte, drawn by Cécile, engraved by Girardet and Séllier, and etched by Réville. (Pl. XXIV). It represents a heroic Egyptian landscape, enframed by elaborate neo-classic borders resting on a base with heraldic and Egyptian ornaments, flanking the Emperor's monogram, a crowned N, encircled by the well-known hieroglyphical representation of a snake biting its tail. (Pl. XXIII, 2a). Matching this monogram are two identical cartouches which we have seen were used in hieroglyphic inscriptions to circumscribe royal names. They are here to match the crowned initial surmounted by the so-called Atef, the royal crown of Osiris. They contain identical inscriptions consisting of only two hieroglyphic signs, a star and a bee. (Pl. XXIII, 2 b). The various representations of the frontispiece are explained in a short commentary printed overleaf. The snake surrounding the monogram is correctly explained as a symbol of eternity. No source is given for this explanation, but we have already seen that it is found as the third hieroglyph in Horapollo's Hieroglyphica (I. 3).

The inscription of the cartouches is merely said to represent 'a symbol characteristic of the Emperor'. However, the star as well as the bee are well-known hieroglyphic symbols. The star is explained by Horapollo (I. 13), who informs us that it signifies 'the God of the World', and it is constantly used by Dürer, Kircher, and other hierogrammates to express the notion of 'divine'. (Pl. XIV, 4). The bee is also described in the 'Hieroglyphica' (I. 62) and explained as 'a people obedient to its legitimate King'. However, in this particular case Napoleon's direct source was not Horapollo, but another hieroglyphic classic, Ammianus Marcellinus, who explicitly states (XVII. 4. 2.) that the hieroglyphic significance of the bee was 'Rex' or 'King', a statement corroborated by Chairemon. This explanation is one of the typical half-truths of the tradition, based on a misinterpretation of the fact that the official title of Egyptian kings in their capacity of rulers of Lower Egypt was in fact written with the picture of a bee. (Pl. XXIII, 1). The enigma of the two cartouches is therefore solved, and the correct interpretation of their inscriptions is 'divus rex' or 'divine king'. It was therefore very wise, probably, only to intimate the meaning vaguely in the commentary. The rather fulsome flattery probably pleased the Emperor, who never outgrew a legitimacy-complex, and it may have amused the Imperial augurs; but as a relapse into the terminology of the 'Roy-Soleil' it would probably have jarred on Jacobine ears. For the same reason the true meaning of the new heraldic emblem was never publicly disclosed, but it is obvious that Napoleon was fully aware of its significance and introduced it deliberately as a venerable monarchical symbol. It is a curious coincidence, quoted by Volkmann in another connection[28], that Louis XII at his entry into Genoa was wearing a crimson robe embroidered with a golden 'Roy d'abeilles' or 'king bee', surrounded by ordinary bees, and a motto which directly refers to Ammianus Marcellinus' explanation of the hieroglyph[29].

With this curious relapse, the romantic period of the hieroglyphic traditions had come to an end. The fortunate discovery of the Rosetta stone at a time when the general development of scientific principles and methods made a new approach possible, resolved the hieroglyphic problems with remarkable rapidity, and already the first systematic attack undertaken by the English scientist Thomas Young (1773-1829) gave unexpected and far reaching results.

A physician by profession, but a physicist by inclination and vocation, Young had a European name as a distinguished scientist long before he made his first contributions to Egyptology in 1814. His discoveries in optics, such as his account of the principle of the interference of light, his elaboration and improvements of Huygen's wave theory of light, his explanation of the muscular activities by which the eye accomodates itself to distance, his hypothesis concerning the colour-perceptive faculties of the eye, and his theory of the tides, were all profoundly original and in advance of their time. He was also a competent classical scholar and accomplished linguist, with knowledge of Hebrew, Persian, and Coptic as well as the modern languages. His interest in the nature of sound, and its manifestation in the human voice and speech, had led him to certain alphabetical reflections, and we are told by himself that it was a note by the German scholar Johann Severin Vater, in his edition of Adelung's compilation 'Mithridates' (Berlin 1806-1817), stating that the unknown language of the Rosetta stone, and the mummy bandages, could be analysed into an alphabet of about thirty letters, which first drew his attention to the hieroglyphs[30]. But his actual researches did not start until about 1814, when he was asked to examine some fragments of a papyrus brought home from Egypt by his friend Sir William Rouse Boughton[31].

Early in the year 1814 he communicated some anonymous remarks on these fragments, together with some comments on Åkerblad's results, to the Society of Antiquaries, and during the summer of the same year, which he spent at Worthing, he subjected the demotic as well as the hieroglyphic inscriptions to a careful study. After a couple of months he had obtained substantial results, and was able to give what he called a 'translation of both texts considered separately'[32]. Unfortunately it was no translation in the ordinary sense of the word. With great diligence and penetration he had succeeded in analysing the two inscriptions into their components of individual words and phrases. His efforts to determine the individual words as graphic groups were remarkably successful, as were his attempts to identify them with equivalents in the Greek text, and insofar he was fully justified in his use of the word translation. But his efforts to analyse the individual graphic groups, and decompose them into their graphic and phonetical elements were mostly failures. In 1815 he published an account of his conception of demotic as such[33], based on a careful study of the texts published in the 'Déscription de l'Égypte'. He had compared the Demotic text of the Rosetta stone with hieratic inscriptions, and come to the important conclusion that there was a direct connection between the two scripts, and that the former 'by means of some intermediate steps' was derived from the latter. A particular account of this comparison of the two systems was contained in two letters, also published in the Museum Criticum (1816, see 'Account' p. 17), and augmented by another important discovery: that the cursive signs were directly derived from the pictorial hieroglyphs, an observation which explained the true relationship between

134

hieroglyphs and hieratic. These results, and the results of his in many ways brilliant efforts to solve the problems presented by the hieroglyphic part of the inscription were published in his article 'Egypt', written for the 'Supplement to the Fourth, Fifth and Sixth editions of the Encyclopaedia Britannica'. A few copies entitled 'Hieroglyphical Vocabulary' appeared as separate offprints already in 1818[34].

Young was able to demonstrate that of the names mentioned in the Greek and demotic texts, one, the name Ptolemaios, was also found in the incomplete hieroglyphic part of the inscription, where it was enclosed in a cartouche. By comparison he was able to prove that also in its hieroglyphical rendering the name was written phonetically, by means of separate alphabetical letters, and this important discovery enabled him to establish the first rudiments of a hieroglyphic alphabet consisting of 14 letters, obtained from a comparative study of proper names. Only five of them, – the letters p, t, j, n, and f – are indisputably correct, but even so the achievement was stupendous and represents the first positive results of a decipherment.

But from then on Young barred his own way by a strange, and to a certain extent tragic, prejudice or misconception. While convinced of the phonetical nature of the script, he refused to admit the existence of alphabetic signs in ordinary hieroglyphic inscriptions, and considered the letters of the hieroglyphical alphabet reserved for the exclusive writing of foreign names and titles. It was a conviction at which he had arrived almost against his will, and nothing, not even the subsequent results of Champollion, could convince him that it was wrong. He defined his position with admirable clarity by stating that, although he had originally hoped to be able to find an alphabet[35], he had gradually been compelled to abandon this expectation, and to admit the conviction that no such alphabet would ever be discovered, because it had never been in existence. And he declared himself unable to find any examples of ordinary words expressed by means of the alphabet employed for foreign names[36].

This is so much the more astonishing as words such as Tefnet and Ptah, written not only with separate uniliteral signs but even with those of which he himself had established the correct values, occur in his vocabulary. It was fortunate, however, that this attitude did not prevent him from carrying on in accordance with his own principles and ideas, and he was still able to obtain important and substantial results. He established the correct meaning of a considerable number of individual hieroglyphic signs such as the signs for 'God', 'letters', 'life', and 'priest', and he was able to isolate several sign-groups, and determine their correct significance, among others the groups representing the words 'Osiris', 'immortal', 'victory', 'year', 'and', and 'likewise'. But he had no idea how the words should be read, and could not explain the principles responsible for the employment of the individual graphic elements inside the different groups; the indisputable deficiencies and the dangerous pitfalls of the method employed, became apparent when the Greek translation induced him to translate a group which actually meant 'of the divine word' with 'sacred', transpose the groups for 'love' and 'Ptah' in the expression 'loved by Ptah', and misinterpret the two signs representing the heraldic emblems of Upper and Lower Egypt as the ordinary adjectives for 'upper' and 'lower'. Le Page Renouf has aptly illustrated the 'mechanical' method employed, with that of a student, who from a translation of the phrase 'arma virumque' would conclude that 'arma' meant 'arms', 'virum' 'and', and 'que' 'man'.

A happy coincidence gave Young the opportunity of still another important contribution to Egyptology.

In 1822 he received from a friend returning from Egypt, a box containing 'several specimens of writing and drawing on papyrus' (Account p. 55). He began studying them immediately, and 'could scarcely believe that he was awake and in his sober senses' (ib. p. 57), when he observed that one papyrus contained a Greek translation of a well-known demotic text recording some business transactions and including extensive lists of proper names. An analysis of these names proved that alphabetic letters were not only used for the writing of foreign but also for native, proper names, and the publication and translation of the Greek text, which appeared in the 'Account' (p. 55), became the last milestone in Young's distinguished Egyptological career.

He continued to make useful contributions to Egyptology, but the time of sensational discoveries was over. In 1819 he formed a small Syro-Egyptian Society[37], which undertook the publication of a collection of hieroglyphical Inscriptions and Manuscripts, called 'Hieroglyphics collected by the Egyptian Society'. The first fascicle appeared in 1819, another in 1823, followed by a last volume in 1829. It contained careful copies of the three texts of the Rosetta stone with a Latin translation, lithographical reproductions of several inscribed monuments and papyri, and a collection of the documents related to the above-mentioned demotic deed.

His famous 'Account of some discoveries' appeared in 1823, as the author's Egyptological testament, a noble and straightforward evaluation of his contributions to the decipherment, and a dignified, if slightly impatient, résumé of his relations to Champollion. Until the very moment of his death he was engaged in Egyptological pursuits, and prepared on his death-bed a small demotic dictionary for publication[38].

The delicate and much disputed problem about Champollion's dependence on the results of Young is not going to occupy us here. It is obvious that the profoundly original and revolutionary result of the latter must necessarily have impressed the former and influenced the course of his activities. But how far, and to what extent, we shall never be able to judge.

As an intellectual achievement a discovery like that of Champollion's is the ultimate result of a prolonged and complicated mental process, by which heterogeneous and disparate elements of knowledge and learning are suddenly, as if by a revelation, merged into one another in a final miracle of understanding. To single out specific incidences in the course of this process, or give prominence to individual agents, would be frivolous as well as futile.

Young's discoveries constituted, in his own words, 'the amusement of a few leisure hours'[39], and were just so many more brilliant achievements in a life rich in a variety of successful exploits. But in Champollion's existence the hieroglyphic problem was destiny, was the sole burning and consuming passion, and its solution was a final blessing and redemption, granted when he had almost succumbed in a superhuman struggle. To put the two scholars up against one another, and judge between them would be vain and futile. As an Apollonian and a Dionysian character, both belong to the harmonious conclusion of the drama. Jean François Champollion (1790-1832) was born at Figeac, a small town in the department of Lot in the South of France. He was a precocious child and received his first education from his devoted elder brother Jacques Joseph, later known as Champollion-Figeac (1778-1867).

Already in 1801, at the tender age of 11 the boy was sent to a boardingschool in Grenoble, and it was in this town that his interest in Egyptology was first aroused.

As a result of the reorganization of the interior administration of France occasioned by Napoleon's election to First Consul, the department of Isère received a new administrator or prefect, the distinguished mathematician Jean Baptiste Joseph Fourier (1768-1830).

After a brilliant career as a teacher and a professor at the 'École Normale' and the 'École Polytechnique' of Paris, he had accompanied Napoleon on the Egyptian expedition, and had achieved great distinction as an engineer as well as a diplomat and a politician.

He was appointed secretary to the 'Institut du Caire', and retained a vivid interest in Egyptological matters, also after his return to France and his appointment as prefect. In his latter capacity he took up residence just outside Grenoble in a charming house in the country, where his 'soirées intimes' became centres of the intellectual life of the community. No administrative duties were permitted to interfere with his literary and scientific activities. He wrote the historical introduction of the 'Déscription de l'Égypte', and gained a European renown by his scientific discoveries concerning the conduction of heat, and his contributions to mathematics. He became almost immediately a member of the local learned society, the 'Académie Delphinate', of which Champollion-Figeac was the secretary, and the latter became very soon his indispensable and confidential assistant, also in administrative affairs. Some time during the autumn of 1802, he expressed the wish to see his secretary's younger brother, and the Egyptological vocation of the latter, and his decision to become the decipherer of the hieroglyphs, dates from the very first meeting of the timid child and the distinguished official, who told the boy about Egypt and showed him his Egyptian collections.

The history of the actual decipherment has been analysed in all its phases and details by Champollion's devoted biographer Hermione Hartleben[40]. It would serve no purpose, therefore, to follow him step by step on his tortuous road through disappointments and mistakes to his final success. A short account of his methods and his progress will suffice for the understanding of his results.

From the very beginning he showed an almost uncanny determination and tenacity of purpose, and all his activities, even his games, were to a great extent determined by his hieroglyphical ambitions. At an incredibly early age he had already acquired the foundations of a solid knowledge of the classical languages, had studied Hebrew and Arabic and had begun to take up Coptic. At the same time he studied ancient History, and even Chinese, inspired by the theories of Barthélémy and de Guignes. His first work was a mythological study concerning the fable of the Giants, based on classical material, and containing some rather youthful etymologies, also of Egyptian names, such as Osiris and Typhon. It was never printed and in later years Champollion generally referred to it as 'ma première bêtise'[41]; but it attracted attention among the members of the local academy and made them realize the remarkable abilities of 'this voracious chicken, demanding triple rations' as Fourier called him[42]. In 1807 he submitted to the Delphinian Academy the plans for an ambitious publication called 'l'Égypte sous les Pharaons', intended as an encyclopaedia on Egypt. As an introduction to the planned geographical section he prepared a useful and remarkably correct map of the country provided with the ancient place names[43], but Fourier and his brother had now come to the conclusion that the time had come to send him to Paris, whither he proceeded in 1807, to study at the 'Collège de France' and the 'École Spéciale des Langues Orientales', under de Sacy and Louis Mathieu Langlès. At the same time he prepared the first, geographical, volume of 'L'Égypte sous les Pharaons' which remained unpublished for nearly seven years. He also intensified his Coptic studies, concentrating on the hitherto rather neglected southern dialect. The study of the hieroglyphs was not neglected, and already in 1808 he made one of his first important discoveries in Egyptian epigraphy.

It was as yet hardly more than a hypothesis, but a comparison of various papyri brought him to the firm conviction that the difference between the three notations was of a graphic and not of a systematic nature[44]. The basic truth of this statement was still obscured by many mistakes. He had not yet discovered the difference between hieratic and demotic, and as far as the demotic text of the Rosetta stone was concerned, he was not yet able to improve the results obtained by Åkerblad. His efforts to translate a papyrus, published in Denon's 'Voyage'[45], proved a failure, and it escaped his attention that it was written in hieratic, and not in demotic.

His stay in Paris came to an abrupt end in 1809, when at the age of 18 he was recalled to be appointed professor at the faculty of Grenoble. His new duties were not permitted to interfere with his egyptological studies. He had become a member of the local Academy already in 1807, and on the 7th of August 1810 he was able to submit a new report, representing another significant step forward.

He had now established the difference between hieratic and demotic, and was able to demonstrate that graphically seen one was dependent on the other. Strangely enough he considered demotic the older system, and hieratic as a secondary derivation, invented for learned and sacerdotal purposes. His conception of the hieroglyphs was still conventional. He thought that they represented two different graphic systems, ordinary 'monumental' hieroglyphs, and 'anaglyphic or symbolical' ones. The symbolical hieroglyphs were philosophical derivations of the ordinary ones, and used for special philosophical purposes, but he was never able to define what he considered the true difference between the two sign-groups. The division was entirely theoretical and made as an effort to reconcile the diverging accounts of Porphyry and Clement of Alexandria.

In spite of the fact that he was able to confirm Åkerblad's observation concerning the pronoun 'f', and made the important observation that it was also found in the hieroglyphic part of the inscription, and written with the hieroglyph which was undoubtedly the direct prototype of the demotic letter, he was still convinced that the ordinary hieroglyphs were essentially unalphabetical, although somehow phonetical.

To explain the difference he developed some rather vague theories concerning the 'monosyllabic' character of the signs, which he tried to illustrate with some untenable theories concerning the 'monosyllabic' character of the Coptic language.

His critical sense was not stupefied by his natural optimism and enthusiasm, and he was fully aware of the insufficiency and the hypothetical character of these explanations, but although he did not actually publish them, he wrote about them in his private correspondence, and they became rather fatal to his reputation as a decipherer. They cost him for a long time the confidence of de Sacy, who began to patronize another pupil, the Étienne Quatremère de Quincy already mentioned. Quatremère was an able oriental and Coptic scholar. In 1808 he had published his 'Recherches critiques et historiques sur la langue et la litérature de l'Égypte', a learned and useful, but not very original, history of the Coptic language and its early studies. In 1811 it was followed by his 'Mémoires géographiques et historiques sur l'Égypte', and in 1812 by 'Observations sur quelques points de la géographie de l'Égypte'.

These publications spurred Champollion to finish the second volume of his geography, which appeared in 1814 as the first – and the last – volume of 'L'Égypte sous les Pharaons' with the subtitle 'Déscription Géographique'. In spite of its indisputable qualities, and its obvious advantages compared with Quatremère's publication, Champollion's book was not a success; and de Sacy's stern and unjust review, in which he more or less directly intimated that Champollion had made unacknowledged use of Quatremère's book, became one more blow to his reputation, and heralded a series of vicissitudes and misfortunes in his existence.

Champollion was unfortunately born in one of those periods of political upheaval and turbulence which are most often fatal to men whose fervour and enthusiasm are not bridled by cunning and circumspection, or an infallible political instinct. After the Jacobin sympathies of his youth he had been carried away by the irresistible wave of Napoleonic enthusiasm, and he found it now exceedingly difficult to submit to the stagnation of the Bourbonic Restoration.

His 'Déscription Géographique' was dedicated to Louis XVIII, but his past was against him, and to the new rulers he remained suspicious and even dangerous. The consequences were not long in following, as his supporters grew cautious, and his enemies bold. Already in 1815 a Coptic grammar and vocabulary submitted to the Académie dès Inscriptions were rejected, and his behaviour during the 'Hundred Days' very nearly involved him in a trial for high treason at the second Restoration. Instead he was exiled from Grenoble and forced to remain at Figeac.

After many vicissitudes he was at last reinstated as a professor, at what was now the 'Collège Royale' at Grenoble, but not for long. He was continually harassed by unscrupulous and ambitious competitors, supported by the ruling clique of former emigrants and 'Ultras', and he was finally dismissed in 1821.

It is obvious that these troubles were equally disturbing for his health, the peace of his mind, and his scientific activities. Deserted by almost everybody, except his noble and faithful brother, he went through a grave mental crisis, and began to doubt the validity even of his best established results. His despair is obvious from his correspondence already from about 1819. He had lost his optimism and hope of success, and had strange relapses to the old superstitions that the hieroglyphs, even the alphabetic signs used for the writing of foreign names, were enigmatical symbols, which should not be read, but philosophically expounded. But he did not give up, and as a reaction and a recreation, he undertook a laborious and meticulous comparison of the sign-forms of all available hieratic and demotic texts, a task facilitated by their contents, which often proved to be parallel passages from funerary texts.

Penniless, and on the verge of a break-down, he came to live with his brother in Paris, and after some months of rest, he was able to submit a new report to the Academy. Generally speaking it was mainly a re-appraisal of his former results, but it contained also some inspired reflections and new ideas. He was able to confirm Young's hypothesis about the direct relations between the hieroglyphs and hieratic, and he recognized the cursive hieroglyphs as an intermediate link between them. He gave up his erroneous idea about demotic as the original script, and was able to demonstrate the correct evolution from hieroglyphs through hieratic to demotic. Also the theory about the enigmatical hieroglyphs was abandoned. He had now come to the conviction that there was no systematic difference between the three notations, all of which he considered phonetical, but unalphabetical. The alphabetic letters were still considered a secondary invention, exclusively used for the writing of names and titles. It will be seen that Champollion had arrived at exactly the same stage as Young, and was up against the same distressing problem that if the alphabetic signs formed no part of the original hieroglyphic system their discovery became of a very secondary importance, and in no way contributed to the actual decipherment of the ordinary texts. The puzzling observation, which had already troubled Young, and was continually stressed by critics and opponents, that various signs were apparently used to express identical sounds, caused him great anxiety and made him again doubt the very existence of alphabetical letters, until he was able to give a plausible explanation of the problem in his theory of homophones, according to which each sign could be used with the alphabetical value of the initial consonant of the Egyptian word for the object it represented.

In spite of its overtones of doubt and confusion, at times almost rising to despair, the report was nevertheless another step forward. It helped Champollion to clarify his ideas, and very soon after he discovered, by a happy inspiration, a method which would enable him to countercheck the alphabetical theories once and for all. His comparisons of the hieratic and the demotic texts had made him familiar with the graphic peculiarities of the two scripts, and we have seen that he realized the latter as a cursive derivation of the former. Theoretically it should be possible, therefore, to transcribe simple words alphabetically written, from one notation into the other; and in making the practical experiment with the word 'Ptolemaios' which from demotic he transcribed first into hieratic and then into cursive hieroglyphs, he found that he arrived at a hieroglyphical spelling of the name which in all essentials was identical with that of the Rosetta stone. This was a far-reaching discovery, which provided the ultimate proof that the readings of the alphabetical values of the letters involved were correct, that his theory of the direct graphic connection of the three scripts was unimpeachable, and that the alphabetic letters also in the hieroglyphical text were used for the writing of foreign names. But he had now grown cautious and wanted further proof. From a demotic text, the so-called papyrus Casati, he knew the demotic writing of the name 'Cleopatra', which he had not yet seen in a hieroglyphic text. By means of the same methods used for the name of Ptolemy he arrived at a theoretical reconstruction of the hieroglyphical form of the name. The next step was to find an original inscription containing the name of the queen to confirm his writing.

141

In 1815 the English traveller William Bankes had visited the island of Philae, and discovered a fallen obelisk carrying a hieroglyphic inscription. Next to it he found what was apparently its base, inscribed with a Greek text, mentioning the names of Ptolemy and Cleopatra.

He had the obelisk transported to England, and re-erected in his park, where it is still to be seen, and in 1821 a lithograph was made of the Greek as well as the hieroglyphic inscriptions. Young saw the pictures and suggested tentatively, as a mere guess, that one of the cartouches might contain the name of Cleopatra, as she was mentioned in the Greek text; but in 1822 the reproductions reached Champollion, and confirmed not only his reconstruction of the name but also the value of the letters P, O, and L, which were used for the same sounds as in the word Ptolemaios.

So far he was now on firm ground and was in Griffith's words, able to turn bewildering investigations into brilliant and continuous decipherment[46]. In a couple of months he was able to give an almost complete list of the hieroglyphical renderings of the names of the Egyptian rulers from Alexander to Antoninus Pius, and in September 1822 the result was submitted to the Académie des Inscriptions, and published in his famous 'Lettre a Mons. Dacier rélative a l'Alphabet des Hiéroglyphes Phonétique' (Paris 1822). The paper contained three plates with no less than 79 reproductions of royal names and their variants, together with a 'List of the phonetic signs in the hieroglyphic and demotic writings of the Ancient Egyptians', comprising twenty letters together with their 'homophones', all of which were in all essentials correctly identified. The communication was deliberately confined to the establishment of these facts, which as far as they went were admirably presented and convincingly demonstrated. But towards the end of his article Champollion intimated a discovery of still greater importance and scope. He expressed the conviction that the phonetic signs were not only used in Hellenistic and Roman times for the exclusive writing of foreign names, and declared that he would soon be able to prove that they were original and integral elements of the hieroglyphical system as such. The actual demonstration and proof of this revolutionary assertion was reserved for a subsequent publication, but it was based on solid evidence, and a brilliant discovery, in fact, the true decipherment. And from this day onwards the profound originality of Champollion's achievement becomes indisputable.

What had happened was this: In September 1822 he received copies of some inscriptions from Abu Simbel, the famous rock temple situated on the Nile between the first and second cataracts. One of the texts contained a cartouche with a royal name written with the picture of the Sun ⊙, a sign 𓏤𓏤𓏤, the reading of which was unknown, and two 𓏤, known to represent an *s*.

From his Coptic studies he knew that the sun was called Rē or Ra, and the un-

142

readable sign ⚏ occurred in the hieroglyphical part of the Rosetta inscription at a place, which made it probable that somehow or other it represented the Greek word for 'bear' or 'engender', the Coptic equivalent of which was 'mīse'.

By a happy inspiration he suddenly realized that the name should probably be read Ra-meses, one of the most famous names from the history of Egypt, known to have been used by several kings of the XIXth and XXth dynasties. At the very same moment his attention was caught by another cartouche, containing the picture of an Ibis, known as a bird of the God Thoth, the sign ⚏, and an s ⟨, and he realized at once that the name was Thoth-mes, a well-known Pharaoh from the XVIIIth dynasty. The understanding had come as a revelation, suddenly and as a shock, but he understood at once that the problem was solved, and the alphabetical nature of the hieroglyphs discovered. In a fever of excitement he was just able to rush to his brother's office at the nearby 'Institut de France', where he threw his papers on his desk, pronounced his famous statement: 'Je tiens l'affaire', 'I have got it', and collapsed.

He remained in a state of absolute lethargy for five consecutive days, after which he was able to get up and continue his work with astounding tenacity and speed. He was present at the meeting at which his letter to Mons. Dacier was read, and had the satisfaction that de Sacy and most of the other members were at last convinced of the validity of his results, while Young, together with Jomard and an influential clique of disappointed decipherers and personal enemies refused to acknowledge their importance. For a while their voices were drowned in the clamour of success, and the following months became turning points in Champollion's existence. His discoveries became topics of conversation all over Paris. His acquaintance with the Duke of Blacas facilitated a reconciliation with the King, and he was no longer harassed by the authorities. His political enemies lost much of their power to make mischief, and he was at long last able to concentrate on his next publication, the incomparable 'Précis du Système Hiéroglyphique', which appeared in Paris 1824, respectfully dedicated to Louis XVIII[47].

At long last he was now to reap the fruits of the painstaking efforts of his youth and was able to proceed with almost miraculous mastery and rapidity.

The principal aim of the book was to prove the now well-defined thesis that phonetical elements were not merely used for the writing of names and titles, but were essential, necessary and inseparable parts of hieroglyphical writing as such (p. 3).

The proofs were furnished with almost overwhelming brilliance. He was able to augment and improve the alphabetical lists and use them for his interpretation of an almost complete list of all the royal names accessible in his material. He realized the difference between ideograms and determinatives, gave correct explanations of several orthographic peculiarities and could already analyse and translate, not merely simple words and phrases but small inscriptions and whole sentences as well. In certain respects his conceptions were erroneous. He took it for granted that the language of the inscriptions could be directly identified with Coptic, a misconception which led to many confused transcriptions of words as well as of letters, and he never grasped the difference between tri-, bi-, and uniliteral signs. Signs such as [hieroglyph] , [hieroglyph] , [hieroglyph] , [hieroglyph] , and [hieroglyph] , were, according to his theory of homophones always uniliteral letters expressing the consonant *m*. But this conception increased the number of homophones alarmingly, and they remained, until their true nature was explained by Lepsius, the principal stumbling block which prevented the general acceptance and propagation of the system.

From a practical point of view these misunderstandings were of minor importance, as they did not prevent Champollion from acquiring an almost uncanny ability to read and translate the texts, nor did they prevent his honest and unbiased colleagues from understanding that the main problem was solved, and the hieroglyphs finally deciphered. (Pl. XXII, 2).

The result was an immediate improvement of his working conditions. Already in 1824 the new King, Charles X, sent him to Italy, to study the rich collections which the Museum of Turin had bought from Bernardo Drovetti, an Italian whom Napoleon had made his Consul General in Egypt, and who, like his English colleague Henry Salt, had undertaken extensive, but not always very responsible, excavations all over Egypt.

Champollion's stay in Turin, and his travels in Italy became of the greatest importance. Some of the results were published in his 'Lettres rélatives au Musée Royale de Turin' (Paris 1824-26). But through his uninterrupted and undisturbed occupation with the rich papyrological and inscriptional material, he made enormous progress in his mastery of the texts, and in the understanding of historical and chronological problems. After his return he acquired, on behalf of the King, a valuable collection of Egyptian antiquities offered for sale by Henry Salt. It was incorporated in the Louvre, and opened to the public in 1827. Champollion, who had already made a useful catalogue of the collection, was appointed its curator.

The following year, 1828, he was sent to Egypt at the head of an archaeological expedition, including his pupil and personal friend Ippolito Rossellini from Pisa. The expedition returned in 1829, and the following year Champollion became at last a member of the Académie des Inscriptions, and received the new chair of Egyptology in the Collège de France. His manuscript and notes bear ample evidence of his almost superhuman industry, but he found little time for publishing his results, many of which did not appear until after his death. As 'Monuments d'Égypte et de Nubie', the results of the Egyptian expedition began to appear in 1829, but the printing was discontinued, and not resumed and finished until 1847.

His 'Grammaire Égyptienne', a masterpiece of learning and erudition, was finished

PLATE XXIV

Frontispiece of 'Déscription de l'Égypte' drawn by Cécile

before 1830, but did not appear until 1836-41. A useful Egyptian vocabulary left partly unfinished was in 1841 prepared for publication by the devoted care of his brother, who also began the publication of other posthumous works 'Notes manuscrites', an undertaking which was not completed until 1872.

One would have thought that his improved conditions, his secured position, and the scientific acknowledgement he received from eminent scholars in England, Germany, and Italy would have made Champollion's last years peaceful and harmonious. Unfortunately this was not the case. For such is the nature of man that every scientific achievement of scope and importance must not merely pass through the unavoidable and indispensable judgement of honest criticism. It must also submit to the disgraceful ordeal and mock-trial of envy, ignorance and stupidity.

The latter process is always painful, and not infrequently fatal to the victim, even if truth prevails, and a small but energetic clique of envious and malicious enemies and defamers succeeded in poisoning the last years of Champollion's existence, by their continual efforts to minimize and ridicule his results, and question his honesty and integrity. His resistance, already impaired by overwork and the vicissitudes of his youth, failed, and he died in Paris on the 4th March 1832 at the age of 42. But Egyptology remains as a monument of his life-work.

Notes

CHAPTER I

1. The basic phonetic character of the original hieroglyphs was first pointed out by Gardiner, Egyptian Hieroglyphic writing, J.E.A. II, (1915), 74.

2. S. Schott, Hieroglyphen. Abh. d. Akad. d. Wissenschaften u. d. Literatur, Geistes und Socialwiss. Kl. Mainz 1950. 46-47. Schott's treatise is the basic authority on which the principles and conceptions of the hieroglyphs entertained in the present chapter are based. The archaeological material for the occurrence of early hieroglyphs will be found in J. Vandier, Manuel d'Archéologie Égyptienne. Paris 1952. I. For a collection of the hieroglyphic signs from the first two dynasties see Hilda Petrie, Egyptian Hieroglyphs of the First and Second Dynasties, London 1927. For a divergent conception of the origin of the script see Kurt Sethe, Das hieroglyphische Schriftsystem. Leipziger ägyptologische Studien. Heft 3. 1935, and: Vom Bilde zum Buchstabe. Unters. zur Geschichte Ägyptens. Bd. 12. 1939.

3. A. Scharff, Archaeologische Beiträge zur Frage der Entstehung der Hieroglyphenschrift. Sitz. Ber. d. Bayrischen Akad. Hist. Abt., 1942.

4. Schott, op. cit.: Merkmale der Entstehungsort, p. 47.

5. For further references v. Scharff, op. cit., p. 70.

6. Zyhlarz, Ursprung und Sprachcharacter des Altaegyptischen. Zeitschrt. f. Eingeborenensprachen 23,1; quoted from Scharff, op. cit., p. 68.

7. Gardiner, J.E.A. II, p. 66.

8. ib., p. 66.

9. Scharff, op. cit., p. 120-121.

10. H. Junker, Über das Schriftsystem im Tempel der Hathor in Dendera. Berlin, 1903.

11. For an example from the fifth dynasty see G. Møller, Die Buchschrift der alten Aegypter. Zeitschrift des Deutschen Vereins für Buchwesen u. Schrifttum (1919). Nr. 7-8. Abb. 9.

12. Petrie, Epigraphy in Egyptian research. Transactions of the statutary ninth International Congress of Orientalists. Woking (1891). I, 315.

13. G. Møller, Hieratische Palaeographie. I-III, Leipzig, 1909-1912. I. Einleitung 1.

14. Møller, Palaeographie I, 2-3.

15. In order to standardize the rendering of hieratic orthography, and to create a uniform method for the reproduction of the texts, it has become customary in modern Egyptology to supply each hieratic text with a hieroglyphic transliteration, in which each hieratic sign as far as possible is substituted by its hieroglyphical prototype, a practical procedure without traditional foundation, but comparable to our substitution of handwritten documents by typescript.

16. Griffith, Catalogue of the Demotic Papyri in the John Rylands Library. Manchester 1909.

17. The name which probably dates from about the 14th century is a European corruption of Arabic 'Kibt' or 'Kubt', which is again a corruption of the Greek word αιγύπτιος, 'Egyptian'. See the introductory chapter in Stern, Koptische Grammatik. Leipzig 1880, and Griffith's article 'Copts' in the Encyclopaedia Britannica.

18. F. Ll. Griffith, Karanòg, The Meroïtic Inscriptions of Shablûl and Karanòg. University of Pennsylvania, Expedition to Nubia, VI. 1911. Cf. also J.E.A. III, IV, XI.

19. For an excellent account of the history of the alphabet see B. F. C. Atkinson's article 'Alphabet', in the latest edition of the Encyclopaedia Britannica. Cf. also D. Diringer, The Alphabet. 1947.

20. Gardiner, The Egyptian origin of the Semitic alphabet. J.E.A. III (1916) 1.

21. W. F. Albright, The vocalization of the Egyptian syllabic orthography. New Haven, 1934. A critical review of Albright's study written by W. F. Edgerton appeared as 'Egyptian Phonetic Writing' in Journal of the American Oriental Society, 60.1940. 473. This was answered by Albright and T. O. Lambdin in 'New Material for the Egyptian Syllabic Orthography', Journal of Semitic Studies, vol. 2, nr. 2. Manchester, 1957. Cf. also E. Edel, 'Neue keilschriftliche Umschreibungen aegyptischer Namen aus der Bogazköytexten'. J.N.E.S., VII. 1948, and 'Neues Material zur Beurteilung der Syllabischen Orthographie'. J.N.E.S., VIII. 1950. W. A. Ward, Notes on Egyptian Group-Writing, J.N.E.S. 16. 1957.

22. Edgerton, J.A.O.S., 60, 486.

23. For examples see Sethe, Die Ächtung feindlicher Fürsten. Abh. d. Preussischen Akad. Phil.-hist. Kl. 1926. Nr. 5, p. 30.

24. Especially in the recurrent use of 〰 for mu.

25. Albright, Vocalization, 10, § 19.

26. ib. 12-13, § 22.

27. Sethe, Die aenigmatischen Inschriften. Northampton-Spiegelberg-Newberry, Report on some excavations in the Theban Necropolis 1898-1899, p. 1. Drioton, Éssay sur la cryptographie privée. Révue d'Égypte, 1 (1933), p. 1. G. Lefebvre, Grammaire de l'Égyptien Classique, § 56. L'Écriture sécrète.

CHAPTER II

1. For a collection of material concerning the non-Christian literary material concerning the classical hieroglyphic tradition, see P. Maréstaing, Les Écritures Égyptiennes et l'Antiquité Classique, Paris 1913.
2. Diodorus, History, I, 69.
3. Herodotus, II, 35. transl. A. D. Godley (Loeb) 1921. I, 319.
4. Herodotus, II, 36.
5. Pythagoras seems to have been an exception. Diogenes Laertius tells us explicitly that he knew the Egyptian language (φωνή). (VIII, 3. Ed. Loeb. 1925. II, 322), and Porphyrius tells us that he knew the language or meaning (φωνή) of Egyptian letters, v. Maréstaing, 105 ff. See also Plutarch, De Iside § 10.
6. Maréstaing, op. et loc. cit.
7. Stromata, V, IV, 20-21.
8. Apuleius, Metamorphoses. XI, 22, transl. W. Adlington, (Loeb) 1915. 579.
9. Philebus, VIII, trans. H. N. Fowler, (Loeb) 1925. 226.
10. Phaedrus, LIX, trans. H. N. Fowler. (Loeb) 1914. I, 560.
11. Cicero, De natura deorum. III, 22.
12. Pliny, Natural history. VII, 56.
13. Diodorus, III, 3.4; but I, 69,5, we are told that the Egyptians considered themselves the inventors of letters.
14. Lucan, The Civil War, III, 220, transl. I. B. Duff, (Heinemann) 1928. 130.
15. Tacitus, The Annals, XI, 14, transl. J. Jackson, (Heinemann), 1937. III, 268.
16. The almost identical accounts of Herodotus (II, 102) and Diodorus (I, 55, 7) concerning the inscriptions of the victorious Sesostris, in which the male and female parts were used for courage and cowardice respectively, are obviously based on misconceptions of the employment of determinatives.
17. Plutarch's statement: 'that the Egyptians, to show the beginning of sunrise, paint a very young baby sitting on a lotus flower' (de Pythia oraculis § 12, transl. F. C. Babbitt, (Loeb) 1936. 400 A p. 290), is not the explanation of a hieroglyph, but a correct iconological interpretation of the well-known representation of the God Nefertum sitting in a lotus flower, and in Egyptian theological commentaries explained as 'the rising sun of the morning'.
18. Diodorus, III, 4, 1-3, transl. C. H. Oldfather. (Loeb) 1935. II, 96.
19. Clement of Alexandria, Stromata V, IV, 20-21. See the commentary of Vergote, Clément d'Alexandrie et l'écriture Égyptienne. Le Muséon. Louvain. 1939. LII, 199.
20. Isis and Osiris. § 10.
21. Plutarch, Moralia, 12 E-F, transl. Babbitt. (Loeb) 1927. 58-61.

22. Stromata, V, IX, transl. W. Wilson, The Writings of Clement of Alexandria. Edinburg, 1871-72, II, 254-55. Ante-Nicene Christian Library. Vol. IV and XII.

23. Enneades V, 8.6. It has been my effort to give a synopsis of what Plotinus has expressed in this and the preceding chapter. The translation of Emile Bréhier in his edition of Plotinus (Collection des Universités de France, Paris, 1931. V, 142) has been my guide.

24. From about the third century A.D., Hermes, – frequently called 'Trismegistus', 'the thrice great', or maybe just 'the very great' and identified with Thoth, the Egyptian God of wisdom and knowledge, – was frequently mentioned as the author of various treatises, generally of a mystic, philosophical character. They did not emanate from any particular sect or school, but represented syncretistical efforts to combine Greek and Oriental mysticism and philosophy.

25. Iamblichus' personal authorship is not established with certainty, but the book came undoubtedly from the school of this Syrian Neo-Platonist, who lived about 300 A.D. He was a pupil of Plotinus, whose commentary on the works of Plato he continued. At the same time he developed the system of his Neo-Platonic predecessors, whose allegorical interpretations he evolved into an established logical system.

26. For the Greek literature dealing with Egyptian subjects, see Walter Otto, Priester und Tempel im Hellenistischen Ägypten, 1905-08, II, 217.

27. The treatise is mentioned by the lexicographer Suidas and by Eusebius, Praep. evang., V, 10.

28. See W. Otto, Priester und Tempel, II, 216[3], 233[4]. It was the English scholar Samuel Birch who first drew attention to Tzetzes' quotations in an article 'On the Lost Book of Chairemon on Hieroglyphs', published in The Transactions of the Royal Society of Literature, 2nd. Ser., IV, 385. 1850.

29. See H. R. Schwyzer, Chairemon. Klassich-phil. Studien, 4. Leipzig, 1932.

30. Parthey, Horapollon von den Hieroglyphen. Monatsschrift der Preuss. Akad. der Wissenschaften zu Berlin, 1871, 110.

31. An excellent account of the book is given in Ranke's article 'Horapollon' in Pauly-Wissowa, Real-Encyclopaedie der Class. Altertumswiss. Neue Bearbeitung. Stuttgart 1913. VIII, 2. For a critical edition of the text v. Sbordone, Hori Apollinis Hieroglyphica, Napoli 1940. Translations: B. v. d. Walle et J. Vergote, Traduction des Hieroglyphica. Chronique d'Egypte XVIII. 1943. 39, ib., 199. G. Boas, The Hieroglyphics of Horapollo. (Bollingen Series XXIII), 1950.

32. The Physiologus is the conventional designation for a book written in Greek in early Christian times by an otherwise unknown Physiologus, treating the nature of a selection of animals, plants, and stones, the mystical qualities of which are applied as allegorical illustrations to the nature of Christ and man. Some of the

information given is in accordance with Horapollo, who also tells us that the lion sleeps with its eyes open (I, 17 and 19). Bestiarius is the Latin *Physiologus* which became translated into most European languages and had great influence on the development of Christian symbolism.

33. It is well worth noticing that, if somebody entirely ignorant of the principles of hieroglyphic writing asked a modern Egyptologist about the meanings of the various signs of a hieroglyphic inscription, merely by pointing at the most characteristic and conspicuous of them, his general impression about their nature would probably come very close to those entertained by Horapollo.

34. Considering that Horapollo was undoubtedly unable to read Egyptian, an oral tradition must almost necessarily connect him with the Egyptian literary sources.

35. The only exceptions are those cases where he tells us that the sun and the moon mean 'always' (I,1), scarab and vulture 'Hephaistos', vulture and scarab 'Afrodite' etc. For other examples of hieroglyphical phrases or sentences see Diodorus I, 55, 7., and especially Plutarch, De Iside § 32.

36. This was already pointed out by Champollion, Précis du Système etc. p. 300.

37. In the classical tradition mainly the literary and philosophic allegory was influenced by these theories, in the Renaissance also that of the visual arts.

38. Rerum gestarum libri XXXI. Book XVII, ch. 4,18.

39. See Ammianus Marcellinus, transl. John C. Rolfe. Intruduction, p. XVI. (Heinemann) 1935.

40. It was Constantine the Great who had taken the initiative in transporting this obelisk from Egypt to Rome, but the project had become delayed by the death of the Emperor. The obelisk had been left for some time at a village outside Rome and Constantine undertook its final erection in the Circus. According to its inscription it was originally dedicated by Tuthmosis III. During the Renaissance (1588) it was re-erected at its present place on the Piazza di St. Giovanni in Laterano.

41. XVII, 4,10. For the translation see Rolfe, op. cit., I, p. 323.

42. XVII, 4,17. There is no doubt that Ammianus is convinced that he speaks about the obelisk now known as the Flaminian. It was originally dedicated by Ramesses the Second to the temple of Heliopolis. In the year 10 B.C. it was transported to Rome by Augustus to celebrate the conquest of Egypt and placed in the Circus Maximus. It had fallen in the time of Valentinianus, (364-375 A.D.) and in 1589 was re-erected on the Piazza del Popolo.

43. Erman, Die Obeliskenübersetzung des Hermapion. Sitzbr. der Preuss. Akademie, Jahrg. 1914, 245.

44. Erman, op. cit., p. 270, came to the conclusion that the obelisk translated by Hermapion was not the Flaminian, but another obelisk of Ramses and Sethos

with a very similar inscription. The present author is not convinced that he was right, and there is no doubt that Ammianus at any rate was convinced of the connection between Hermapion's translation and this obelisk.

45. For the cults of Isis and Serapis see Roeder's articles Isis and Serapis in Pauly-Wissowa, Real-Encyclopaedie; Walter Otto, Priester und Tempel; and Černy, Ancient Egyptian Religion.

46. Černy, Religion, 85.

47. Černy, Religion, 141.

48. Giehlow, p. 29. See chap. III, note 1.

49. Erman, Römische Obelisken. Abhdl. d. Preuss. Akad., phil.-hist. Klasse (1917), Nr. 4, p. 7. Note 2.

50. The inscription of the small obelisk now in the Museo Nazionale in Naples is probably also of local origin.

51. Ernesto Scamuzzi, La 'mensa Isiaca' del Regio Museo di Antichitá a Torino, Roma 1949. Publicazioni Egittologiche del R. Museo di Torino, V.

52. Three 'cartouches' or royal rings, generally used to circumscribe royal names, are found on the table. Scamuzzi has demonstrated that the hieroglyphs they contain represent what is probably to be taken as very imperfect renderings of the name of Claudius Tiberius and his title Autocrator Caesar. But even if this identification is correct, it seems very doubtful whether the signs were actually meant to be read, or just mechanical copies taken from a genuine inscription carrying the name of the Emperor, and used for ornamental purposes like the rest of the signs of the table.

53. Trismegistus to Asclepius. Asclepius III,24 b. Hermetica, ed. and transl. by Walter Scott. 1924. I,340.

CHAPTER III

1. The main authorities on the hieroglyphical traditions of the Renaissance are still Karl Giehlow, Die Hieroglyphenkunde des Humanismus in der Allegorie der Renaissance. Jahrbuch der Kunsthistorischen Sammlungen, XXXII, Heft 1. Wien 1915, quoted as Giehlow, and Volkmann, Bilderschriften der Renaissance, Leipzig 1923, quoted as Volkmann. For more recent discussions of the emblematic and allegorical problems involved, see M. Praz, Studies in Seventeenth-Century Imagery (Studies of the Warburg Institute, III). London 1939 and 1947. J. Seznec, The Survival of the Pagan Gods (Bollingen Series XXXVIII), New York, 1953. Guy de Tervarent, Les Énigmes de l'art. Bruges s. d., and Guy de Tervarent, Attributs et Symbols dans l'Art profane. 1958. See also W. S. Hek-

scher's and K. A. Wirth's articles 'Emblem. Emblembuch' in Reallexicon zur deutschen Kunstgeschichte, V, 1959, col. 85 ff., and E. H. Gombrich, 'Icones Symbolicae: The Visual Image in Neo-Platonic Thought', Journal of the Warburg and Courtauld Institutes, XI, 1943, p. 163 ff. E. Panofsky, Idea. Leipzig 1924. E. Panofsky, Meaning in the Visual Arts, New York. 1955.

2. Eusebius, Praeparatio Evangelica, III, V. Translated by E. H. Gifford, Eusebii Pamphili evangelicae praeparationis libri XV. Oxford 1903. III^1, 104.

3. ib.

4. See page 47 above.

5. Martin Schantz, Geschichte der Römischen Literatur IV, 2, 1084. Handbuch der Altertumswissenschaft, $VII,4^2$.

6. Max Manitius, Die Lateinische Literatur des Mittelalters. I,3, p. 52. Handbuch der Altertumswissenschaft. $IX,2^1$.

7. Julius Honorius, Cosmographia, ed. Riese, Geographi latini minores. Heilbronn, 1878, p. 51. B,45. Honorius was a Roman orator from the IVth or the Vth century. See Handbuch der Altertumswissenschaft VIII,4,2, § 1060. The tradition is also mentioned about 814 by the Irish grammarian Dicuil, in his Liber de mensura orbis terrae, ed. Parthey, Berlin 1870. 6,13,2.

8. H. Jordan, Topographie der Stadt Rom im Alterthum. Berlin 1871. II, 182. Michaelis, Le Antichita della città di Roma descritte da Nicolas Muffel. Bulletino dell' Imperiale Instituto archeologico Germanico. III, Tome 1888. Giehlow. 16.

9. Giehlow, p. 22, and W. Scott, Hermetica, Oxford 1924, I,31-33.

10. Scott, op. cit., p. 33.

11. This is the obvious interpretation of the two figures of which one is seen in a Greek, the other in an oriental costume like Hermes himself. To explain them as the Sages of the East and the West is made impossible by the inscription, which explicitly calls them Egyptians. For the pavement – probably made by Giovanni di Maëstro Stefano – see Cust, The Pavement Masters of Siena (1901).

12. Černy, Ancient Egyptian Religion. London 1952. p. 148.

13. Giehlow, p. 80.

14. Roberto Valturio, De re militari. Verona 1472. Bk. XII. De signis militaribus.

15. For his biography see Wachler's article Annius, in Ersch und Gruber, Allgemeine Encyclopaedie der Wissenschaften und Künste. Bd. 4.

16. Antiquitatum variarum volumina XVII. 1498?

17. The paintings were completed in 1495 before the publication of Annius' book (1498), but Giehlow has demonstrated their indisputable dependence on his theories. Op. cit. p. 45.

18. Giehlow, p. 23.

19. For Plotinus' definition see page 45 above.

20. Sbordone, op. cit. LX.

21. The medal was modelled by Matteo de' Pasti, see pl. X, 2 a–b.

22. De re aedificatoria, X, VIII,4.

23. Voigt, Die Wiedererlebung des classischen Altertums 1893. II, 277.

24. Hautecoeur, Rome et la Renaissance Italienne, p. 104. After 1525 the Isiac table must be added to this material. Cf. also Tory's remarks quoted on page 81. For the obelisks see H. Jordan, Topographie der Stadt Rom. I, Dritte Abtheilung. Register.

25. Published by H. Stuart Jones, A Catalogue of the Ancient Sculptures preserved in the Municipal Collections of Rome. The Sculptures of the Museo Capitolino. Oxford 1912. No. 99, (100), 102, (104), (105), (107), p. 258 ff. Pl. 61-62.

26. For a useful, if not complete, list of the various copies, see Hülsen und Egger, Die Römischen Skizzenbücher von Marten Heemskerck. Berlin 1913-1916. Tekstband I,29, fol. 53 and 21. For Herwarth von Hohenburg's edition see pl. VI, 2.

27. Curtius, Das Antike Rom. Vienna 1944. Pl. 6-7.

28. Francesco Colonna, Hypnerotomachia Poliphili. Venice 1499. A French translation with an extensive commentary is published by Claudius Popelin, Le Songe de Poliphile, I-II. Paris 1883. An incomplete English translation called 'The strife of Love in a Dream' appeared in 1593. A useful recent bibliography is found in an article by Linus Birchler: Über die Hypnerotomachia Poliphili. Librarium, I,1. 1958, p. 37. For the relation between the illustrations and Donatello's lost frescos in Treviso, and those of Bernardo Parentius in Padua, see Léon Dorez, Études Aldines, II; 'Des Origines et de la Diffusion du Songe de Poliphile', in Révue des Bibliotheques, VI. 1896, p. 239. In the intricate problems concerning the mutual relationships of these representations I have followed Giehlow, also in those cases where he differs from Dorez.

29. Text and translation is found on page C in the original edition. Colonna's Latin translation runs: 'Ex labore Deo naturae sacrifica liberaliter, paulatim reduces animum Deo subiectum. Firmam custodiam vitae tuae misericorditer gubernando tenebit, incolumemque servabit'.

30. The word rebus with the meaning of 'what is written with things' i. e. instead of with letters, is framed as a result of the hieroglyphic activities. See Giehlow, p. 34. For its use in 'Les Bigarrures' by Étienne Tabourat who translates it 'des choses', see Volkmann, p. 71. It is also used by Tory who provides it with another etymology.

31. Giehlow, p. 47 and 59.

32. They are almost obliterated on the original, but they are clearly to be seen on Huybert's later print which appeared in Samuel Clarke's magnificent edition of Caesar's works. London 1712.

33. See 'The Riddle of the New-Old Pyramids', p. 21 in Leslie Hotson's 'Shakespeare's Sonnets dated'. London 1949.

34. The Burlington Magazine, January 1958, p. 15.

35. Fol. q. 6 verso.

36. For examples see Volkmann, p. 41 ff.

37. Volkmann, p. 23 and 24, where a full reproduction of Francesco Mengardi's very rare print of the frescos will be found. For the problem of their date see Giehlow p. 70 and 122.

38. It should be mentioned that occasional references to the existence of a 'vulgar' Egyptian system of writing do occur. It is f. inst. mentioned by Valerianus in Book XXXVII, 'Literae Aegyptiacae', and Giehlow mentions an unpublished sixteenth century manuscript in Vienna (Hofbibliothek Codex Nr. 269) containing representations of 23 letters of an 'Alphabetum Egyptiorum'. Giehlow p. 123, note 4.

39. Giehlow p. 109.

40. ib. 114.

41. Michaud, Biographie Universelle XLII, artcl. 'Valerianus'.

42. The title page of the Italian edition (Venice 1625) enumerates the contents of the various books thus: 'Ne'quali, con l'occasione de' Ieroglifica, si tratta delle natura di molti Animali, Terrestri, Maritimi, et volatili: della Piante, dell'Herbe, de' Fiori, e de'Frutti: delle Pietre delle Gioie, e Metalli: de' Fonti, de' Fiumi, de' Mari, e dell'Acque tutte de' cieli, delle Stelle, e de' Pianeti; delle Monti, & Medagli: de' vestimenti, & Arme: de Gl'Instrumenti Musicali, Bellici, & usatili: de' Numeri, de'Segni de' Cenni, de'Sogni, e delle Fauole, & altri cose curiose, e degne.

43. Not the 26th as Volkmann has it, p. 37.

44. An uncle, Domenico Grimani, was the owner of a famous collection of antiquities, and a brother, Marco, travelled extensively in the Near East. He visited Egypt in 1555 and brought from Cairo numerous drawings and plans, later used by Serlio. Giehlow p. 122.

45. For more examples see Volkmann, p. 37-39.

46. Biographie Universelle XLII, p. 464.

47. Already the Swiss edition from 1567 was augmented with two books by Coelius Augustinus (also known as Curio or Curione) (1503-1569). This edition appeared for the first time in 1567, and not in 1575 as Volkmann has it, p. 75.

48. For a short sketch of his life see Henry Green's introduction to his publication 'Alciati Emblematum Fontes Quattuor'. London 1870.

49. Volkmann p. 41.

50. G. Whitney, A choice of Emblemes and other Devises. Leyden 1586. Edited in

facsimile by H. Green. London 1866. p. 138. The front page of Green's edition is curiously enough adorned with temple-frieze ornaments, borrowed from Colonna's Hypnerotomachia, another example of the strange persistence of this tradition.

51. Andreae Alciati Emblematum Fontes Quattuor, ed. Henry Green. London 1870.

52. The translation is Green's from his above-mentioned edition of Alciati, p. 5.

53. De verborum significatione. Lyon 1530. Quoted from Volkmann p. 41.

54. For the history of the various editions see Green's introduction to his edition 'Andreae Alciati Emblematum Flumen Abundans.' London 1871.

55. Les Sculptures ou Gravures Sacrées, traduites du Latin en Francois. Paris 1543, and, with the Greek and Latin texts, Hori Apollinis Niliaci de sacris notis et sculpturis libri duo. Paris 1551.

56. Heyden-Weldt. Basel 1554. Part III. Hori eins vor dreytausent jare, in Aegypten Kunigs und Priesters/gebildte waarzeichen/ durch wölliche vorerfundnen buchstaben/alle heymlicheyt der geystlichen und weldtglerten zuverston geben/ auch anzeigt worden.

57. Volkmann p. 81.

58. Chiliades adagiorum. II, no. 1.

59. It must not be forgotten that the modern offshoots of these movements, even in their most debased and vulgar forms, are legitimate offspring of genuine Neo-Platonic traditions.

60. Ed. Chmelarz, Die Ehrenpforte des Kaiser Maximilians I. Jahrbücher der Kunsthistorischen Sammlungen des Allerhöchsten Kaiserhauses. Bd. IV. Vienna 1886. p. 289.

61. See note 1.

62. See pl. XIV, 4.

63. For quotations from Horapollo in 'Annotationes in Vitruvium' by Guillaume Philandrier (Philander), Rome 1544, see Volkmann p. 68.

64. Léon Dorez, Songe de Poliphile. 349, note 1. Études Aldines, II: Des Origines et de la Diffusion de 'Songe de Poliphile'. Révue des Bibliothèques, VI. (1896).

65. L. Dorez, op. cit. p. 249.

66. ib., pl. III-X, p. 247 ff.

67. Volkmann, p. 60.

68. Champfleury. Paris 1529. f. LXXVII verso.

69. ib. f. LXXIII recto.

70. ib. f. LXXIII verso.

71. ib. f. LXXIII recto.

72. ib. f. LXXXIII recto. For these fragments and their relations to other contemporary sources especially those of Anonymus Magliabechianus see Giehlow p. 17-18, (note 5 on p. 17).

73. 'La grenoille, la teste de boeuf' and 'les violettes', are either free inventions by the copyist himself or else mistakes in Tory's description. All the other signs occur in the Hypnerotomachia exactly as he describes them, and in the same order and sequence.

74. It is represented on page LXXX in the original edition of the Champfleury, and explained on page XLIII recto.

75. Rabelais, La Vie Très Horrifique du Grand Gargantua. I, IX.

76. C'est l'ordre qui a tenu la nouvelle et joyeuse entrée que le Roy Henri ..... a faicte en sa bonne ville de Paris. Paris 1549. That Goujon made the cuts has been demonstrated by Maurice Roy, Revue du Seizième Siècle, 1917-1918, V. Cf. Francois Courboin, Histoire Illustrée de la Gravure en France. Paris 1923. I, 93. I have not seen Goujon's other contributions to the hieroglyphic tradition: 'Hiéroglyfique (sic) de la vertu sous la figure du lyon'. Lyon 1608, and 'Hiéroglyphe royal d'Henry le Grand. Lyon 1610.

77. Henri Gauthier, Un Prédesseur de Champollion. Bulletin de l'Institut Francais d'Archáéologie Orientale V,1,65. Le Caire 1906. I have not seen the two books; but from Gauthier's description it is obvious that they are just ordinary offshoots of the general tradition. The second one is apparently an extract from Valerianus' Hieroglyphica. The 'Discours des Hiéroglyphes', Paris 1554, mentioned as no. 1409 on page 121 in Jolowicz' Bibliotheca Aegyptiaca, is undoubtedly the same book. See ib. no. 1204 on page 103. It has evidently got a wrong date.

78. According to the printing licence the author was a doctor of theology and councillor of the King's chapel. The preface, dedicated to the Princess of Conty by an anonymous Lady, makes it clear that the author had died long before the book was printed. He is mentioned without any data, solely as the author of this book, in the Biographie Universelle.

79. The title page of the original edition is adorned with obelisks and 'hieroglyphic' inscriptions, engraved by the well-known artist Leonard Gaultier, born about 1561.

80. P. 104 ff.

81. Walter Mönch, Die italienische Platonrenaissance und ihre Bedeutung für Frankreichs Literatur- und Geistesgeschichte (1450-1550). Römische Studien, Heft 40. 1936.

82. For the early history of the English emblematic literature, see the dissertation in Green's facsimile edition of Whitney's emblems, London 1866, and Rosemary Freeman, English Emblem Books. London 1948.

83. I have only seen the edition from 1574.

84. It is typical that the whole ensemble is re-used in Bocchi's fifth book, as devise and motto for Symb. CXLVII: 'Ex Mysticis Aegyptiorum Literis'.

85. For Shakespeare's references to emblematic material see Essay IV (p. 293) in Green's above mentioned edition of Whitney.

86. A translation of Asclepius was added to the second edition 1657.

87. Charlotte Fell Smith, John Dee. London 1909. P. 165. This Dr. Hannibal is probably Hannibal Rossel, who published a ponderous commentary on select passages of 'Pymander'. Cracow 1585-1590.

88. The book was dedicated to the emperor Maximilian, and published in Antwerp 1564. I have had no opportunity to see it.

89. The Cambridge History of English Literature. VII,318.

90. There are scanty references to 'Tarphan, the Egyptian', in the appendix to the chapter called 'Of the sixth seal', p. 64.

91. The book was published by Domenico Basa in Rome. Some critical remarks by the learned critic Latino Latini (1513-1593), made Mercati publish a supplement called 'Consideratatini sopra gli avvertimenti del Signor Latino Latini (1590).

92. Cap. XI, delle lettere Hieroglyphice, p. 82.

93. See page 41 above.

94. See page 55 above. The first edition of Pignorius' book appeared in Venice in 1605 under the title 'Vetustissimae Tabulae Aenae explicatio'. For subsequent editions see note 96 below.

95. A copy of Vico's print made by another engraver, Giacomo Franco, appeared in Venice in the year 1600.

96. The book was rapidly reprinted and saw several new editions. With the title 'Characteres Aegyptii' it was published in 1608 by Matthias Becker in Frankfurt with prints made by the brothers de Bry, and an engraving of the table which had been lacking in the first edition. Another edition called 'Mensa Isiaca' was published in Amsterdam 1670 (1669).

97. The book is without a date, but from the dating of the various plates it would appear that it was published soon after 1607.

98. According to a note in A. G. Hofmann's article in Ersch und Gruber's Encyclopaedie (Bd. XXIV. 1845. 438), the commentary is published by his son J. F. Herwarth in 'Admiranda ethnicae theologiae Mysteria propalata' (Munich 1626), a rare book which I have had no opportunity to see. The same book is said to propound for the first time the afterwards popular theory that the Egyptian Gods represented personifications of natural phenomena, see Biographie Universelle, XIX, p. 364.

99. He was born 1526, and died sometime after 1613.

100. See pl. XXI, 1.

101. Charles Paschal 1547-1625, a renowned diplomat and antiquarian. He visited England in 1589 as French ambassador to the court of Queen Elizabeth.

102. The Burlington Magazine, September 1958, p. 324.

103. See above page 66.

104. See note 98 above.

CHAPTER IV

1. Origines Antwerpianae, lib. IX. 1572. Opera posth., Antwerp. 1580. See Volk-mann, 110. That the tradition also made its influence felt in the artistic field is clear from the sepulchral monument of Hubert Mielemanns in the Church of the Holy Cross in Liège. It dates from about 1558 and has a hieroglyphical inscrip-tion the signs of which are borrowed from the Hypnerotomachia and Horapollo. It is one of the very few original neo-hieroglyphical stone-inscriptions still in exi-stence. It was published by J. Philippe and L. Deroy, Le Monument Funéaire du Chanoine Hubert Mielemanns a l'Église Sainte Croix a Liège. Liège 1948. Mons. Deroy's untenable expounding of the hieroglyphs was contested by Guy de Ter-varent in an article: Les hieroglyphes de la Renaissance, in Chronique Archéo-logique du Pays de Liège. 40 Année, no. 1.1949, p. 8, in which he demonstrated their dependence on Horapollo and the Hypnerotomachia. See pl. XIX, 2.

2. Olaus Magnus, Historia de gentibus septentrionalibus, lib. I. cap. XXXVI, 58. Quoted from Axel Friberg's delightful and useful book 'Den svenske Hercules'. Lund 1945. Pag. 20-22.

3. Olaus Rudbeck, Atlantica. Upsala 1698. See Ersch und Gruber, Allgemeine En-cyclopaedie, XXIV, 438.

4. Melchior Guilandinus, Papyrus, hoc est commentarius in tria C. Plinii maioris de papyro capita. Venice 1572. The commentary refers to the natural history, XIV, XXI.

5. The book was probably published in Oppenheim 1614. Some copies printed with a special, engraved title-page, and a separate leaf for the writing of dedications have given rise to the erroneous assumption that a second edition appeared in London in the same year.

6. P. Maréstaing, Un Égyptologue du XVIIe siècle: Le Père Kircher. Recueil de Traveaux Rélatifs à la Philologie et à L'Archéologie Égyptiennes, XXX, 1908, 22. See also Jozef Janssen's article: Athanase Kircher 'Égyptologue', in Chroni-que d'Égypte, 18, 1943, 240.

7. P. Guillaume Hahn, La theorie des microbes est -telle récente? Révue médicale de Louvain, 1884.

8. Vansleb (Wansleben), Nouvelle Rélation en forme de Journal d'un Voyage fait en Égypte en 1672-1673. Paris 1677. 363.

9. Steindorf, Lehrbuch der Koptischen Grammatik. Chicago 1951.1.

10. Étienne Quatremère, Recherches Critique et Historique sur la Langue et la Littérature de l'Égypte. Paris 1808. 43.

11. Gesner's quotations are obviously taken from the Latin translation of Myrepsis made by Leonhard Fuchs. Basel 1549. 110.

12. See the list of his contributions to the Vatican library: G. Levi della Vida, Ricerche sulla Formazione del Piú Antico Fondo dei Manoscritti Orientali della Bibliotheca Vaticana. Studi e Testi. Vol. 92. Citta del Vaticano 1939. 200-255. For the history of the separate Coptic volumes in the same library see also 'Codices Coptici Vaticani Barberiani Borgiani Rossiani'. Tom. I. Ed. Hebbelynck and van Lantschoot. Citta del Vaticano 1937.

13. Della Vida op. cit. 224.

14. ib. 230.

15. ib. 264.

16. Quatremère op. cit. 46.

17. They were later to be seen in Dresden. See Maréstaing op. cit. 26. Note 22.

18. From Girolamo Aleandro's report to Peiresc, quoted by Francis W. Gravit, 'Peiresc et les Études Copte en France au XVIIᵉ Siècle'. Bulletin de la Societé d'Archéologie Copte. IV. 1938. 4. See also the article by van Lantschoot quoted below, note 19.

19. A. van Lantschoot, 'Un précurseur d'Athanase Kircher: Thomas Obicini'. Bibliothèque de Muséon. Vol. 22. Louvain 1948. Mr. L. has found Obicini's translations of one of the grammars and one of the vocabularies.

20. No less than six volumes of his letters, which form only a small part of the existing material, have been published by Tamizey de Larroque, in Collection dès Documents inédits sur l'Histoire de la France 1888-1896.

21. La Grande Encyclopaedie XXVI. Artcl. 'Peiresc'.

22. His collections included also a mummy, probably the one drawn by Rubens in 1636 see N. Pevsner and S. Lang, The Egyptian Revival. The Architectural Review, Vol. 119. No. 712. May 1956. 242.

23. Gravit, op. cit. 2.

24. ib. 7.

25. 'Noua & insolita methodo' as the title-page of the first edition has it. Rome 1636.

26. Page 139. See also Maréstaing's remarks on page 22 in the article quoted above.

27. The words of the scalae are arranged in categories just as we find them in the ancient glossaries.

28. Between 1636 and 1650 he published various translations of Coptic texts: 'Eulogium targumicum'. 1638. 'Tristicon tricolon'. 1644. 'Rituale ecclesiae aegyptiacae sive cophticarum'. 1647. I have not seen these publications but quote from Maréstaing op. cit. 25.

29. Page 333.

30. Maréstaing's article is one of the honourable exceptions.

31. The recurrent accusations against Kircher, that he had inserted words of his own fabrication in the lists to support his theories, are utterly unfounded. See Maréstaing, op. cit. 29.

32. Kircher's classification of the various categories of letters is based on an Arabic manuscript, purportedly written by Barachias – in Prodromus p. 254 called Barachias Albenephi. It would be of great interest to know what had happened to this manuscript, which seems to have disappeared. For a similar Arabic text published by Hammer-Purgstall see below page 130.

33. Oedipus Aegyptiacus, III, 556.

34. An augmented catalogue was published by Bonanni, Museum Kircherianum. Rome 1709.

35. For the history of the Coptic studies at this stage of their development, see Quatremère, op. cit. p. 54 ff. For a contemporary résumé of the material before Kircher's publications see Thomas Bangius, Exercitatio Literariae Antiquitates, III, de Hieroglyphicis. Copenhagen 1641. and IV, Hieroglyphico Schemate. ib. 1643.

36. Robert Huntington (1637-1701). His 'Letter from Dublin' (see above p. 157) was published in 'Philosophical Transactions', No. 161. July 1684, p. 624.

37. Quatremère op. cit. 53. The dissertation of Rasmus Vinding which Q. deplores not to have seen, contains a refutation of Kircher's theory, with the final conclusion, that there is no connection between Egyptian and Greek, p. 24.

38. I. XV. 66.

39. Quatremère, op. cit. 57.

40. Dissertatio de nomine patriarchae Josephi a Pharaone imposito. Rome 1696. Bonjour, distinguished for his Coptic and Sinological studies, had written several Egyptological works: 'Explication de la légende d'une pierre gravée Égyptienne', a treatise called 'Epochi Aegyptiacis', and in manuscript a 'Histoire des dynasties d'Égypte'. I have seen none of these books, but cf. Biographie Universelle, V. 14.

41. Fundamenta linguae Copticae. Leipzig 1716. It includes Hebrew etymologies of f. inst. ⲗⲁⲥ 'tongue', ⲁⲣⲟ 'river', ⲓⲟⲙ 'sea', and ⳉⲟⳉⲉⲛ 'lily'.

42. In a dissertation called 'De lingua Aegyptiaca', on the authority of Tromler quoted by Quatremère, op. cit. 79. I know neither the man nor the book.

43. For this résumé of Leibniz' contributions to the Egyptological debate see Maréstaing's article quoted above (p. 124, note 2), where the reference to Leibniz' correspondence will be found. For the Armenian theories not mentioned by M. see above. From Quatremères' remarks (p. 72-73) it would seem as if Leibniz had later changed his ideas about the theories.

44. Ficoroni had it engraved, and it was published, first by Montfaucon and later by Ficoroni himself in 'Le Vestigia et Raritá di Roma antica'. Rome 1744. 80.
45. L. Hautecoeur, Rome et la renaissance de l'antiquité. Paris 1912. 104.
46. Montfaucon, L'Antiquité expliquée et representée en Figures. I-XV. Paris 1719-1724.
47. The English traveller called 'Fontaine', whose collection M. saw in Paris, and from which he gave many reproductions, was undoubtedly Sir Andrew Fountaine, a well-known virtuoso and numismatologist, who, curiously enough, was rudely attacked by Pope in the 'Dunciade' under the name of 'the antiquary Annius'. Cf. Dict. of National Biography., XX. 75. For the English collections of the period, such as that of Sloane, see Michaelis, Ancient Marbles p. 52, and for the French, such as that of the Duc de Sully, later acquired by Caylus, see Hautecoeur op. cit. p. 104.
48. Liv. II, pl, CXL, Text p. 346.
49. Tom. I. Preface IV.
50. M.'s edition is found in 'Collectio nova patrum et scriptorum graecorum'. Paris 1706. The passage in question is tom. II, 1707.
51. Lib. II, chapt. VII, p. 350.
52. Preface, IV.
53. English edition from 1730, translated by Th. Lediard. Reprinted 1737.
54. See I, pl. XVI where he proceeds to the Persian monuments 'apres la simplicité des pyramides d'Égypte'.
55. The Burlington Magazine, September 1958. 325.
56. Isaac Newton, The Chronology of Ancient Kingdoms Amended. London 1728.
57. Introduction p. 8.
58. The hieroglyphic section of W.'s book was published separately in a French translation under the title 'Essay sur les Hiéroglyphes'. Paris 1744.
59. Cf. The Cambridge History of English Literature. 1920. Vol. IX. 296-297. It should be pointed out that W.'s book was a contribution to a very heated contemporary controversy, whether 'the Messian message was a revocation of the Mosaic' and if 'a belief in Jesus made Moses an impostor'. For W.'s reference to this debate see especially book II, Dedication to the Jews, p. XI.
60. Book IV, sect. VI. 281 (Vol. II, part 1).
61. The following résumé has as far as possible been quoted in W.'s own words. See especially IV, sect. IV, 1 ff.
62. A typical example is where he talks about epistologic writing and states that the signs here used 'stood for words, formed by the letters of an alphabet' (p. 97). Seen in its proper context this statement loses much of its originality, and is merely a repetition of the old theories concerning the existence of a 'vulgar'

Egyptian alphabet. It would be entirely wrong to use this vague and theoretical statement to declare W. the discoverer of the phonetic nature of the hieroglyphs.

63. At its best his style is almost suggestive of Gibbon.

64. For W.'s authority it is interesting to see that Diderot's article on the hieroglyphs in the French 'Encyclopédie' (ed. 1775) is directly based on 'The divine legation'.

65. The renowned author of 'L'Art des Emblèmes' (1684) and 'La Science et L'Art des Dévises', in which much hieroglyphical material survived.

66. See above page 98.

67. The book is a typical example of the strange confusion of mythological and hieroglyphical problems.

68. I have not seen these publications. Winckelmann quotes them in his 'Allegorie' (p. 6) as one of the 'last' efforts to read the hieroglyphs. They are also mentioned in Nichols' Literary Anecdotes V, 1812. 336, together with another publication of Gordon's called 'Twenty-five plates of all the Egyptian Mummies and other Egyptian Antiquities in England about 1739'. Bugde says (Rosetta Stone p. 189-190) that the essay was actually the work of the antiquarian Gough.

69. See W. R. Dawson, An Eighteenth-Century Discourse on Hierolgyphs, Studies presented to Fr. L. Griffith. 1932. See also the same author's article 'Louis Poinsinet de Sivry on Hieroglyphs'. Mélanges Maspero 1934. I. 367.

70. Given as lectures at the 'Académie des Inscriptions', and later published in the Mémoires (tom. XXXII. 1761) as 'Éxplication d'une Bas-Rélief Égyptian et d'une Inscription Phénicienne qui l'accompagne', and 'Réflexions générale sur les Rapports des Langues Égyptienne, Phénicienne et Grècque' (ib. 1763). The Phoenician inscriptions in question had been published by R. Pococke in his 'Description of the East'. I. LIV and LV.

71. The publications in question are 'Mémoire dans lequel .... on essaye d'établir que le charactère hiéroglyphique .... dès Égyptiens se retrouve dans les charac-tères des Chinois'. Mémoires de Litérature tirés des Reg. de L'Académie R. des Inscriptions. Tom. XXIX 1764. 'Essay sur le Moyen de Parvenir a la Lecture et à L'Intelligence des Hiéroglyphes Égyptiens' Ib. Tom. XXXIV 1770. 'Mémoi-res dans lequel on prouve que les Chinois sont une colonie Égyptienne'. Paris 1769. Cf. also Corneille de Pauw, Recherches sur les Égyptiens et les Chinois. Berlin. 1773.

72. Drawings of some Ruins and Colossal Statues at Thebes in Egypt. London 1741. The plates are engraved after Norden's originals by Tuscher, Norden himself, and Virtue, but they are not of the same quality as those of the final edition of the 'Voyage'.

73. 'Voyage d'Égypte et de Nubie'. I-II. Copenhagen 1755. The text was translated from Norden's journals by Des Roches de Parthenay. An English edition ap-

peared in 1757 translated by P. Templeman. The plates were made after Norden's original drawings by his friend M. Tuscher.

74. They were rather severely criticized by d'Anville.

75. Especially the inscription from the obelisk of Sesostris (pl. XXXIX) and that from the Canopic jar on pl. LV are remarkably well copied.

76. Nichols' Literary Anecdotes V, 1812. 334.

77. Some are remarkably careless and out of style, such as those found on pl. XLII. Others, such as the four pictures called 'statues of Isis and Osiris' (pl. LX-LXIII) are almost the most charming representations of Egyptian statuary made until then.

78. The following remarks will be found in his 'Reisebeschreibung nach Arabien', Copenhagen 1774. 200 ff. The reproductions are found tab. XXX-XLI.

79. Tab. 39, and pages 203 and 207.

80. His description of the big and the smaller signs becomes clear when it is realized that he describes the representation seen on tab. XXXIX.

81. Tab. 31-35, and page 206.

82. As Hautecoeur has pointed out this is even the case with the frontispiece of Norden's Travels.

83. Hautecoeur, op. cit. 103.

84. ib. 131.

85. A temple by Kléber in the parc of Étupes (1787). The salon in the house of a famous financier (1786). Dance's designs for Stilbourne House include a fireplace with Egyptian figures (1779). Soane published an Egyptian temple in his 'Designs in Architecture (1778). These examples are from Pevsner's and Lang's article quoted above note 22, where several additional examples will be found.

86. See the article by Pevsner and Lang, where illustrations of these pictures will be found.

87. A list of the Egyptian antiquities in Rome to which Winckelmann had access, and on which his knowledge of Egyptian art was based is found in C. Justi, 'Winckelmann', 2nd. ed. Leipzig 1872. II, § 125, 180.

88. Geschichte der Kunst, chapt. 1.

89. ib. chapt. 2.

90. Quoted from Justi's 'Winckelmann', p. 266.

91. Valerianus, Cesare Ripa, and Baudart are criticized and ridiculed in an unjust and not very understanding way. See especially p. 23.

92. Based on a quotation from Plutarch's 'Isis and Osiris'.

93. Allegorie, p. 6.

94. L'Architecture égyptienne considerée dans son origine, ses principes et son gout, et comparée sous les mèmes rapports à l'architecture Grècque.

95. Published in 1803.

96. Déscription des pierres gravées du feu Baron de Stosch. 1760.

97. Numi Aegyptii Imperatorii praestantes in Museo Borgiano Veletris. Rome 1787. It is a reasoned catalogue containing a profusion of useful historical information.

98. Rome 1807-1808. The engravings were made by Tomasso Piroli and executed in the calcographical institute of Pietro Piranesi.

99. Monumenti Antichi Inediti, Rome 1767. The engravings include some representations of Egyptian antiquities, but are of inferior quality and execution.

100. Historische Architectur, II, XX.

101. For Mercati see above page 84. Bandini published in 1750 'De obelisco Augusti Caesaris', which contained the most careful and correct copy of a more extensive hieroglyphical text until then published. It was drawn and engraved by James Stuart, after the publication of his famous book 'The Antiquities of Athens' know as 'Athenian Stuart' (1762). An extensive memoir on the hieroglyphs contained in a letter from S. to Charles Wentworth, was also published in Bandini's above mentioned book. Epistola XIII, p. LXXIII.

102. Among the works and articles not considered separately here are: Gibert, 'Observations sur l'obélisque interpreté par Hermapion'. Mém. de L'Acad. d. Inscript. XXV. 670. De Brosses, 'Traité de la formation mécanique des langues'. 1765. In a previous publication called 'Du Culte des dieux fetiches'. Genève 1760 B. had attacked the Neo-Platonic, symbolic, conception of Egyptian religion. See Biographie Universelle, V, 616-617. A. Court de Gébelin, Le monde primitif. Paris 1772. Tychsen, Über die Buchstabenschrift der alten Aegypter. Göttingische Bibliothek 1789. No. 6, and several other works of minor importance.

103. He supports this opinion with a reference to Bandini, Istoria universale. III, 109. XXIX, 411.

104. It is unjust to reproach Z. for his introduction of these parallels which for a long time had been topical in the debate.

105. Such as signs representing strokes, geometrical figures, utensils, plants, parts of mammals, human beings etc.

106. P. Netl, Mozart und die königliche Kunst. Berlin 1932. 104. F.'s architechtural descriptions and his symbolical inscriptions recall the Hypnerotomachia to such an extent that it would be tempting to assume a direct connection between the two books.

107. It was reprinted in 1766 in the author's collected works under the title 'Danuca'.

108. That it originally appeared in 1770 is explicitly stated in an editor's note found in Stahlbaum's edition, Berlin 1778.

109. Italienische Reise. September 1787. Sämmtliche Werke ed. Geiger. XXVII,

105. For G.'s judgement of the drawings and the plans which the French architect Cassas had brought back from his journey to the Orient, see ib. p. 115.

110. It is only a fragment called 'Der Zauberflöte zweiter Teil'. Sämmtl. Werke. VIII. 291. It was published for the first time in 1802 (ib. f. 363).

111. Netl, op. cit. The frequently mentioned novel by T. E. Rambach called 'Aylo and Dschadina oder die Pyramiden' (Leipzig 1793-1794) is a novel from Islamic Egypt.

112. E. A. Waite, A New Encyclopaedia of Freemasonry. London 1921. I, 90. II, 98.

113. 'Nachricht von der Berüchtigten Cagliostros Aufenthalt in Mitau im Jahre 1779 und von dessen dortigen magischen Operationen'. See H. Conrad, Der Graf Cagliostro. Stuttgart 1921.

114. 'Šaman Sibirskih', The Siberian Shaman. 1786. 'Obmanscik', The Impostor 1785-1786. 'Obol'ščennyh', The Beguiled. 1785-1786.

CHAPTER V

1. For Leibniz' scheme see Onno Klopp, Leibniz' Vorschlag einer französichen Expedition nach Aegypten. Hannover 1864.

2. The author was born about 1668, and was still alive in 1747. See C. v. Wurzbach, Biographisches Lexicon des Kaisertums Oesterreich. X. 1863, p. 112, and J. M. Quérard, La France Littéraire. IV. 1830, p. 217. Jauna's book also contains a 'Dissertation sur les hiéroglyphes', with a description of the mummy cloth, which had been discussed by d'Arvieu, Bonjour and several others. Ibid., II, 1392.

3. A copy of the preliminary report called 'Consilium Aegyptiacum' was sent him from Hannover in 1803. See Hartleben, Champollion I.63, note 4.

4. Budge, The Rosetta Stone. 1929. 17.

5. Two brothers of this name took part in the expedition. The younger, Alyre (1778-1850), was the author of a famous 'Flore d'Égypte' and several other papers on Egyptian botany. The elder was an engineer, and probably the maker of the cast.

6. The Gentleman's Magazine. Supplement for the Year 1801. 1194.

7. Budge, The Rosetta Stone. 27.

8. ib. 28.

9. ib. 31.

10. ib. 33.

11. Inscriptionis phoeniciae oxoniensis nova interpretatio. Paris 1802.

12. Published in the Magasin Encyclopédique. Année VII. V. 1801. 490.

13. I have not seen this publication.

14. I do not know his subsequent publications, 'De l'étude des Hiéroglyphes', Paris, 1812. 'Supplément aux Fragmens', (s. l. et a.). 'Nouvelles Recherches', Florence, 1830.

15. For typical examples of his method see the explanation of the snake and the hare. Essay 13,18.

16. Hartleben, Champollion I, 419.

17. Alphabets and Hieroglyphic characters explained. London 1806. His explanations of the pictures from a hieratic copy of the Book of the Dead published by Fontana in Vienna 1822 and called 'Copie Figurée d'un Papyrus', are based on the same principles.

18. Magasin Encyclopédique. 1810. VI. 145.

19. Further references to similar texts will be found in de Sacy's above-mentioned review.

20. Hartleben, Champollion. I, 455.

21. For his biography and the titles of several other Egyptological papers see Biographie Universelle, XXIV. 134.

22. I have only seen the first three volumes. 1809-1810.

23. For a list of the more notorious publications, see Hartleben, Champollion I. 366. It is worth noticing, however, that Grotefend, the famous decipherer of cuneiform writing, correctly identified a small inscription as written in hieratic. His efforts to explain its individual characters were not successful. See Fundgruben des Orients. IV. 240.

24. Hartleben, Champollion, I, 367, where more attempts are enumerated.

25. First published in Déscription de l'Égypte. Mémoires, II. 67.

26. His Egyptological papers were published separately under the title Recueil sur l'Égypte. I-IV. Paris, s. a.

27. In his above-mentioned article in the Architectural Review. See chap. IV, note 22.

28. Volkmann, 42.

29. According to the phrasing of Volkmann's text one would expect his source to be Paolo Giovio's 'Dialogo dell'Imprese Militari et Amoroso', but I have been unable to find the account in either of the two editions at my disposal. The original text of the motto is quoted by G. de Tervarant in 'Attributs et Symboles dans l'Art Profane', I, but without further reference.

30. Th. Young, An account of some Recent Discoveries. London 1823. Preface, XIV.

31. ib. XV.

32. ib. 11

33. It was published in Museum Criticum.

34. I have not seen the article, but have used Young's own detailed account of it as published in his 'Account'.

35. 'Account', 13. It is irrelevant that Young speaks about the enchorial text, as he was rightly convinced of the basic conformity of all three writings.

36. Op. et loc. cit.

37. Griffith, The Centenary of Egyptology, The Times Literary Supplement, Febr. 2. 1922. 65.

38. Griffith, op. cit. 66, col. 2.

39. 'Account', XIV.

40. Hermione Hartleben, Champollion, sein Leben und sein Werk. I-II, Berlin, 1906.

41. Hartleben, I, 45.

42. Adolf Erman, Die Entzifferung der Hieroglyphen, Sitzungsber. d. Preus. Akademie, 26. Januar 1922.

43. The part comprising Lower Egypt was subsequently published in 'L'Égypte sous les Pharaons', Déscription Géographique I, XXVI. Paris, 1814.

44. In a letter to Champollion Figeac quoted by Hartleben, I, 108.

45. Dominique Dénon, Voyage dans la Basse et la Haute Égypte, I-II, Paris 1802. III, 138.

46. The Times Literary Supplement, February 1922, No. 2. 66, col. 1.

47. A revised edition in two volumes appeared in 1828.

List of Illustrations

PLATE VII

    1   Cut by Th. de Bry in Boissard's Topographia. II, N 2

    2   Domenico Fontana, Della Trasportatione Dell'Obelisco Vaticano. Roma 1590, fol. B, 2

    3   Print from the seventeenth century

PLATE VIII

    1   The photograph has been placed at my disposal by E.N.I.T.

PLATE IX

    1 a-c C. Boito, La Basilica di San Marco. Venice 1888-91. Tav. XX

    2   W. Scott, Hermetica. Oxford 1924. Frontispiece

    3   Photo Anderson, Roma

PLATE X

    1   Additamenta 275. 4°

    2   G. F. Hill, A Corpus of Italian Medals of the Renaissance. London 1930. Pl. 30, 161

    3   Livre des Édifices Romains. Paris 1584

PLATE XI

    1-4 Colonna, Hypnerotomachia Poliphili. Venice 1499

PLATE XII

    1   Photo Anderson, Roma

    2   Fol. b VII verso

PLATE XIII

    1   Reproduction by Jean Goujon in C'est l'ordre qui a esté ténu à la nouvelle et joyeuse entrée que le Roy Henri II a faicte en sa bonne Ville de Paris. Paris 1549

PLATE XIV

    1   Hieroglyphica. 1567. XXXIV, 246

    2   Ib. XXXI, 219

    3   Giehlow, Hieroglyphenkunde, p. 216

PLATE XV

   1 National Gallery, Copenhagen

PLATE XVI

   1 Giehlow, Hieroglyphenkunde, p. 184
   2 De Sacris Aegyptiorum notis. Paris 1574. Fol. 12 verso
   3 Hori Apollinis Selecta hieroglyphica, Roma 1599, p. 44
   4 Fischer v. Erlach, Entwurf einer historischen Architectur. Vienna 1721.
       I, 14

PLATE XVII

   1 I. Boissard, Romanae urbis topographia. Pars V. Frankfurt 1600. A I recto

PLATE XVIII

   1 Ib., pars VI. Frankfurt 1602. Pl. 6
   3 J. T. Needham, De inscriptione quadam Aegyptiaca ... epistola. Roma
       1761, pl. 1

PLATE XIX

   1 Volkmann, Bilderschriften, fig. 18-19
   2 Guy de Tervarent, Attributs et Symboles dans l'Art Profane. Genève 1958.
       I, fig. 3
   3 The Architectural Review. Vol. CXIX. May 1956, p. 247, 24
   4 Oedipus Aegyptiacus. Roma 1653. I. Elogium XXVII

PLATE XX

   1 Piranesi, Diverse Maniere d'Adornare i Cammini. Roma 1769, pl. 38
   2 Ib., pl. 46

PLATE XXI

   1 Cesare d'Onofro, Le Fontane di Roma. Roma 1957, fig. 70
   2 Nordens original drawings are in the possession of the Royal Academy in
       Copenhagen
   3 Luigi Canina, Le nuove fabbriche della Villa Borghese, Roma 1829

PLATE XXII

   1 Photograph from the British Museum
   2 Champollion, Lettre à Mons. Dacier

PLATE XXIII

    1 Hieroglyphs from the bed-canopy of Queen Hetepheres. Dyn. IV.
        W. S. Smith, A History of Egyptian Sculpture in the old Kingdom. London
        1946, pl. 37

    2 a-b The book is Maxim du Camp's Égypte, Nubie, Palaestine et Syrie,
        dessins photographique. Paris 1852

PLATE XXIV

    1 'Déscription de l'Égypte', Frontispiece

Index

The first numbers refer to the pages, those preceded by Roman numerals to the
chapters and the numbers of the notes

Pluto, 52
Pococke, Edward, Pl. III, 3
Pococke, Richard, 109, 110, 116, 129; IV, 70
Poggio see Bracciolini
Polia, 67
Poliphilo see Colonna
Poliziano, Angelo, 62
Pomponne, Simon Arnauld de, 126
Pope, Alexander, IV, 47
Popelin, Claudius, III, 28
Porphyry, 41, 139; II, 5
Praz, M., III, 1
Ptah, 52, 135, 137
Ptolemy I, 52
Ptolemy V Epiphanes, 128, 135
Pythagoras, 45, 60, 76, 85, 94, 97, 105; II, 5

QUARLES, Francis, 83
Quatremère de Quincy, Étienne, 99, 116, 117, 139, 140; IV, 10, 16, 35, 39, 43
Querard, J.M., V, 2
Querini, Angelo, 112

RABELAIS, 81; 81; III, 75
Rafféneau Delile, Alyre (?), 127
Raimondi, Battista, 91, 92
Rameau, 122
Ramesses II, 143; II, 42, 44
Ramesses III, Pl. II, 2, 3
Ranke, H., II, 31
Raphael, Pl. XIX, 3
Re, 51, 52
Recke, Elisa v. d., 122
Renouf, P. Le Page, 136
Reville, Jean Bapt., 132
Reuchlin, Johan, 76, 77
Rhodiginus see Ricchieri
Ricchieri, Ludovico (Coelius Rhodiginus), 70, 80
Richelieu, 106
Rigord, Jean Pierre, 100, 106
Roeder, G., II, 45
Rosicrucians, 77, 121

Rossel, Hannibal, 84; III, 87
Rossellini, Ippolito, 144
Roy, Maurice, III, 76
Rubens, IV, 22
Rudbeck, Olof, 88; IV, 3

SABELLICO, Marcantonio, 70
Sacy, Silvestre de, 128-130, 138, 140, 143; V, 19
Saint Germain, comte de, 121
Sallustius, 53, 69; Pl. XIV, 1
Salt, Henry, 144
Saumaise, Claude de, 92
Sbordone F., II, 31; III, 20
Scamuzzi, Ernesto, II, 51, 52
Schantz, M., III, 5
Scharff, A., 3, 5, 6, 9
Schikaneder, Emanuel, 122
Schiller, 122
Scholtz, Christian, 98
Schott, S., I, 2, 4
Schrepfer, Johann Georg
Schumacher, Johan Heinrich, 106
Schwyzer, H.R., II, 29
Scott, W., III, 9, 10
Sellier, Louis, 132
Sepibus, Georg de, 98
Serapis, 51-53; II, 45
Sesostris, 102; II, 16; IV, 75; Pl. XIV, 2
Seth, 37, 95
Sethe, Kurt, I, 2, 23, 27
Sethos, 122; II, 44
Seznec, J., III, 1
Sforza, Bianca Maria, 75
Shakespeare, 69; III, 33, 85
Shaw, Dr. (?), 109
Sisac, 102
Sivry, Louis Poinsenet de, IV, 69
Sloane, Hans, IV, 47
Smith, Charlotte Fell, III, 87
Sobieski, John, 124
Soliman, 124
Sothis, 102
Spiegelberg, W., I, 27
Spiess, Christian Heinrich, 122

Springinklee, Hans, 77
Stabius, 77, 78
Stahlbaum, IV, 108
Stefano, Giovanni di Maëstro, III, 11
Steindorf, Georg, IV, 9
Stern, Ludvig, I, 17
Stosch, Philip de, 108, 117; IV, 96
Stuart, James, IV, 101
Stukeley, William, 107
Suidas, II, 27
Sully, duc de, IV, 47
Swedenborg, Emmanuel, 121

TABOURAT, Étienne, III, 30
Tacitus, 43; II, 15
Tamizey de Larroque, J.P., IV, 20
Tandeau, St. Nicolas de, 131
Tannevot, Alexandre, 122
Tefnet, 133
Télémaque see Fénélon
Templeman, P., IV, 73
Terrason, Jean, 121
Tervarent, G. de, III, 1; IV, 1; V, 29
Tesi, Mauro, 113
Theseus, 68
Thoth, 25, 42, 55, 60, 143; II, 40; Pl. VI, 1
Thuthmosis III, 143; II, 40; Pl. II, 1
Tiberius, II, 52
Titus, 54, 76
Tory, Geoffroy, 80, 81; III, 24, 73
Tromler, Carl Heinrich, IV, 42
Tuki, Raphael, 98
Tuscher, M. IV, 72, 73; Pl. XXI, 2
Tychsen, Thom. Christ., IV, 102
Typhon, 95, 138
Tzetzes, 46, 59; II, 28

URBANO see Valeriano
Usar-Hapi, 52

MYTHOS: The Princeton/Bollingen Series in World Mythology

J. J. Bachofen / MYTH, RELIGION, AND MOTHER RIGHT

George Boas, trans. / THE HIEROGLYPHICS OF HORAPOLLO

Anthony Bonner, ed. / DOCTOR ILLUMINATUS: A RAMON LLULL
READER

Jan Bremmer / THE EARLY GREEK CONCEPT OF THE SOUL

Joseph Campbell / THE HERO WITH A THOUSAND FACES

Henry Corbin / AVICENNA AND THE VISIONARY RECITAL

F. M. Cornford / FROM RELIGION TO PHILOSOPHY

Mircea Eliade / IMAGES AND SYMBOLS

Mircea Eliade / THE MYTH OF THE ETERNAL RETURN

Mircea Eliade / SHAMANISM: ARCHAIC TECHNIQUES OF ECSTASY

Mircea Eliade / YOGA: IMMORTALITY AND FREEDOM

Garth Fowden / THE EGYPTIAN HERMES

Erwin R. Goodenough (Jacob Neusner, ed.) / JEWISH SYMBOLS IN THE
GRECO-ROMAN PERIOD

W.K.C. Guthrie / ORPHEUS AND GREEK RELIGION

Jane Ellen Harrison / PROLEGOMENA TO THE STUDY OF GREEK
RELIGION

Joseph Henderson & Maud Oakes / THE WISDOM OF THE SERPENT

Erik Iversen / THE MYTH OF EGYPT AND ITS HIEROGLYPHS IN
EUROPEAN TRADITION

C. G. Jung & Carl Kerényi / ESSAYS ON A SCIENCE OF MYTHOLOGY

Carl Kerényi / ELEUSIS: ARCHETYPAL IMAGE OF MOTHER AND
DAUGHTER

Stella Kramrisch / THE PRESENCE OF ŚIVA

Roger S. Loomis / THE GRAIL: FROM CELTIC MYTH TO CHRISTIAN
SYMBOL

Bronislaw Malinowski (Ivan Strenski, ed.) / MALINOWSKI AND THE
WORK OF MYTH

Erich Neumann / AMOR AND PSYCHE

Erich Neumann / THE GREAT MOTHER

Maud Oakes with Joseph Campbell / WHERE THE TWO CAME TO
THEIR FATHER

Dora & Erwin Panofsky / PANDORA'S BOX

Paul Radin / THE ROAD OF LIFE AND DEATH

Otto Rank, Lord Raglan, Alan Dundes / IN QUEST OF THE HERO

Gladys Reichard / NAVAHO RELIGION

Géza Róheim (Alan Dundes, ed.) / FIRE IN THE DRAGON

Robert A. Segal, ed. / THE GNOSTIC JUNG

Philip E. Slater / THE GLORY OF HERA

Daisetz T. Suzuki / ZEN AND JAPANESE CULTURE

Jean-Pierre Vernant (Froma I. Zeitlin, ed.) / MORTALS AND
    IMMORTALS

Jessie L. Weston / FROM RITUAL TO ROMANCE

Heinrich Zimmer (Joseph Campbell, ed.) / THE KING AND THE
    CORPSE: TALES OF THE SOUL'S CONQUEST OF EVIL

Heinrich Zimmer (Joseph Campbell, ed.) / MYTHS AND SYMBOLS IN
    INDIAN ART AND CIVILIZATION